DICTIONARY OF
PSEUDONYMS
AND PEN-NAMES

Other books by Frank Atkinson

The public library
Yesterday's money (with John Fines)
Librarianship
Illustrated teach yourself coins (with J Matthews)

DICTIONARY OF

PSEUDONYMS

AND PEN-NAMES

a selection of popular modern writers in English

FRANK ATKINSON

CLIVE BINGLEY
LONDON

LINNET BOOKS
HAMDEN · CONN

FIRST PUBLISHED IN THE UK BY CLIVE BINGLEY LTD
16 PEMBRIDGE ROAD LONDON W11
SIMULTANEOUSLY PUBLISHED IN USA BY LINNET BOOKS
AN IMPRINT OF THE SHOE STRING PRESS INC
995 SHERMAN AVENUE HAMDEN CONNECTICUT 06514
SET IN 10 ON 12 POINT JOURNAL ROMAN
PRINTED AND BOUND IN THE UK BY
REDWOOD BURN LTD TROWBRIDGE AND ESHER
COPYRIGHT © FRANK ATKINSON 1975
ALL RIGHTS RESERVED
BINGLEY ISBN: 0-85157-199-9
LINNET ISBN: 0-208-01540-X

In memory of Otis Criblecoblis

ACKNOWLEDGEMENTS

Many authors, and colleagues in libraries and the book trade, have given me information and clues to information about writers' names and I am grateful to them all. My special thanks are due to John Gittins of Robert Hale and Company for his generous assistance and also, as always, to my wife for her constant help and support.

Broad Oak   Frank Atkinson
Heathfield Sussex
April 1975

CONTENTS

INTRODUCTION

We had a bottle of port for dinner, and drank dear Willie's health. He said, 'Oh, by the by, did I tell you I've cut my first name William, and taken the second name Lupin? In fact, I'm only known at Oldham as Lupin Pooter. If you were to 'Willie' me there, they wouldn't know what you meant'.

That which we call a rose, by any other name would smell as sweet— that is, it would now, of course. Even so, it wouldn't *sound* very attractive if it were called Old Man's Beard, or Bladderwort, or Witch's Oatmeal. And who knows, had it been called say, Nastythumbpricker, from the start, it might now be a despised weed with a smell like last week's *borsch*. So it is with personal names. Look how Uriah Heap turned out. (The law of libel precludes mention of any of the real, living Uriahs.)

The names wished on us by our parents don't always please, and lots of people fiddle about varying the order of the components to suit them- selves better; or they manage to get themselves nicknamed. The Grossmiths, in the piece quoted above from *The diary of a nobody*, satirised this harmless foible—but quite gently. And they did allow young W L Pooter, who could not come to terms with life as a Willie, to prosper as Lupin. His champagne flows at the end of the book.

Choosing a pen-name

Authors are great name fiddlers, and many have performed quite drastic nomenectomies in order to achieve a satisfactory pseudonym. Arthur Elliott Elliott-Cannon lopped off Arthur and the spare Elliott; Reginald David Stanley Courtney-Browne excised his three forenames, and most understandably, Richard Nathaniel Twisleton-Wykeham-Fiennes writes as Richard Fiennes.

Many people would like to adopt an entirely new name, but most of them are inhibited by family and friends, business and other encum- brances. In the separate world of books, however, writers please them- selves. They choose the name, it is solemnised on the title-page and perpetuated in lists, catalogues and the less-probing bibliographies.

Generally speaking, there is no deep thought, and little ingenuity, in the devising of pseudonyms. Obvious punning and word association provide one popular method: for example, Cecil John Street became

John Rhode; Morris West about faced to Michael East and Owen Seaman thought up Nauticus. Very basic anagrams or part anagrams, such as Melusa Moolson for Samuel Solomon, John Gannold for John Langdon and Walter De la Mare's Walter Ramal, come a close second.

Producing a more profound pseudonym takes a little longer. *Life* magazine carried a letter from Edward Stratemeyer, author of the Rover Boys stories in the 1920s, explaining how he got his pseudonym of Arthur M Winfield:

One evening when writing, with my mother sitting near sewing, I remarked that I wanted an assumed name—that I wasn't going to use my own name on the manuscript. She thought a moment and suggested Winfield. 'For then', she said, 'you may win in that field.' I thought that good. She then supplied the first name saying, 'You are going to be an author, so why not make it Arthur?'

Stratemeyer added the M himself, reasoning that as M stood for thousand, it might help to sell thousands of books.

Corey Ford, in his *Time of laughter*, quotes this Stratemeyer letter, and also gives a highly dubious version of how he selected a pseudonym for himself. 'Unfortunately,' he writes, 'I did not have Mr Stratemeyer's mother to help me out. So I shut my eyes, opened the New York telephone directory at random and put my finger on a name. The name turned out to be Runkelschmelz, so I threw the phone book away and thought up John Riddell.'

Part of the package

It is not always personal preference alone that motivates an author's name change. Often it is done to match a particular type of book, on the grounds that any product sells better under a familiar label. Westerns, for example, should appear to be the work of lean and saddle-sore cowpokes, a six-shooter in either hand—with which, presumably, after bacon and beans round the ole campfire, they whack their typewriter keys.

So, when offering their readers *Rustlers and powder-smoke, Hopalong Cassidy, The big corral*, or similar horsesweat, the respective authors Charles Horace Snow, Louis L'Amour and Archibald Lynn Joscelyn, become Charles Ballew, Tex Burns and Al Cody.

Romantic fiction, on the other hand, is not expected to be penned by the Bucks and Hanks of this world. That *genre* requires authors' names suggestive of crisp, clean blouses and commonsense, yet with a hint of madcap moments; names like Elaine Carr, Phyllis Marlow and Caroline Holmes—all three of which are pseudonyms of one Major Charles Mason.

Tandem names

When two writers work together and decide to share a pseudonym, they rarely come up with an Ellery Queen. (And even Dannay and Lee took some time to drop Barnaby Ross in favour of the peerless Ellery.) Usually, like married couples naming their house Marjalf or Gladern, they make one name from bits of the two. Kelley Roos is made up from two surnames (Audrey Kelley and William Roos), as is Manning Coles (Adelaide Manning and Cyril Coles).

The two first names of Constance and Gwenyth Little, lopped fore and aft, form this couple's pseudonym of Conyth Little; while David Eliades and Robert Forrest Webb decided on David Forrest for their joint works.

Hilary Aidan St George Saunders and John Leslie Palmer, on the other hand, settled firstly for Francis Beeding as a joint pseudonym and later for David Pilgrim, simply because they liked these names.

The game of the name

All of this suggests that the pseudonym business is a bit of a lark. For the most part, as far as British and American writers are concerned, it is. Although some of them are compelled (or find it politic) for professional or contractual reasons not to publish under their real names, very few can be in fear of serious prosecution or persecution.

It is often said that some writers adopt pseudonyms in order to deceive the taxman. At best, this could only be playing for time. Death and taxes are still the two certainties of life.

So it really is a game—a mixture of fantasising, crossword puzzling and riddle-me-ree. When the game gets a good grip on a writer he may soon, like John Creasey, Michael Angelo Avallone Jr, or a number of others, clock up a double-figure pseudonym total. Some real fanatics for false names have acquired bumper collections. François Marie Arouet is usually cited as the top man in this field. In addition to the pseudonym Voltaire, he is credited with some 136 others; but most of them he used only for signing letters. Within the scope of this work, however, Lauran Paine leads the field with sixty five discovered pen-names.

What a tangled web

The real name-pseudonym area of research is more full of snags than most. In the first place there is the writers' intention to deceive. This may be an ephemeral and relatively lighthearted intention—as witnessed by the number of authors who freely declare their pen-names in the various biographical reference works. Or it may be a serious and long-standing determination such as that of the former librarian Eric Leyland, of whom Lofts and Adley, in their *Men behind boys' fiction*, say: 'Written nearly 150 books for young people . . . and another 100 books under various pen-names which are strictly private.'

Shifts do occur, from the second group to the first, as circumstances change—usually for business reasons. The commercial success of a writer often leads to her, or his, pseudonyms being blazoned on dust jackets and in advertisements.

Secondly, there are the publishers. With few exceptions, those contacted in the course of compiling this work may be divided into two groups. One group considers authors' pseudonyms to be such close and vital secrets that any enquiry after them is treated, at best, as an impertinence but, more often, as attempted subversion. The other group consists of firms carrying on business in cheerful ignorance of the true identity of many of those whose work they publish. Enquiries there cause amused surprise that anybody should be interested. As to practical help, well that's not possible because no-one really knows and then, you see, royalties are mostly paid to authors' agents and no-one, apparently, cares.

Call me Sappho, call me Chloris

Of the writers who kindly replied to our enquiries, a number were vague about the various names under which they had written. Of those who were certain, two gave spellings of their pseudonyms which differed from those on the title-pages of their books. It is not surprising, then, that the great catalogues of the British Museum and the Library of Congress, and the *British national bibliography* and the *Cumulative book index*, are sometimes at odds with one another as to whether a name is real or assumed. For the period 1900-1950, volume eight of Halkett and Laing's *Dictionary of anonymous and pseudonymous English literature* is a further contender except, of course, when it quotes the British Museum catalogue as its authority. Since 1968, the *British national bibliography* has not distinguished between real names and pseudonyms.

A few threads teased out

This dictionary is limited to writers in English and the selection has been made from those writing in the years 1900 to date. It is hoped that it will help librarians and booksellers to answer some of the many questions which are asked about authors—particularly contemporary authors—who write under more than one name. It may also assist in solving some of the queries about pseudonymous contributors to newspapers and magazines during the early decades of this century.

On a less practical, but equally justifiable level, there is the intention to satisfy people's curiosity. W P Courtney called his book on British anonymous and pseudonymous writings which was published in 1908, *The secrets of our national literature*. In the first paragraph he wrote: 'The pleasure of finding out the secrets of our neighbours appeals to most minds.'

Many readers are even more curious about their favourite authors than they are about their neighbours. This book may give them some small pleasure.

REAL NAMES

ABRAHALL, Clare Hoskyns
    Drury, C M
    Drury, Clare
ABRAHAMS, Doris Caroline
    Brahms, Caryl
ACWORTH, Marion W
    Neon
ADAM, C G M
    Stewart, C R
ADAM, Robin
    MacTyre, Paul
ADAM, Ronald
    Blake
ADAM SMITH, Janet Buchanan
    Carleton, Janet
ADAMS, Agnes
    Logan, Agnes
ADAMS, Charles William Dunlop
    Montrose
ADAMS, Cleve Franklin
    Spain, John
ADAMS, Clifton
    Randall, Clay
ADAMS, Franklin Pierce
    F P A
ADAMS, Samuel Hopkins
    Fabian, Warner
ADDIS, E E
    Drax, Peter
ADDIS, Hazel Iris
    Adair, Hazel
    Heritage, A J
    Mao
ADLER, Irving
    Irving, Robert
AGATE, James
    Prentis, Richard
AGELASTO, Charlotte Priestley
    Watson, C P
AIKEN, John
    Paget, John

AINSWORTH, Mary Dinsmore
    Salter, Mary D
    Salter Ainsworth, Mary D
AITKEN, Andrew
    Arnold, Wilcox
AITKEN, E H
    E H A
AKERS, Elizabeth
    Percy, Florence
ALBANESI, Effie Maria
    Rowlands, Effie Adelaide
ALBERT, Harold A
    Priestly, Mark
ALDRED, Margaret
    Saunders, Anne
ALEXANDER, Colin James
    Jay, Simon
ALEXANDER, Janet
    McNeill, Janet
ALEXANDER, Joan
    Pepper, Joan
ALEXANDER, Robert William
    Butler, Joan
ALGER, Leclaire Gowans
    Macleodhas, Sorche
ALINGTON, Argentine Francis
    Talbot, Hugh
ALLAN, Mabel Esther
    Estoril, Jean
    Pilgrim, Anne
ALLAN, Philip Bertram Murray
    Cabochon, Francis
    Phillip, Alban M
ALLDRIDGE, John Stratten
    Stratton, John

> Who gave you this name?
> My godfathers and god-
> mothers. — Church of
> England Catechism

ALLEGRO, John Marco
  McGill, Ian
ALLEN, Henry
  Fisher, Clay
  Henry, Will
ALLEN, John E
  Danforth, Paul M
ALLEN, Stephen Valentine
  Allen, Steve
  Stevens, William Christopher
ALLEN-BALLARD, Eric
  Allen, Eric
ALLFREE, P S
  Blackburn, Martin
ALMOND, Brian
  Vaughan, Julian
ALPERS, Mary Rose
  Campion, Sarah
AMBLER, Eric and RODDA,
 Charles
  Reed, Eliot
AMES, Francis
  Watson, Frank
AMIS, Kingsley
  Markham, Robert
AMY, William Lacey
  Allan, Luke
ANDERS, Edith Mary
  England, Edith M
ANDERSON, (Lady) Flavia
  Portobello, Petronella
ANDERSON, Martin
  Cynicus
ANDERSON, Poul
  Craig, A A
  Karageorge, Michael
  Sanders, Winston P
ANDREWS, Claire and ANDREWS,
 Keith
  Claire, Keith
ANDREWS, Naomi Cornelia
  Madgett, Naomi Long
ANSELL, Edward Clarence
 Trelawney
  Crad, Joseph

ANSLE, Dorothy Phoebe
  Conway, Laura
  Elsna, Hebe
  Lancaster, Vicky
  Snow, Lyndon
ANTHONY, Barbara
  Barber, Antonia
ANTHONY, E
  Parr, Dr John Anthony
APPLEBY, Carol McAfee
  Morgan, Carol McAfee
APPLEMAN, John Alan
  Daley, Bill
  Montrose, James St David
APPLIN, Arthur
  Swift, Julian
APPS, Edwin and DEVANEY,
 Pauline
  Wraith, John
ARDEN, Adrian
  Ariel
ARMSTRONG, Douglas
  Douglas, Albert
  Windsor, Rex
ARMSTRONG, Richard
  Renton, Cam
ARMSTRONG, T I F see
 FYTTON ARMSTRONG, T I
ARSHAVSKY, Abraham Isaac
  Shaw, Artie
ARTER, Wallace E
  Kay, Wallace
ARTHUR, Frances Browne
  Cunningham, Ray
ARTHUR, Ruth M
  Huggins, Ruth Mabel
ASHFORD, F C
  Charles, Frederick
ASHLEY, Ernest
  Vivian, Francis
ASHMORE, Basil
  Marlin, Roy
ASHTON, (Lady)
  Garland, Madge

14

ASHTON, Winifred
  Dane, Clemence
ASHTON-WARNER, Sylvia
  Henderson, Sylvia
  Sylvia
ASIMOV, Isaac
  Dr A
  French, Paul
ASTON, (Sir) George
  Amphibian
  Southcote, George
ATKINS, Frank A
  Ash, Fenton
  Aubrey, Frank
ATKINSON, Frank
  Shallow, Robert
ATKINSON, John
  Aye, John
ATTENBOROUGH, Bernard
George
  Rand, James S
AUBREY-FLETCHER, (Sir)
Henry Lancelot
  Wade, Henry
AUCHINCLOSS, Louis
  Lee, Andrew
AUSTIN, John and AUSTIN,
Richard
  Gun Buster
AVALLONE, Michael Angelo Jr
  Carton, Nick
  Conway, Troy
  Dalton, Priscilla
  Dane, Mark
  De Pre, Jean-Anne
  Michaels, Steve
  Nile, Dorothea
  Noone, Edwina
  Stanton, Vance
  Stuart, Sidney
AVENELL, Donne
  King, Charles
AVERY, Harold
  Westridge, Harold

AVEY, Ruby D
  Page, Vicki
AYCKBOURNE, Alan
  Allen, Ronald
AYRES, Paul and RONNS,
Edward
  Aarons, Edward Sidney

BABCOCK, Frederick
  Mark, Matthew
BACKUS, Jean L
  Montross, David
BAILEY, Gordon
  Gordon, Keith
BAILY, Francis Evans
  Wilson, Ann
BAIN, K B F
  Findlater, Richard
BAKER, Anne
  Cross, Nancy
BAKER, Betty
  Renier, Elizabeth
BAKER, Laura
  Minier, Nelson
BAKER, Louise Alice
  Alien
BAKER, Marjorie
  McMaster, Alison
BAKER, Mary Gladys Steel
  Stuart, Sheila
BAKER, Ray Stannard
  Grayson, David
BAKER, William Howard
  Ballinger, W A
BALCHIN, Nigel
  Spade, Mark
BALDWIN, Dorothy
  Jones, Clara
BALDWIN, Gordon C
  Gordon, Lew
BALDWIN, Oliver
  Hussingtree, Martin
BALFOUR, William
  Russell, Raymond

BALL, Brian N
   Kinsey-Jones, Brian
BALLARD, Willis Todhunter
   Ballard, P D
   Ballard, Todhunter
   Bonner, Parker
   Bowie, Sam
   Hunter, John
BALLINGER, William Sanborn
   Sanborn, B X
BALOGH, Penelope
   Fox, Petronella
BAMBERGER, Helen R
   Berger, Helen
BAMFIELD, Veronica
   Wood, Mary
BANBURY, Olive Lethbridge
   Lethbridge, Olive
BANDY, Eugene Franklin Jr
   Franklin, Eugene
BARBER-STARKEY, Roger
   Shropshire Lad
BARCLAY, George
   Kinnoch, R G B
BARCLAY, Oliver Rainsford
   Triton, A N
BARCLAY, Vera C
   Beech, Margaret
BARFIELD, Arthur Owen
   Burgeon, G A L
BARKER, Clarence Hedley
   Seafarer
BARKER, Dudley
   Black, Lionel
BARKER, E M
   Jordan, Nell
BARKER, Leonard Noel
   Noel, L
BARKER, Michael
   Barker, Jack
BARKER, Ronald Ernest
   Ronald, E B
BARKER, S Omar
   Canusi, Jose
   Squires, Phil

BARKER, Will
   Demarest, Doug
BARLTROP, Mabel
   Octavia
BARNARD, Marjorie Faith and
   ELDERSHAW, Flora Sydney
   Eldershaw, M Barnard
BARNES, Patricia
   Abercrombie, Patricia Barnes
BARNITT, Nedda Lemmon
   Lamont, N B
BARNSLEY, Alan
   Fielding, Gabriel
BARONAS, Aloyzas
   Aliunas, S
BARR, Patricia
   Hazard, Laurence
BARRADELL-SMITH, Walter
   Bird, Lilian
   Bird, Richard
BARRAUD, E M
   Johns, Hilary
BARRE, Jean
   Lindsay, Lee
BARRETT, Alfred Walter
   Andom, R
BARRETT, Geoffrey John
   Anders, Rex
   Blaine, Jeff
   Cole, Richard
   Kilbourn, Matt
   Macey, Carn
   Rickard, Cole
   Royal, Dan
   Sanders, Brett
   Summers, D B
   Wade, Bill
BARRETT, Hugh Gilchrist
   Bellman, Walter
BARRINGTON, E
   Moresby, Louis
BARRINGTON, Howard
   Stone, Simon
BARRINGTON, Pamela
   Barling, Charles

Barling, Muriel Vere
Barling, Pamela
BARROW, Albert Stewart
Sabretache
BARTLETT, Marie
Lee, Rowena
Rift, Valerie
BARTLETT, Stephen
Slade, Gurney
BARTLETT, Vernon
Oldfield, Peter
BASHAM, Daisy
Aunt Daisy
BASHFORD, (Sir) Henry
Howarth
Carp, Augustus
BASS, Clara May
Overy, Claire May
BASTIN, John
Sturgus, J B
BATEMAN, Robert Moyes
Moyes, Robin
BATES, Herbert Ernest
Flying Officer X
BATTYE, Gladys
Lynn, Margaret
BAUMANN, Arthur A
A A B
BAUMANN, Margaret
Lees, Marguerite
BAX, (Sir) Arnold
O'Byrne, Dermot
BAXTER, Elizabeth
Holland, Elizabeth
BAYBARS, Taner
Bayliss, Timothy
BAYLISS, John Clifford
Clifford, John
BAYNES, Dorothy Julia
Creston, Dormer
BAYS, J W
Roadster
BEADLE, Gwyneth Gordon
Gordon, Glenda

BEAR, Joan E
Mayhew, Elizabeth
BEARDMORE, George
Stokes, Cedric
Wolfenden, George
BEAUCHAMP, Kathleen Mansfield
Mansfield, Katherine
BECHOFFER ROBERTS, C E
Ephesian
BECK, Eliza Louisa Moresby
Barrington, E
Beck, Lily Adams
BECKER, Peter
Vul' Indlela
BECKETT, Ronald Brymer
Anthony, John
BEEBE, Elswyth Thane
Thane, Elswyth
BEESTON, L J
Camden, Richard
Davies, Lucian
BEETON, D R
Barratt, Robert
BEITH, John Hay
Hay, Ian
Junior Sub
BELL, Alexander
Young, Filson
BELL, Eric Temple
Taine, John
BELL, Gerard
Landis, John
BELL, John Keble
Howard, Keble
Methuen, John
BELL, Martin
Oates, Titus
BELLASIS, Margaret Rosa
Marton, Francesca
BENARY, Margot
Benary-Isbert, Margot
BENCHLEY, Robert
Fawkes, Guy
BENDER, Arnold
Philippi, Mark

BENDIT, Gladys
  Presland, John
BENJAMIN, Lewis S
  Melville, Lewis
BENNETT, Arnold
  King, Sampson
BENNETT, Dorothy
  Kingsley, Laura
BENNETT, Geoffrey Martin
  Sea-Lion
BENNETT, J J
  Jackstaff
BENNETT, William E
  Armstrong, Warren
BENSON, Michael
  Thomas, Michael
BENTLEY, Edmund Clerihew
  Clerihew, E
BENTLEY, Frederick Horace
  Wilson, D M
BENTLEY, James W B
  Claughton-James, James
  Nostalgia
BENTLEY, Phyllis
  A Batchelor of Arts
BENTON, Peggie
  Burke, Shifty
BERESFORD, Leslie
  Pan
BERGER, Josef
  Digges, Jeremiah
BEST, Allena
  Berry, Erick
BEST, Carol Anne
  Ashe, Susan
  Darlington, Con
  Martin, Ann
  Wayne, Marcia
BEST, Rayleigh Breton Amis
  Amis, Breton
  Bentinck' Ray
  Haddow, Leigh
  Hughes, Terence
  Roberts, Desmond
  Wilde, Leslie

BETHELL, Leonard Arthur
  Cailloux, Pousse
  Severn, Forepoint
BETTANY, F G
  N O B
BETTERIDGE, Anne
  Newman, Margaret
  Potter, Margaret
BEVAN, Aneurin
  Celticus
BEVAN, Tom
  Bamfylde, Walter
BHATIA, June
  Edwards, June
  Rana, J
BICKHAM, Jack M
  Clinton, Jeff
  Miles, John
BICKLE, Judith
  Tweedale, J
BIDWELL, Marjory Elizabeth
  Sarah
  Gibbs, Mary Ann
BIGG, Patricia Nina
  Ainsworth, Patricia
BINGLEY, David Ernest
  Adams, Bart
  Benson, Adam
  Bridger, Adam
  Canuck, Abe
  Carver, Dave
  Chatham, Larry
  Chesham, Henry
  Coltman, Will
  Coniston, Ed
  Dorman, Luke
  Fallon, George
  Horsley, David
  Jefford, Bat
  Kingston, Syd
  Lynch, Eric
  Martell, James
  North, Colin
  Plummer, Ben
  Prescott, Caleb

18

Remington, Mark
Roberts, John
Romney, Steve
Silvester, Frank
Starr, Henry
Tucker, Link
Wigan, Christopher
Yorke, Rogers
BINNS, Ottwell
  Bolt, Ben
BIRCH, Jack Ernest Lionel and
  MURRAY, Venetia Pauline
  Flight, Francies
BIRD, Dennis Leslie
  Noel, John
BIRD, William Henry Fleming
  Fleming, Harry
BIRKENHEAD, Elijah
  Birkenhead, Edward
BIRT, Francis Bradley
  Bradley, Shelland
BISHOP, Stanley
  Edgar, Icarus Walter
BISSET-SMITH, G T
  Bizet, George
BLACK, Dorothy
  Black, Kitty
BLACK, Hazleton
  Graham, Scott
BLACK, Ladbroke Lionel Day
  Day, Lionel
  Urquhart, Paul
BLACK, Maureen
  Black, Veronica
  Darby, Catherine
  Peters, Maureen
  Rothmann, Judith
  Whitby, Sharon
BLACK, Oliver
  Black, Jett
BLACKBURN, James Garford
  Garford, James
BLACKETT, Veronica
  Heath, Veronica

BLACKMORE, Anauta
  Anauta
BLAGBROUGH, Harriet
  Eastertide
BLAIR, Dorothy
  Bolitho, Ray D
BLAIR, Dorothy and
  PAGE, Evelyn
  Scarlett, Roger
BLAIR, Eric
  Orwell, George
BLAIR, Kathryn
  Brett, Rosalind
  Conway, Celine
BLAIR, Norma Hunter
  Hunter, Alison
BLAIR, Pauline Hunter
  Clare, Helen
  Clarke, Pauline
BLAIR-FISH, Wallace Wilfrid
  Blair
BLAIKLOCK, Edward
  Grammaticus
BLAKE, Leslie James
  Tabard, Peter
BLAKE, Sally Mirliss
  Sara
BLATCHFORD, Robert
  Nunquam
BLAUTH-MUSZKOWSKI, Peter
  Blauth, Christopher
BLECH, William J
  Blake, William
  Blake, William James
BLIXEN-FINECKE, Karen
  Christence (Baroness)
  Blixen, Karen
  Dinesen, Isak
BLOFELD, John
  Chu Feng
BLOOD, Marje
  McKenzie, Paige
BLOOM, Jack Don
  Donne, Jack

BLOOM, Ursula
  Burns, Sheila
  Essex, Mary
  Harvey, Rachel
  Mann, Deborah
BLOOM, Ursula and EADE,
  Charles
  Prole, Lozania
BLOOMER, Arnold
  More, Euston
BLOOMFIELD, Anthony John
  Westgate
  Westgate, John
BLUNDELL, V R
  Nixon, Kathleen
BLYTH, Harry
  Meredith, Hal
BLYTON, Enid
  Pollock, Mary
BOATFIELD, Jeffrey
  Jeffries, Jeff
BODENHAM, Hilda
  Boden, Hilda
BODINGTON, Nancy Hermione
  Smith, Shelley
BOGGS, Winifred
  Burke, Edmund
BOLSTER, (Sister) M Angela
  Bolster, Evelyn
BOLTON, Miriam
  Davis, Stratford
  Sharman, Miriam
BOND, Gladys Baker
  Mendel, Jo
  Walker, Holly Beth
BOND, Grace
  Todhunter, Philippa
BOON, Violet Mary
  Williams, Violet M
BOOTH, Philip Arthur
  Werner, Peter
BORBOLLA, Barbara
  Martyn, Don
BORDEN, Deal
  Borden, Leo

BORG, Philip Anthony John
  Borg, Jack
  Pickard, John Q
BORNEMAN, Ernest
  McCabe, Cameron
BORNEMANN, Eva
  Geisel, Eva
BOSHELL, Gordon
  Bee
BOSWORTH, Willan George
  Borth, Willan G
  Leonid
  Worth, Maurice
BOULTON, A Harding
  Harding, Richard
BOURQUIN, Paul
  Amberley, Richard
BOWDEN, Jean
  Barry, Jocelyn
  Curry, Avon
  Dell, Belinda
BOWER, John Graham
  Klaxon
BOWMAN, Gerald
  Magnus, Gerald
BOYD, Elizabeth Orr
  MacCall, Isabel
BOYD, Martin à Beckett
  Mills, Martin
BOYLE, John Howard Jackson
  Dawson, Michael
BRADBURY, Parnell
  Dermott, Stephen
  Lynn, Stephen
BRADBY, Rachel
  Anderson, Rachel
BRADLEY, Marion Z and
  COULSON, Juanita
  Wells, John J
BRADY, Jane Frances
  White, Jane
BRADSHAW-JONES, Malcolm
  Henry
  Jones, Bradshaw

BRAEME, Charlotte Monica
  Clay, Bertha M
BRAMBLEBY, Ailsa
  Craig, Jennifer
BRANDENBERG, Alyce Christina
  Aliki
BRAND, Charles Neville
  Lorne, Charles
BRAUN, Wilbur
  Albert, Ned
  Brandon, Bruce
  Fernway, Peggy
  Ring, Basil
  Warren, Wayne
BRAYBROOKE, Patrick
  P B
BRENAN, Edward Fitzgerald
  Beaton, George
  Brenan, Gerald
BRENNAN, John
  Welcome, John
BRENT, Peter Ludwig
  Peters, Ludovic
BRETHERTON, C H
  Algol
BRETON-SMITH, Clare
  Boon, August
  Caldwell, Elinor
  Vernon, Claire
  Wilde, Hilary
BRETT, Leslie Frederick
  Brett, Michael
BRIDGES, Thomas Charles
  Beck, Christopher
  Bridges, Tom
BRIGHOUSE, Harold and
  WALTON, John
  Conway, Olive
BRINSMEAD, Hesba
  Brinsmead, H F
  Hurgerford, Pixie
BRINTON, Henry
  Fraser, Alex
BROCKIES, Enid Florence
  Magriska, Hélène (Countess)

BRODEY, Jim
  Femora
  Taylor, Ann
BRODIE, John
  Guthrie, John
BRODIE, Julian Paul and GREEN,
  Alan Baer
  Denbie, Roger
BROOKE, Peter
  Carson, Anthony
BROOKES, Ewart Stanley
  Tyler, Clarke
BROOKMAN, Laura L
  Wilson, Edwina H
BROOKS, Edwy Searles
  Gray, Berkeley
  Gunn, Victor
BROOKS, Ern
  Orion
BROOKS, Jeremy
  Meikle, Clive
BROOKS, Vivian Collin
  Mills, Osmington
BROSIA, D M
  D'Ambrosio, Raymond
BROWN, George Douglas
  Douglas, George
BROWN, Howard
  Evans, John
BROWN, Ivor
  I B
BROWN, John
  Browning, John
BROWN, John Ridley
  Castle, Douglas
BROWN, Kay
  Back-Back
BROWN, L Rowland
  Grey, Rowland
BROWN, Laurence Oliver
  Oliver, Laurence
BROWN, Margaret Elizabeth
  Snow
  Brown, Marel

BROWN, May
   Blake, Vanessa
   Brown, Mandy
BROWN, Morna Doris
   Ferrars, E X
   Ferrars, Elizabeth
BROWN, Rosalie
   Moore, Rosalie
BROWN, Zenith
   Ford, Leslie
   Frome, David
BROWNE, Charles Farrar
   Ward, Artemus
BROWNE, Harry T
   John o' the North
BROWNJOHN, Alan
   Berrington, John
BRUFF, Nancy
   Gardner, Nancy Bruff
BRUNNER, John
   Woodcott, Keith
BRYANS, Robert Harbinson
   Bryans, Robin
   Harbinson, Robert
BRYSON, Charles
   Barry, Charles
BUCHAN, Anna
   Douglas, O
BUCKLAND—WRIGHT, Mary
   Hume, Frances
BUCKLEY, Fergus Reid
   Crumpet, Peter
BUDD, John
   Prescot, Julian
BUDD, William John
   Budd, Jackson
BUDDEE, Paul
   Richards, Paul
BULLEID, H A V
   Collins, D
BULLETT, Gerald
   Fox, Sebastian
BUMPUS, Doris Marjorie
   Alan, Marjorie

BUNCE, Oliver Bell
   Censor
BUNCH, David R
   Groupe, Darryl R
BURBRIDGE, Edith Joan
   Cockin, Joan
BURDEN, Jean
   Ames, Felicia
BURFORD, Roger d'Este
   East, Roger
BURG, David
   Dolberg, Alexander
BURGE, Milward Rodon
   Kennedy
   Kennedy, Milward
BURGESS, Thornton W
   Thornton, W B
BURGIN, G B
   Smee, Wentworth
BURKE, John Frederick
   Burke, Jonathan
   George, Jonathan
   Jones, Joanna
   Miall, Robert
   Morris, Sara
   Sands, Martin
BURKHARDT, Eve and
   BURKHARDT, Robert
Ferdinand
   Bliss, Adam
   Eden, Rob
BURNE, Clendennin Talbot
   Hawkes, John
BURNETT, Hallie
   Hutchinson, Anne
BURNETT, Hugh
   Phelix
BURNETT-SMITH, Annie S
   Swan, Annie S
BURNS, Bernard
   Auld, Philip
BURNS, Vincent
   Burns, Bobby
BURROUGHS, William
   Lee, William

22

BURROWS, Hermann
　　Rag Man
BURTON, Alice Elizabeth
　　Kerby, Susan Alice
BUSH, Christopher
　　Home, Michael
BUSH-FEKETE, Marie Ilona
　　Fagyas, Maria
BUSSY, Dorothy
　　Olivia
BUTLER, Arthur Ronald
　　Butler, Richard
BUTLER, Bill
　　Sabbah, Hassan i
BUTLER, Teresa Mary
　　Hooley, Teresa
BUTTERS, Paul
　　Williamson, Paul
BUTTERWORTH, Frank Nestle
　　Blundell, Peter
BUTTON, Margaret
　　Leona
BUXTON, Anne
　　Maybury, Anne
　　Troy, Katherine
BYERS, Amy
　　Barry, Ann
BYROM, James
　　Bramwell, James

CADELL, Elizabeth
　　Ainsworth, Harriet
CAESAR, Richard Dynely and
　MAYNE, William J C
　　James, Dynely
CALLARD, Thomas
　　Ross, Sutherland
CAMERON, Elizabeth Jane
　　Duncan, Jane
CAMERON, William Ernest
　　Allerton, Mark
CAMPBELL, Barbara Mary
　　Cam
CAMPBELL, Gabrielle
　Margaret Vere

Bowen, Marjorie
Paye, Robert
Preedy, George
Preedy, George R
Shearing, Joseph
Winch, John
CAMPBELL, John Lorne
　　Chanaidh, Fear
CAMPBELL, John Wood Jr
　　Stuart, Don A
CAMPBELL, R O
　　Staveley, Robert
CAMPBELL, Walter Stanley
　　Vestal, Stanley
CAMPBELL, William Edward
　　March
　　March, William
CAMPION, Sidney
　　Swayne, Geoffrey
CANADAY, John
　　Head, Matthew
CANAWAY, W H
　　Canaway, Bill
　　Hamilton, William
　　Hermes
CANNING, Victor
　　Gould, Alan
CAPSTICK, Elizabeth
　　Scott, Elizabeth
CARAS, Roger
　　Sarac, Roger
CARDENA, Clement
　　De Laube
CAREW-SLATER, Harold James
　　Carey, James
CAREY, Joyce
　　Mallory, Jay
CARLISLE, R H
　　Hawkeye

Oh Amos Cottle! —
Phoebus what a name
To fill the speaking trump
of future fame. — Byron

23

CARLTON, Grace
  Garth, Cecil
CARNEGIE, Raymond Alexander
  Carnegie, Sacha
CARR, Barbara Irene Veronica
  Comyns
  Comyns, Barbara
CARR, John Dickson
  Dickson, Carr
  Dickson, Carter
CARR, Margaret
  Carroll, Martin
  Kerr, Carole
CARRIER, Robert and DICK,
  Oliver Lawson
  Oliver, Robert
CARRINGTON, Charles
  Edmonds, Charles
CARTER, Bryan
  Carter, Nick
CARTER, Compton Irving
  Carter, John L
CARTER, Ernest
  Giffin, Frank
CARTER, Felicity Winifred
  Bonett, Emery
CARTER, John Franklin
  Diplomat
  Franklin, Jay
  Unofficial Observer
CARTER, Thomas
  Wood, J Claverdon
CARUSO, Joseph
  Barnwell, J O
CARY, Joyce
  Cary, Arthur
  Joyce, Thomas
CASEMENT, Christina
  Maclean, Christian
CASEY, Michael T and CASEY,
  Rosemary
  Casey, Mart
CASSELEYR, Camille
  Danvers, Jack

CASSON, Frederick
  Beatty, Baden
CASTLE, Brenda
  Ferrand, Georgina
CASTLE, Frances Mundy
  Whitehouse, Peggy
CASWELL, Anne
  Orr, Mary
CATALANI, Victoria
  Haas, Carola
CATHERALL, Arthur
  Channel, A R
  Hallard, Peter
CATTO, Maxwell Jeffrey
  Catto, Max
  Kent, Simon
CAULFIELD, Max
  McCoy, Malachy
CAVERHILL, William Melville
  Melville, Alan
CHADWICK, Joseph
  Barton, Jack
  Callahan, John
  Conroy, Jim
CHALKE, Herbet
  Blacker, Hereth
CHALLANS, Mary
  Renault, Mary
CHALMERS, Patrick
  P C
CHALONER, John Seymour
  Chalon, Jon
CHAMBERS, Aidan
  Blacklin, Malcolm
CHANCE, John Newton
  Chance, Jonathan
  Drummond, John
  Lymington, John
  Newton, David C
CHANDLER, Arthur
  Whitley, George
CHAPMAN, Mary I and CHAPMAN,
  John Stanton
  Chapman, Mariston

24

CHAPMAN, Raymond
  Nash, Simon
CHAPPELL, George S
  Traprock, Walter E
CHARLES, Richard
  Awdry, R C
CHARLTON, Joan and others
  Heptagon
CHARNOCK, Joan
  Thomson, Joan
CHAUNDLER, Christine
  Martin, Peter
CHEETHAM, James
  Cheetham, Hal
CHESHIRE, Gifford Paul
  Merriman, Chad
  Pendleton, Ford
CHESTERTON, G K
  Arion
  G K C
CHETHAM-STRODE, Warren
  Douglas, Noel
  Hamilton, Michael
CHEYNE, (Sir) Joseph
  Munroe, R
CHI LIEN
  Wong, Elizabeth
CHILD, Philip A G
  Wentworth, John
CHIPPERFIELD, Joseph
  Craig, John Eland
CHISHOLM, Lilian
  Alan, Jane
  Lorraine, Anne
CHITTY, (Sir) Thomas Willes
  Hinde, Thomas
CHOSACK, Cyril
  Maclean, Barry
CHOVIL, Alfred Harold
  Brook, Peter
CHRISTIE, (Dame) Agatha
  Mallowen, Agatha Christie
  Westmacott, Mary
CHRISTIE, Douglas
  Campbell, Colin

CITOVICH, Enid
  Baldry, Enid
CLAIR, Colin
  Nicholai, C L R
CLAMP, Helen M E
  Leigh, Olivia
CLARK, Alfred Alexander Gordon
  Hare, Cyril
CLARK, Charles Heber
  Adeler, Max
CLARK, Douglas
  Ditton, James
CLARK, Frederick Stephen
  Dalton, Clive
CLARK, Mabel Margaret
  Storm, Lesley
CLARK, Maria
  Clark, Mary Lou
CLARK, Marie Catherine Audrey
  Curling, Audrey
CLARKE, Brenda
  Honeyman, Brenda
CLARKE, David
  Waldo, Dave
CLARKE, J Calvitt
  Grant, Richard
CLARKE, (Lady)
  Fitzgerald, Errol
CLARKE, Percy A
  Frazer, Martin
  Lander, Dane
  Lytton, Jane
  Nielson, Vernon
CLAYTON, Richard H M
  Haggard, William
CLEARY, C V H
  Day, Harvey
  Duncan, A H
  Norris, P E
CLEAVER, Hylton Reginald
  Crunden, Reginald
CLEGG, Paul
  Vale, Keith
CLEMENS, Brian
  O'Grady, Tony

CLEMENS, Paul
  Cadwallader
CLEVELY, Hugh Desmond
  Claymore
  Claymore, Tod
CLINE, Norma
  Klose, Norma Cline
CLOPET, Liliane M C
  Bethune, Mary
CLUTTERBUCK, Richard
  Jocelyn, Richard
COAD, Frederick R
  Sosthenes
COATES, Anthony
  Mandeville, D E
COBB, Ivo Geike
  Weymouth, Anthony
COCKBURN, Claud
  Helvick, James
  Pitcairn, Frank
COERR, Eleanor Beatrice
  Hicks, Eleanor
  Page, Eleanor
COFFEY, Edward Hope
  Hope, Edward
COFFMAN, Virginia
  Du Vaul, Virginia
COHEN, Morton N
  Moreton, John
COHEN, Victor
  Caldecott, Veronica
COKE, Desmond
  Blinders, Belinda
COLE, Margaret A
  Renton, Julia
  Saunders, Ione
COLEMAN, William Lawrence
  Coleman, Lonnie
COLEMAN-COOKE, John C
  Ford, Langridge
COLES, Albert John
  Stewer, Jan
COLES, Cyril Henry and
  MANNING, Adelaide Frances
  Oke

Coles, Manning
  Gaite, Francis
COLES, Phoebe Catherine
  Fraser, Peter
COLEY, Rex
  Ragged Staff
COLLIE, Ruth
  Stitch, Wilhelmina
COLLINGS, Edwin
  Blackwell, John
COLLINGS, I J
  Collings, Jillie
  George, Vicky
COLLINGS, Joan
  Sutherland, Joan
COLLINS, Mildred
  Collins, Joan
COLLINSON OWEN, H
  C O
COLLOMS, Brenda
  Cross, Brenda
  Hughes, Brenda
COMBER, Elizabeth
  Han Suyin
COMBER, Lillian
  Beckwith, Lillian
COMBER, Rose
  Star, Elison
COMPTON, D G
  Compton, Guy
CONE, Molly
  More, Caroline
CONE, P C L
  Clapp, Patricia
CONNOR, Joyce Mary
  Marlow, Joyce
CONNOR, (Sir) William
  Cassandra
CONRAD, Isaac
  Conrad, Jack
COOK, Dorothy Mary
  Cameron, D Y
  Clare, Elizabeth
COOK, Ida
  Burchell, Mary

26

COOK, Ramona Graham
    Graham, Ramona
COOK, William Everett
    Cook, Will
    Everett, Wade
    Keene, James
COOKE, C H
    Bickerdyke, John
COOKE, Diana
    Witherby, Diana
COOKSON, Catherine
    Fawcett, C
    Marchant, C
COOLBEAR, Marian H
    Colbere, Hope
COOMBS, Joyce
    Hales, Joyce
    Scobey, Marion
COOPER, Edmund
    Avery, Richard
COOPER, John
    Finch, John
    Lloyd, John
COOPER, Mae Klein and KLEIN,
  Grace
    Farewell, Nina
COPPEL, Alfred
    Gilman, Robert Cham
    Marin, A C
    Marin, Alfred
COPPER, Dorothy
    Carter, Diana
    Dickens, Irene
    Grant, Carol
    Green, Linda
CORDES, Theodor K
    Casey, T
    Daedalus
    Erskine-Gray
CORK, Barry
    Causeway, Jane
CORLEY, Edwin and MURPHY,
  John
    Buchanan, Patrick

CORNISH, Doris Mary
    Lisle, Mary
CORNWELL, David John Moore
    Le Carré, John
CORTEZ-COLUMBUS, Robert
  Cimabue
    Kennedy, R C
CORY, Desmond
    McCarthy, Shaun
COSTA, Gabriel
  Callisthenes
COULSON, John
    Bonett, John
COULSON, Juanita and
  BRADLEY, Marion Z
    Wells, John J
COULSON, Robert Stratton
  and DE WEESE, T Eugene
    Stratton, Thomas
COURAGE, John
    Goyne, Richard
COURSE, Pamela
    Becket, Lavinia
    Mansbridge, Pamela
COURTNEY-BROWNE,
  Reginald D S
    Browne, Courtney
COUSINS, Margaret
    Johns, Avery
    Masters, William
    Parrish, Mary
COWLISHAW, Ranson
    Wash, R
    Woodrook, R A
COWPER, Francis
    Roe, Richard
COVE, Joseph Walter
    Gibbs, Lewis
COX, A B
    Berkeley, Anthony
    Iles, Francis
COX, Edith Muriel
    Goaman, Muriel
COX, Euphrasia Emeline
    Cox, Lewis

COX, John
  Cox, Jack
  Roberts, David
COXALL, Jack Arthur
  Dawson, Oliver
CRADOCK, Phyllis Nan Sortain
  Cradock, Fanny
  Dale, Frances
CRADOCK, Phyllis Nan Sortain
  and CRADOCK, John
  Bon Viveur
CRAIG, Edward Anthony
  Carrick, Edward
CRAGIE, Dorothy
  Craigie, David
CRAWFORD, Sallie
  Trotter, Sallie
CREASEY, Jeanne
  Crecy, Jeanne
  Williams, J R
  Williams, Jeanne
CREASEY, John
  Ashe, Gordon
  Cooke, M E
  Cooke, Margaret
  Cooper, Henry St John
  Deane, Norman
  Fecamps, Elise
  Frazer, Robert Caine
  Gill, Patrick
  Halliday, Michael
  Hogarth, Charles
  Hope, Brian
  Hughes, Colin
  Hunt, Kyle
  Mann, Abel
  Manton, Peter
  Marric, J J
  Marsden, James
  Martin, Richard
  Mattheson, Rodney
  Morton, Anthony
  Ranger, Ken
  Reilly, William K
  Riley, Tex
  York, Jeremy
CREBBIN, Edward Horace
  Sea-wrack
CRICHTON, Eleanor
  McGavin, Moyra
CRICHTON, Kyle
  Forsythe, Robert
CRICHTON, Lucilla Matthew
  Andrews, Lucilla
CRICHTON, Michael
  Hudson, Jeffrey
  Lange, John
CRISP, S E
  Crispie
CRITCHLOW, Dorothy
  Dawson, Jane
CROFT-COOKE, Rupert
  Bruce, Leo
CRONIN, Brendan Leo
  Cronin, Michael
  Miles, David
CROSBIE, Hugh Provan
  Carrick, John
  Crosbie, Provan
CROSS, John Keir
  MacFarlane, Stephen
CROSSEN, Kendell Foster
  Chaber, M E
  Monig, Christopher
  Richards, Clay
CROUDACE, Glyn
  Monnow, Peter
CROWE, (Lady)
  Lunn, Peter
CRYER, Neville
  Fern, Edwin
CUMBERLAND, Marten
  O'Hara, Kevin
CUMMINGS, Bruce Frederick
  Barbellion, W N P
CUMMINS, Mary Warmington
  Melville, Jean

CUNNINGHAM, Virginia Myra
  Mundy
    Mundy, V M
CURRY, Thomas Albert
  Jefferis, Jeff
CUST, Barbara Kate
  Fanshawe, Caroline
  Ward, Kate

DA CRUZ, Daniel
  Ballentine, John
  Cross, T T
DAINTON, William
  Dainton, Courtney
DAKERS, Elaine
  Lane, Jane
DALE, Margaret
  Miller, Margaret J
DALLY, Ann
  Mullins, Ann
DALRYMPLE-HAY, Barbara
  and DALRYMPLE-HAY, John
  Hay, John
DALTON, Gilbert
  Carstairs, Rod
  Norton, Victor
DANIEL, Glyn Edmund
  Rees, Dilwyn
DANIELL, Albert Scott
  Bowood, Richard
  Daniell, David Scott
DANNAY, Frederic
  Nathan, Daniel
DANNAY, Frederic and LEE,
  Manfred B
  Queen, Ellery
  Ross, Barnaby
DANSON, Frank Corse
  Dickson, Frank C
DAREFF, Hal
  Foley, Scott
DARGAN, Olive
  Burke, Fielding

DAUGHTREY, Olive Lydia
  Earle, Olive L
DAUKES, Sidney Herbert
  Fairway, Sidney
DAVENTRY, Leonard John
  Alexander, Martin
DAVID, Julia
  Draco, F
DAVIDSON, Edith May
  May, Roberta E
DAVIDSON, Margaret
  Compere, Mickie
  Davidson, Mickie
DAVIES, D Jacob
  Jacob, Herbert Mathias
DAVIES, David Margerison
  Margerison, David
DAVIES, Edith
  Jay, Joan
DAVIES, Joan Howard
  Drake, Joan
DAVIES, John
  Whitaker, Ray
DAVIES, John Evan Watson
  Mather, Berkely
DAVIES, Leslie Purnell
  Berne, Leo
  Blake, Robert
  Bridgeman, Richard
  Evans, Morgan
  Jefferson, Ian
  Peters, Lawrence
  Philips, Thomas
  Thomas, G K
  Vardre, Leslie
  Welch, Rowland
DAVIS, Arthur Hoey
  Rudd, Steele
DAVIS, Frederick Clyde
  Ransome, Stephen
DAVIS, Hope Hale
  Hale, Hope

DAVIS, Lily May and DAVIS,
  Rosemary
  Davis, Rosemary L
DAVIS, Lois Carlile
  Lamplaugh, Lois
DAVIS, Robert Prunier
  Brandon, Joe
DAVIS, Rosemary and DAVIS,
  Lily May
  Davis, Rosemary L
DAY, George Harold
  Quince, Peter
DAY LEWIS, Cecil
  Blake, Nicholas
DE BANZIE, Eric and RESSICH,
  John S M
  Baxter, Gregory
DE BELLET, Liane
  De Facci, Liane
DE CAIRE, Edwin
  Moodie, Edwin
DE CRISTOFORO, R J
  Cristy, R J
DE FREYNE, George
  Bridges, Victor
DE JONG, David Cornel
  Breola, Tjalmar
DE LA MARE, Walter
  Ramal, Walter
DE LA PASTURE, Edmée E M
  Delafield, E M
DE LAUNAY, André Joseph
  Launay, André
  Launay, Droo
DE LEEUW, Cateau W
  Hamilton, Kay
  Lyon, Jessica
DE MENDELSSOHN, Hilde
  Spiel, Hilde
DE SCHANSCHIEFF, Juliet
  Dymoke
  Dymoke, Juliet
DE WEESE, T Eugene and
  COULSON, Robert Stratton
  Stratton, Thomas

DEAN, Mary
  Mee, Mary
DEE, Stephanie
  Plowman, Stephanie
DEGHY, Guy and WATERHOUSE,
  Keith
  Froy, Herald
  Gibb, Lee
DEGRAS, Henry Ernest
  Benney, Mark
DEINDORFER, Robert G
  Bender, Jay
  Dender, Jay
  Greene, Robert
DELANEY, Mary Murray
  Lane, Mary D
DELVES-BROUGHTON, Josephine
  Bryan, John
DEMING, Richard
  Franklin, Max
  Moreno, Nick
DENHOLM, David
  Forrest, David
DENNEY, Diana
  Ross, Diana
DENNIS-JONES, Harold
  Hamilton, Paul
  Hessing, Dennis
DENNISON, Enid
  Lloyd, Willson
DENNISTON, Elinore
  Foley, Rae
DENT, Anthony
  Amplegirth, Anthony
  Lampton, Austen
DENVIL, Jane Gaskell
  Gaskell, Jane
DERN, Erolie Pearl
  Courtland, Roberta
  Dern, Peggy
  Gaddis, Peggy
DEVANEY, Pauline and APPS,
  Edwin
  Wraith, John

DEWAR, Hubert Stephen Lowry
  Wessex Redivivus
DICK, Oliver Lawson and
  CARRIER, Robert
  Oliver, Robert
DICK-ERIKSON, Cicely Sibyl
  Alexandra
  Dick, Alexandra
  Hay, Frances
DICK-HUNTER, Noel
  N D H
DICK-LAUDER, (Sir) George
  Lauder, George Dick
DICKINSON, Anne Hepple
  Hepple, Anne
DIENES, Zoltan
  Zed
DIETZ, Howard
  Freckles
DILCOCK, Noreen
  Christian, Jill
  Ford, Norrey
  Walford, Christian
DILLARD, Polly Hargis
  Hargis, Pauline
  Hargis, Polly
DILLON, E J
  Lanin, E B
DINGLE, Aylward Edward
  Cotterell, Brian
  Sinbad
DINNER, William
  Smith, Surrey
DIVINE, Arthur Durham
  Divine, David
DIXON, Arthur
  Whye, Felix
DIXON, Ella Hepworth
  Wynman, Margaret
DOHERTY, Ivy Ruby
  Hardwick, Sylvia
DONN-BYRNE, Brian Oswald
  Byrne, Donn
DONNELLY, Augustine
  Bear, Bullen

DONSON, Cyril
  Hartford, Via
  Kidd, Russell
  Mackin, Anita
  Pinder, Chuck
DORLING, Henry Taprell
  Taffrail
DOUGLAS, Archibald C
  Nemo
DOUGLAS, Mary
  Tew, Mary
DOUGLAS, Norman and
  FITZGIBBON, Elsa
  Normyx
DOUGLASS, Percival Ian
  Bear, I D
  Crane, Henry
DOWNEY, Edmund
  Allen, F M
DRACKETT, Phil
  King, Paul
DRAGO, Harry Sinclair
  Ermine, Will
  Lomax, Bliss
DRESSER, Davis
  Halliday, Brett
DRESSER, Davis and
  ROLLINS, Kathleen
  Debrett, Hal
DREW, Jane B
  Fry, Jane
DRIVER, Christopher
  Archestratus
DRUMMOND, Alison
  Schaw, Ruth
DRUMMOND, Cherry
  Evans, Cherry
DRUMMOND, Edith
  Carman, Dulce
DRUMMOND, Humphrey
  Ap Evans, Humphrey
DU BOIS, Theodora
  McCormick, Theodora

DUDDINGTON, Charles Lionel
  Campbell, Berkeley
  Nightingale, Charles
DUDLEY-SMITH, Trevor
  Black, Mansell
  Fitzalan, Roger
  Hall, Adam
  North, Howard
  Rattray, Simon
  Scott, Warwick
  Trevor, Elleston
DUFF, Douglas Valder
  Mainsail
  Savage, Leslie
  Stanhope, Douglas
  Wickloe, Peter
DUFFIELD, Dorothy Dean
  Duffield, Anne
DUFFY, Agnes Mary
  Vox, Agnes Mary
DUGGAN, Denise Valerie
  Egerton, Denise
DUGGLEBY, Jean Colbeck
  Kennedy, Diana
DUKE, Anita
  Hewett, Anita
DUKE, Madelaine
  Duncan, Alex
DUKENFIELD, William Claude
  Bogle, Charles
  Criblecoblis, Otis
  Fields, W C
  Jeeves, Mahatma Kane
DUNCAN, Actea
  Thomas, Carolyn
DUNCAN, Kathleen
  Simmons, Catherine
  Simmons, Kim
DUNCAN, Robert Lipscomb
  Roberts, James Hall
DUNCAN, William Murdoch
  Cassells, John
  Dallas, John
  Graham, Neill

  Malloch, Peter
  Marshall, Lovat
DUNK, Margaret
  Duke, Margaret
DUNKERLEY, Elsie Jeanette
  Oxenham, Elise Jeanette
DUNKERLEY, William Arthur
  Oxenham, John
DUNLOP, Agnes M R
  Kyle, Elisabeth
  Ralston, Jan
DUNN, Mary
  Faid, Mary
DUNNETT, Dorothy
  Halliday, Dorothy
DUNSING, Dee
  Mowery, Dorothy
DURBRIDGE, Francis and
  MC CONNELL, James
  Douglas Rutherford
  Temple, Paul
DURGNAT, Paymond
  Green, O O
DURRELL, Lawrence
  Norden, Charles
DURST, Paul
  Bannon, Peter
  Chelton, John
  Cochran, Jeff
  Shane, John

EADE, Charles and BLOOM,
  Ursula Harvey
  Prole, Lozani
EAGLESTONE, Arthur Archibald
  Dataller, Roger
EAMES, Helen Mary
  Mercury
EARNSHAW, Patricia
  Mann, Patricia
EASTWOOD, Helen
  Baxter, Olive
  Ramsay, Fay
EBBETT, Eve
  Burfield, Eva

EBBS, Robert
 Pitchford, Harry Ronald
 Severn, Richard
EDGAR, Alfred
 Lyndon, Barrie
EDGLEY, Leslie
 Bloomfield, Robert
EDMISTON, Helen J M
 Robertson, Helen
EDMONDS, Helen
 Kavan, Anna
EDMONDSON, Sybil
 Armstrong, Sybil
EDMUNDSON, Joseph
 Burton, Conrad
 Jody, J M
EDWARD, Ann
 West, Anna
EDWARD, Irene
 Barr, Elisabeth
EDWARDS, Florence
 Edwards, Laurence
 Jolly, Susan
EDWARDS, Frederick Anthony
 Edwards, Charman
 Van Dyke, J
EDWARDS, George Graveley
 Graveley, George
EHRENBORG, (Mrs) C G
 Trew, Cecil G
EHRLICH, Bettina
 Bettina
EISENSTADT-JELEZNOV,
 Mikhail
 Argus, M K
ELDERSHAW, Flora Sydney and
 BARNARD, Marjorie Faith
 Eldershaw, M Barnard
ELGIN, Betty
 Kirby, Kate
ELIADES, David and WEBB,
 Robert Forrest
 Forrest, David
ELLERMAN, Annie Winifred
 Bryher

ELLIOTT-CANNON, Arthur
 Elliott
 Cannon, Elliott
 Forde, Nicholas
 Martyn, Miles
ELLIS, Oliver
 Briony, Henry
ELLISON, Joan
 Robertson, Elspeth
ELWART, Joan Frances
 Elwart, Joan Potter
 Trawle, Mary Elizabeth
ELY, George Herbert and
 L'ESTRANGE, C James
 Strang, Herbert
EMMS, Dorothy
 Charques, Dorothy
ENGEL, Lyle Kenyon
 Kenyon, Larry
ENGLISH, Jean Ellen
 French, Ellen Jean
EPSTEIN, Beryl
 Williams, Beryl
EPSTEIN, Samuel
 Campbell, Bruce
ESCHERLICH, Elsa Antoine
 Falk, Elsa
EVANS, Constance May
 Gray, Jane
 O'Nair, Mairi
EVANS, George
 Geraint, George
EVANS, Gwynfil Arthur
 Gwynne, Arthur
 Western, Barry
EVANS, Hilary Agard
 Agard, H E
EVANS, Jean
 Shaw, Jane
EVANS, Julia
 Hobson, Polly
EVANS, Kathleen
 Kaye, Evelyn
EVANS, Kay and EVANS, Stuart
 Tracey, Hugh

33

EVANS, Marguerite Florence
  Barcynska, Hélène (Countess)
  Sandys, Oliver
EVANS, Stuart and EVANS, Kay
  Tracey, Hugh
EVELYN, John Michael
  Underwood, Michael
EVENS, George Bramwell
  Romany
EWART, Ernest Andrew
  Cable, Boyd
EYLES, Kathleen Muriel
  Tennant, Catherine
EYSSELINCK, Janet Gay
  Burroway, Janet

FABRY, Joseph B
  Fabrizius, Peter
FADIMAN, Edwin J
  Mark, Edwina
FAIRBAIRN, R H
  R H F
FAIRBURN, Eleanor
  Carfax, Catherine
FAIRCHILD, William
  Cranston, Edward
FAIRLIE, Gerard
  Sapper
FALK, Katherine and others
  Heptagon
FALK, Millicent and others
  Heptagon
FALLA, Frank
  Sarnian
FARGUS, Frederick John
  Conway, Hugh
FARJEON, Eve
  Jefferson, Sarah
FARMERS, Eileen
  Lane, Elizabeth
FARRELL, Anne Elisabeth
  Allaben, Anne E
FARRIS, John Lee
  Bracken, Steve

FARROW, R
  Vincent, John
FAST, Howard
  Cunningham, E V
FAUST, Frederick
  Austin, Frank
  Baxter, George Owen
  Bolt, Lee
  Brand, Max
  Butler, Walter C
  Challis, George
  Dawson, Peter
  Dexter, Martin
  Evan, Evin
  Evans, Evan
  Frederick, John
  Frost, Frederick
  Lawton, Dennis
  M B
  Manning, David
  Morland, Peter Henry
  Owen, Hugh
  Silver, Nicholas
  Uriel, Henry
FAY, Judith
  Nicholson, Kate
FEAR, William H
  Reynolds, John
FEARSON, Percy
  Poy
FEEHAN, (Sister) Mary Edward
  Clementia
FEILDING, Dorothy
  Fielding, A
FEIWEL, Raphael Joseph
  Fyvel, T R
FELDMAN, Eugene P R
  Burroughs, Margaret
FELLOWES-GORDON, Ian
  Collier, Douglas
  Gordon, Ian
FELLOWS, Dorothy Alice
  Collyer, Doric
  Hunt, Dorothy

FELSTEIN, Ivor
  Steen, Frank
FELTON, Ronald Oliver
  Welch, Ronald
FENN, George Manville
  Manville, George
FENWICK-OWEN, Roderic
  Owen, Roderic
FERGUSSON HANNAY, (Lady)
  Leslie, Doris
FERGUSON, Marilyn
  Renzelman, Marilyn
FERNEYHOUGH, Roger
 Edmund
  Hart, R W
FETHERSTONHAUGH,
 Patrick William Edward
  Fetherston, Patrick
FETTER, Elizabeth Head
  Lees, Hannah
FEW, Eunice Beatty
  Few, Betty
FICKLING, Forrest E and
 FICKLING, Gloria
  Fickling, G G
FIELD, M J
  Freshfield, Mark
FIELDING, Alexander
  Fielding, Xan
FINK, Merton
  Finch, Matthew
  Finch, Merton
FINKEL, George
  Pennage, E M
FINLAY, Ian
  Philaticus
FINN, (Sister) Mary Paulina
  Pine, M S
FINNEY, Jack
  Braden, Walter
FINNIN, Mary
  Hogarth
FIRTH, Violet Mary
  Fortune, Dion

FISH, Robert L
  Pike, Robert L
FISHER, Dorothea F C
  Canfield, Dorothy
FISHER, Douglas George
  Douglas, George
FISHER, John
  Piper, Roger
FISHER, Veronica Suzanne
  Veronique
FITCHETT, W H
  Vedette
FITZGERALD, Beryl
  Hoffman, Louise
FITZ-GERALD, S J A
  Hannaford, Justin
FITZGIBBON, Elsa and
 DOUGLAS, Norman
  Normyx
FITZHARDINGE, Joan Margaret
  Phipson, Joan
FLANAGAN, Ellen
  Raskin, Ellen
FLANNER, Janet
  Genêt
FLEISCHER, Anthony
  Hofmeyer, Hans
FLETCHER, Constance
  Fleming, George
FLETCHER, Harry L Verne
  Fletcher, John
  Garden, John
  Hereford, John
FLEXNER, Stuart
  Fletcher, Adam
FLOREN, Lee
  Austin, Brett
  Franchon, Lisa
  Hall, Claudia
  Harding, Matt
  Lang, Grace
  Nelson, Marguerite
  Sterling, Maria Sandra
  Thomas, Lee

Turner, Len
Watson, Will
FLUHARTY, Vernon L
Carder, Michael
O'Mara, Jim
FLYNN, (Sir) J A
Oliver, Owen
FLYNN, Mary
Livingstone, Margaret
FOCKE, E P W
Ernest, Paul
FOLSOM, Franklin Brewster
Brester, Benjamin
Gorham, Michael
Nesbit, Troy
FOOT, Michael
Cassius
FOOT, Michael; HOWARD,
 Peter and OWEN, Frank
Cato
FOOTE, Carol
Odell, Carol
FOOTE, Carol and GILL, Traviss
Odell, Gill
FORBES, Stanton
Wells, Tobias
FORD, Corey
Riddell, John
FORD, T Murray
Le Breton, Thomas
FORD, T W
Clay, Weston
Shott, Abel
FORDE, Claude Marie
Claude
FOSTER, Donn
Saint-Eden, Dennis
FOSTER, George Cecil
Seaforth
FOSTER, Jess Mary Mardon
White, Heather
FOULDS, Elfrida Vipont
Vipont, Charles
Vipont, Elfrida

FOWKES, Aubrey
Boy
FOWLER, Eric
Mardle, Jonathan
FOWLER, Helen
Foley, Helen
FOWLER, H W
Egomet
Quilibet
Quillet
FOWLER, Kenneth A
Brooker, Clark
FOX, Charles
Jeremy, Richard
FOX, James
Holmes, Grant
FOX, Mona Alexis
Brand, Mona
FOX, Winifred and others
Heptagon
FOXALL, P A
Vincent, Jim
FRAENKEL, Heinrich
Assiac
FRANCE-HAYHURST,
 Evangeline
France, Evangeline
FRANCIS, Arthur Bruce
Charles
Bruce, Charles
FRANCIS, Stephen D
Williams, Richard
FRANCK, Frederick S
Fredericks, Frank
FRANKLIN, Cynthia
Neville, C J
FRANKLIN, Stella Maria Sarah
Miles
Brent, (of Bin Bin)
FRASER-HARRIS, D
Grange, Ellerton
FRAZER, James Ian Arbuthnot
Frazer, Shamus

FREDE, Richard
   Frederics, Jocko
   Macdowell, Frederics
FREEGOOD, Morton
   Godey, John
FREELING, Nicolas
   Nicholas, F R E
FREEMAN, Kathleen
   Cory, Caroline
   Fitt, Mary
FRENCH, Alice
   Thanet, Octave
FREWER, Glyn
   Lewis, Mervyn
FREY, Charles Weiser
   Findley, Ferguson
FRIEDBERG, Gertrude
   Tonkongy, Gertrude
FRIEDLANDER, Peter
   French, Fergus
FRIEDMAN, Eve Rosemary
   Tibber, Robert
   Tibber, Rosemary
FRIEND, Oscar Jerome
   Jerome, Owen Fox
FRY, Clodagh Micaela Gibson
   Gavin, Amanda
FTYARAS, Louis George
   Alexander, L G
FULLBROOK, Gladys
   Hutchinson, Patricia
FULLER, Harold Edgar
   Fuller, Ed
   Fulman, Al
FULLER, Henry B
   Page, Stanton
FULLER, James Franklin
   Ignotus
FURLONG, Vivienne
   Welburn, Vivienne
FYTTON-ARMSTRONG, T I
   Gawsworth, John

GAINES, Robert
   Summerscales, Rowland
GALSWORTHY, John
   Sinjohn, John
GANDLEY, Kenneth Royce
   Jacks, Oliver
   Royce, Kenneth
GANTNER, Neilma B
   Sidney, Neilma
GARBER, Nellia B
   Berg, Ila
GARD, Joyce
   Reeves, Joyce
GARDINER, Alfred George
   Alpha of the plough
GARDNER, Erle Stanley
   Fair, A A
   Green, Charles M
   Kendrake, Carleton
   Kenny, Charles J
GARDNER, Jerome
   Gilchrist, John
GARGILL, Morris and HEARNE,
 John
   Morris, John
GARNETT, David S
   Lee, David
GARRATT, Alfred
   Garratt, Teddie
GARRETT, Winifred Selina
   Dean, Lyn
GARROD, John William and
 PAYNE, Ronald Charles
   Castle, John
GARVEY, Eric William
   Herne, Eric
GARVIN, J L
   Calehas
GARWOOD, Godfrey Thomas
   Thomas, Gough

> What are names but air?
> — Coleridge

GASE, Richard
  GALE, John
GASPAROTTI, Elizabeth
  Seifert, Elizabeth
GASTON, William J
  Bannatyne, Jack
GAUNT, Arthur N
  Nettleton, Arthur
GEEN, Clifford
  Berkley, Tom
GEISEL, Theodor Seuss
  Dr Seuss
  Lesieg, Theo
GELB, Norman
  Mallery, Amos
GEORGE, Robert Esmonde
  Gordon
  Sencourt, Robert
GERAHTY, Digby George
  Standish, Robert
GERMANO, Peter
  Cord, Barry
  Kane, Jim
GERSHON, Karen
  Tripp, Karen
GERSON, Noel Bertram
  Edwards, Samuel
  Vail, Philip
  Vaughan, Carter
GESSNER, Lynne
  Clarke, Merle
GIBBS, Norah
  Boyd, Prudence
  Garland, Lisette
  Ireland, Noelle
  Merrill, Lynne
  Ritchie, Claire
  Shayne, Nina
  Wayne, Heather
  Whittingham, Sara
GIFFORD, James Noble
  Noble, Emily
  Saxon, John
GILBERT, Ruth
  Ainsworth, Ruth

GILBERT, William Schwenck
  Bab
  Tomline, F Latour
GILBERTSON, Mildred
  Gilbert, Nan
  Mendel, Jo
GILCHRIST, Alan
  Cowan, Alan
GILDEN, Katya and GILDEN,
  Bert
  Gilden, K B
GILDERDALE, Michael
  Flemming, Sarah
GILL, Winifred and others
  Heptagon
GILLHAM, Elizabeth Wright
  Enright
  Enright, Elizabeth
GILMER, Elizabeth Meriwether
  Dix, Dorothy
GILZEAN, Elizabeth Houghton
  Houghton, Elizabeth
  Hunton, Mary
GIRDLESTON, A H
  A H G
GITTINGS, Jo
  Manton, Jo
GLASKIN, G M
  Jackson, Neville
GLASSCO, John
  Colman, George
  Okada, Hideki
  Underwood, Miles
GLEADOW, Rupert
  Case, Justin
GLEN, Duncan Munro
  Munro, Ronald Eadie
GLENTON, Stella Lennox
  King, Stella
GLIDDEN, Frederick Dilley
  Short, Luke

GLIDDEN, Jonathan H
  Dawson, Peter
GLOVER, Modwena
  Sedgwick, Modwena
GOAMAN, Muriel
  Cox, Edith
GODFREY, Frederick M
  Cronheim, F G
GODFREY, Lionel Robert
 Holcombe
  Kennedy, Elliott
  Mitchell, Scott
GOGGAN, John Patrick
  Patrick, John
GOHM, Douglas Charles
  O'Connell, Robert Frank
GOLBERG, Harry
  Grey, Harry
GOLDEN, Dorothy
  Dennison, Dorothy
GOLDIE, Kathleen Annie
  Fidler, Kathleen
GOLDING, Louise
  Davies, Louise
GOLDMAN, William
  Longbaugh, Harry
GOLDSTON, Robert
  Conroy, Robert
GOLLER, Celia Margaret
  Fremlin, Celia
GOLSWORTHY, Arnold
  Holcombe, Arnold
  Jingle
GOMPERTZ, Martin Louis Alan
  Ganpat
GOOD, Edward
  Oyved, Moysheh
GOODAVAGE, Joseph F
  Greystone, Alexander A
  Savage, Steve
GOODCHILD, George
  Dare, Alan
  Templeton, Jesse
GOODEY, P E
  Condon, Patricia

GOODMAN, George Jerome and
 KNOWLTON, Winthrop
  Goodman, Winthrop
GOODWIN, Geoffrey
  Gemini
  Telstar
  Topicus
GOODYEAR, Stephen Frederick
  Taylor, Sam
GORDON, Alan Bacchus
  Ordon, A Lang
GORDON, Charles William
  Connor, Ralph
GORDON, Jan
  Gore, William
GOSLING, Veronica
  Henriques, Veronica
GOSSMAN, Oliver
  Clyde, Craig
GOTTLIEBSEN, Ralph J
  Scott, O R
GOTTSCHALK, Laura Riding
  Riding, Laura
GOVAN, Mary Christine
  Allerton, Mary
  Darby, J N
GOWING, Sidney Floyd
  Goodwin, John
GOYDER, Margot and JOSKE,
 Neville
  Neville, Margot
GRABER, George Alexander
  Cordell, Alexander
GRAHAM, Charles
  Montrose, David
GRAHAM, James Maxtone
  Anstruther, James
GRANT, Donald and WILSON,
 William
  Ness, K T
GRANT, Hilda Kay
  Grant, Kay
  Hilliard, Jan
GRANT, M H
  Linesman

GRANT, (Lady) Sybil
  Scot, Neil
GRAVES, Clotilda Inez Mary
  Dehan, Richard
GRAY, Dorothy K
  Haynes, Dorothy K
GRAY, K E
  Grant, Eve
GRAY, Simon
  Reade, Hamish
GRAYDON, William Murray
  Gordon, William Murray
  Murray, William
GRAYLAND, Valerie M
  Belvedere, Lee
  Subond, Valerie
GREALEY, Tom
  Southworth, Louis
GREAVES, Michael
  Callum, Michael
GREEN, Alan Baer and BRODIE,
  Julian Paul
  Denbie, Roger
GREEN, Dorothy
  Auchterlonie, Dorothy
GREEN, Elisabeth Sara
  Tresilian, Liz
GREEN, Evelyn Everett
  Adair, Cecil
GREEN, Lalage Isobel
  March, Hilary
  Pulvertaft, Lalage
GREEN, Maxwell
  Cabby with camera
GREEN, Peter
  Delaney, Denis
GREEN, T
  Ramsey, Michael
GREENAWAY, Gladys
  Manners, Julia
GREENE, Sigrid
  De Lima, Sigrid
GREENHILL, Elizabeth Ann
  Giffard, Ann

GREENLAND, W K
  King, W Scott
GREENWOOD, Augustus George
  Archer, Owen
GREENWOOD, Julia E C
  Askham, Francis
GREENWOOD, T E
  McCabe, Rory
GREGG, Hilda
  Grier, Sydney C
GREIG, Maysie
  Ames, Jennifer
  Barclay, Ann
  Warre, Mary D
GRIBBEN, James
  James, Vincent
GRIBBLE, Leonard Reginald
  Cody, Stetson
  Denver, Lee
  Grant, Landon
  Grex, Leo
  Grey, Louis
  Marlowe, Piers
  Muir, Dexter
  Sanders, Bruce
GRIERSON, Walter
  Enquiring Layman
GRIEVE, Christopher Murray
  MacDiarmid, Hugh
GRIEVESON, Mildred
  Flemming, Cardine
  Mather, Anne
GRIFFIN, Jonathan
  Thurlow, Robert
GRIFFITHS, Aileen Esther
  Passmore, Aileen E
GRIFFIN, Vivian Cory
  Crosse, Victoria
GRIFFITHS, Charles
  Bold, Ralph
GRIFFITHS, Jack
  Griffith, Jack
GRIMSTEAD, Hettie
  Manning, Marsha

GRINDAL, Richard
  Grayson, Richard
GUARIENTO, Ronald
  Parks, Ron
GUEST, Enid
  Quin, Shirland
GUGGISBERG, (Sir) F G
  Ubique
GUIGO, Ernest Philip
  Holt, E Carleton
GUINNESS, Maurice
  Brewer, Mike
  Gale, Newton
GUIRDHAM, Arthur
  Eaglesfield, Francis
GULICK, Grover C
  Gulick, Bill
GUTHRIE, Thomas Anstey
  Anstey, F
GUYONVARCH, Irene
  Pearl, Irene
GWINN, Christine
  Kelway, Christine
GWYNN, Audrey
  Thomson, Audrey
GWYNN, Ursula Grace
  Leigh, Ursula
GYE, Harold Frederick Neville
  Gye, Hal
  Hackston, James

HAARER, Alec Ernest
  Shanwa
HADFIELD, Alan
  Dale, Robin
HAGAN, Stelia F
  Hawkins, John
HALDANE, Robert Aylmer
  Square, Charlotte
HALE, Kathleen
  McClean, Kathleen
HALE, Sylvia
  Barnard, Nancy
HALEY, W J
  Sell, Joseph

HALL, Emma L
  St Claire, Yvonne
HALL, Frederick
  Hall, Patrick
HALL, Irene
  Gough, Irene
HALL, Marie
  Boas, Marie
HALL, Oakley Maxwell
  Manor, Jason
HAMILTON, Alex
  Pooter
HAMILTON, Cecily
  Hamilton, Max
  Rae, Scott
HAMILTON, Charles Harold
 St John
  Clifford, Martin
  Conquest, Owen
  Redway, Ralph
  Richards, Frank
  Richards, Hilda
HAMILTON, Leigh Brackett
  Brackett, Leigh
HAMILTON, Mary Margaret Kaye
  Kaye, Mary Margaret
HAMILTON-WILKES, Edwin
  Hamilton-Wilkes, Monty
  Uncle Monty
HAMMETT, Dashiell
  Collinson, Peter
HAMMOND, Lawrence
  Francis, Victor
HAMMOND-INNES, Ralph
  Hammond, Ralph
  Innes, Hammond
HAMON, Louis (Count)
  Cheiro
HAMPDEN, John
  Montagu, Robert
HANKINSON, Charles J
  Holland, Clive
HANLEY, Clifford
  Calvin, Henry

41

HANLEY, James
  Bentley, James
  Shone, Patric
HANNA, Frances
  Nichols, Fan
HANNAY, James Owen
  Birmingham, George A
HARBAGE, Alfred
  Kyd, Thomas
HARBAUGH, Thomas Chalmers
  Holmes, (Captain) Howard
HARDINGE, George
  Milner, George
HARDINGE, Rex
  Capstan
HARDISON, O B
  Bennett, H O
HARDWICK, Richard
  Holmes, Rick
  Honeycutt, Richard
HARDY, Jane
  Boileau, Marie
HARDY, Marjorie
  Hardy, Bobbie
HARE, Walter B
  Burns, Mary
HARKINS, Peter
  Adams, Andy
HARLAND, Henry
  Luska, Sidney
HARPER, Edith
  Flamank, E
HARRELL, Irene Burk
  Amor, Amos
  Waylan, Mildred
HARRIS, Ida Fraser
  Proctor, Ida
HARRIS, John
  Hebden, Mark
HARRIS, John Beynon
  Wyndham, John
HARRIS, Marion Rose
  Young, Rose
HARRIS, Pamela
  Meinikoff, Pamela

HARRIS, William
  Harris, Peter
HARRISON, Chester William
  Hickok, Will
HARRISON, Elizabeth C
  Cavanna, Betty
  Headley, Elizabeth
HARRISON, John Gilbert
  Gilbert, John
HARRISON, Michael
  Downes, Quentin
HARRISON, Philip
  Carmichael, Philip
HARRISON, Richard Motte
  Motte, Peter
HART, Caroline Horowitz
  Winters, Mary K
HARTIGAN, Patrick Joseph
  O'Brien, John
HARTLEY, Ellen R
  Raphael, Ellen
HARTMANN, Helmut Henry
  Seymour, Henry
HARVEY, Charles
  Willoughby, Hugh
HARTHOORN, Susanne
  Hart, Susanne
HARVEY, Peter Noel
  Day, Adrian
  Peters, Noel
HARVEY, William
  Denovan, Saunders
HASSON, James
  De Salignac, Charles
HASWELL, C J D
  Foster, George
  Haswell, Jock
HAUCK, Louise Platt
  Landon, Louise
HAWKINS, (Sir) Anthony Hope
  A H
  Hope, Anthony
HAWTON, Hector
  Curzon, Virginia

42

HAYNES, John Harold
    Wake, G B
HAYNES DIXON, Margaret Rumer
    Godden, Rumer
HAZLEWOOD, Rex
    Delta
    Keneu
HEADLEY, Elizabeth
    Allen, Betsy
HEAL, Edith
    Page, Eileen
    Powers, Margaret
HEARD, Henry Fitzgerald
    Heard, Gerald
HEARNE, John and GARGILL,
    Morris
    Morris, John
HEAVEN, Constance
    Fecher, Constance
HEBERDEN, Mary Violet
    Leonard, Charles L
HECTOR, Barbara
    Barrie, Hester
HEELIS, Beatrix
    Potter, Beatrix
HEINEY, Donald William
    Harris, Macdonald
HEINLEIN, Robert A
    Macdonald, Anson
HEISS, John Stanger
    Asche, Oscar
HEMING, Dempster E
    Dempster, Guy
HEMING, Jack C W
    Western-Holt, J C
HENDERSON, Donald Landels
    Bridgwater, Donald
    Landels, D H
    Landels, Stephanie
HENDERSON, Le Grand
    Le Grand
HENDRY, Frank Coutts
    Shalimar
HENHAM, E J
    Trevena, John

HENKLE, Henrietta
    Buckmaster, Henrietta
HENLEY, Art
    Eric, Kenneth
    Jones, Webb
HEPBURN, Thomas Nicoll
    Setoun, Gabriel
HEPPELL, Mary
    Clare, Marguerite
    Heppell, Blanche
HERBERT, (Sir) Alan P
    A P H
HERBERT, John
    Simple, Peter
HERN, Anthony
    Hope, Andrew
HERTZBERG, Nancy
    Keesing, Nancy
HETHERINGTON, Keith James
    Conway, Keith
    Keith, James
HEWITT, Cecil Rolph
    Rolph, C H
HEWSON, Irene Dale
    Ross, Jean
HIBBERT, Eleanor Alice Burford
    Burford, Eleanor
    Carr, Philippa
    Ford, Elbur
    Holt, Victoria
    Kellow, Kathleen
    Plaidy, Jean
    Tate, Ellalice
HIBBS, John
    Blyth, John
HICKEN, Una
    Kindler, Asta
HICKEY, Madelyn E
    De Lacy, Louise
    Eastlund, Madelyn
    Hickey, Lyn
    Sullivan, Eric Harrison
HIGGINBOTHAM, Anne D
    Higginbotham, Anne T
    McIntosh, Ann T

HIGGINS, Charles
   Dall, Ian
HIGGINS, Margaret
   O'Brien, Bernadette
HIGGINSON, Henry Clive
   Theta, Eric Mark
HIGGS, Alec S
   Stansbury, Alec
HILL, Brian
   Magill, Marcus
HILL, Douglas
   Hillman, Martin
HILL, John Alexander
   Skeever, Jim
HILLS, Frances E
   Mercer, Frances
HILLYARD, Mary Dorothea
   Kellway, Mary D
HILTON, James
   Trevor, Glen
HILTON, John Buxton
   Stanley, Warwick
HINCKS, Cyril Malcolm
   Coulsdon, John
   Dayle, Malcolm
   Gee, Osman
   Howard, John M
   Malcolm, Charles
HINES, Dorothea
   De Culwen, Dorothea
HIRD, Neville
   Meyer, Henry J
HIRST, Gillian
   Baxter, Gillian
HISCOCK, Eric
   E H
   Whitefriar
HITCHENS, Dolores
   Olsen, D B
HITCHIN, Martin
   Mewburn, Martin
HOAR, Peter
   Amberley, Simon
HOBSBAWM, E J
   Newton, Francis

HODDER-WILLIAMS,
  Christopher
   Brogan, James
HODGE, Horace Emerton
   Hodge, Merton
HODGES, Barbara
   Cambridge, Elizabeth
HODGES, Doris Marjorie
   Hunt, Charlotte
HOFDORP, Pim
   Geerlink, Will
HOFF, Harry Summerfield
   Cooper, William
HOFFMAN, Anita
   Fettsman, Ann
HOGAN, Ray
   Ringold, Clay
HOGARTH, Grace
   Gay, Amelia
HOGBIN, Herbert
   Hogbin, Ian
HOGG, Michael
   Simple, Peter
HOGUE, Wilbur Owings
   Shannon, Carl
HOLBECHE, Philippa
   Shore, Philippa
HOLDAWAY, Neville Aldridge
   Temple-Ellis, N A
HOLDEN J R
   Joystick
HOLDEN, Raymond
   Peckham, Richard
HOLLIDAY, Joseph
   Bosco, Jack
   Dale, Jack
HOLMES, Llewellyn Perry
   Stuart, Matt
HOLMES, Peter
   Fenwick, Peter
HOLMSTROM, John Eric
   Gellert, Roger
HOLROYD, Ethel Mary
   Cookridge, John Michael
   Marshall, Beverley

HOME-GALL, Edward Reginald
  Clive, Clifford
  Dale, Edwin
  Hall, Rupert
  Home-Gall, Reginald
HOOK, Alfred Samuel
  Colton, A J
HOOK, H Clarke
  Harvey, Ross
HOPE, Charles Evelyn Graham
  Pelham, Anthony
HOPP, Signe
  Zinken
HOPSON, William L
  Sims, John
HORLER, Sydney
  Cavendish, Peter
  Heritage, Martin
  Standish, J O
HORNBY, John W
  Brent, Calvin
  Grace, Joseph
  Summers, Gordon
HORNE, Geoffrey
  North, Gil
HOSIE, Stanley William
  Stanley, Michael
HOSKEN, Alice Cecil Seymour
  Stanton, Coralie
HOSKEN, Clifford James
 Wheeler
  Keverne, Richard
HOUGH, Richard
  Carter, Bruce
HOUGH, Stanley Bennett
  Gordon, Rex
  Stanley, Bennett
HOUNSFIELD, Joan
  Wheezy
HOUSEMAN, Lorna
  Westall, Lorna
HOVICK, Rose Louise
  Lee, Gypsy Rose
HOWARD, Felicity
  Longfield, Jo

HOWARD, Herbert Edmund
  Philmore, R
HOWARD, Munroe
  St Clair, Philip
HOWARD, Peter; FOOT, Michael
 and OWEN, Frank
  Cato
HOWARTH, Patrick John Fielding
  Francis, C D E
HOWE, Doris
  Munro, Mary
  Nash, Newlyn
HOWELL, Douglas Nayler
  Hancock, Robert
HOWITT, John Leslie Despard
  Despard, Leslie
HOYT, Edwin Palmer Jr
  Martin, Christopher
HUBBARD, L Ron
  Elron
  Esterbrook, Tom
  La Fayette, Rene
  Northrop, (Capt) B A
  Rachen, Kurt von
HUDSON, H Lindsay
  Lindsay, H
HUEFFER, Ford Madox
  Ford, Ford Madox
HUFF, Darrell
  Hough, Don
  Nelson, Chris
  West, Mark
HUGGETT, Berthe
  Brook, Esther
HUGHES, Ivy
  Hay, Catherine
HUGHES, Valerie Anne
  Carrington, V
HUGHES, Walter Dudley
  Derventio
HUGHES, Walter Llewellyn
  Walters, Hugh
HUGHES, William
  Northerner

HUGILL, John Anthony
  Crawford
  Crawford, Anthony
HUGILL, Robert
  Gill, Hugh
HULBERT, Joan
  Rostron, Primrose
HULL, Richard
  Sampson, Richard Henry
HUMPHREYS, Eliza M J
  Rita
HUMPHRIES, Elsie Mary
  Forrester, Mary
HUMPHRIES, Sydney
  Vane, Michael
HUMPHRYS, Leslie George
  Condray, Bruno
  Humphrys, Geoffrey
HUNT, E Howard
  Baxter, John
  Davis, Gordon
  Dietrich, Robert
  St John, David
HUNT-BODE, Gisele
  Hunt, Diana
HUNTER, Alfred John
  Brenning, L H
  Drummond, Anthony
  Hunter, Jean
  Hunter, Joan
HUNTER, Bluebell Matilda
  Guildford, John
HUNTER, Christine
  Hunter, John
  Steer, Charlotte
HUNTER, Eileen
  Clements, E H
  Laura
HUNTER, Elizabeth
  Chace, Isobel
HUNTER, Evan
  Collins, Hunt
  McBain, Ed
  Marsten, Richard

HURREN, Bernard
  Nott, Barry
HURWOOD, Barnhardt J
  Knight, Mallory
HUTCHINSON, Barbara Beatrice
  Fearn, Roberta
HUSKINSON, Richard King
  King, Richard
HUTCHINSON, Juliet Mary
  Phoenice, J
HUTCHINSON, Robert Hare
  Hare, Robert
HUTCHISON, Graham Seton
  Seton, Graham
HUTTON, Andrew Nielson
  Olympic
HUXLEY, Julian Sorell
  Balbus
HUXTABLE, Marjorie
  Dare, Simon
  Stewart, Marjorie
HYDE, Edmund Errol Claude
  Rejje, E
HYDE, Lavender Beryl
  Ashe, Elizabeth
HYMERS, Laura M
  West, Laura M

IBBOTT, Arthur Pearson
  Bertram, Arthur
IDELL, Albert Edward
  Rogers, Phillips
INGAMELLS, F G
  Home Guard
IRISH, Betty M
  Arthur, Elisabeth
  Bell, Nancy
IRWIN, Constance
  Frick, C H
IVISON, Elizabeth
  Towers, Tricia
  Wilson, Elizabeth

JACOB, Piers Anthony
   Anthony, Piers
JACOBS, Charles
   Humana, Charles
JACOBS, Helen Hull
   Hull, H Braxton
JACOBS, Thomas Curtis Hicks
   Carstairs, Kathleen
   Curtis, Tom
   Dower, Penn
   Howard, Helen
   Pender, Marilyn
   Pendower, Jacques
   Penn, Ann
JACOT DE BOLNOD, B L
   Jacot, Bernard
JAFFE, Gabriel
   Poole, Vivian
JAMES, Charles
   Coronet
JAMES, Godfrey Warden
   Broome, Adam
JAMES, J G W
   Norham, Gerald
JAMESON, Annie Edith
   Buckrose, J E
JAMIESON, Kathleen Florence
   Janes, Kathleen F
JANNER, Greville
   Mitchell, Ewan
JAQUES, Edward Tyrrell
   Tearle, Christian
JAY, Marion
   Spalding, Lucille
JEFFERIES, Greg
   Collins, Geoffrey
JEFFERIES, Ira
   Morris, Ira J
JEFFERY, Graham
   Brother Graham
JEFFREY-SMITH, May
   Aunt Maysie
   Thornton, Maimee

JEFFRIES, Graham Montague
   Bourne, Peter
   Graeme, Bruce
   Graeme, David
JEFFRIES, Roderic Graeme
   Ashford, Jeffrey
   Graeme, Roderic
JELLY, Oliver
   Fosse, Alfred
JENKINS, Alan Charles
   Bancroft, John
JENKINS, Sara Lucile
   Sargent, Joan
JENKINS, William Fitzgerald
   Leinster, Murray
JENNINGS, E C
   Jay
JENNINGS, Hilda and others
   Heptagon
JENNINGS, John
   Baldwin, Bates
JEROME, Owen Fox
   Friend, Oscar Jerome
JERVIS, Vera Murdock Stuart
   England, Jane
JOHN, Owen
   Bourne, John
JOHNSON, Annabel I and
 JOHNSON, Edgar R
   Johnson, A E
JOHNSON, H
   Robertson, Muirhead
JOHNSON, Henry T
   Thomson, Neil
JOHNSON, Lilian Beatrice
   Johnson, Lee
JOHNSON, Marion
   Masson, Georgina

> Sam Johnson is hardly a
> name for a great writer.
> — George Bernard Shaw

JOHNSON, Nancy Marr
  Marr, Nancy J
JOHNSON, Victor
  Bell, John
JOHNSTON, George Henry
  Shane, Martin
JOHNSTON, Robert Thomson
  Forsyth, R A
JONES, A Miles
  Bullingham, Ann
JONES, Frank H
  Mentor
JONES, Harry Austin
  Jons, Hal
JONES, Jack
  Reynolds, Jack
JONES, (Lady) Roderick
  Bagnold, Enid
JONES, Le Roi
  Baraka, Imamu Amiri
JONES, P D
  Denham, Peter
JONES, Robert Maynard
  Jones, Bobi
  Probert, Lowri
  Siôn, Mari
JORDAN, June
  Meyer, June
JOSCELYN, Archie Lynn
  Cody, A R
  Cody, Al
  Westland, Lynn
JOSKE, Neville and GOYDER, Margot
  Neville, Margot
JUDD, Frederick
  Lester-Rands, A

KAGEY, Rudolf
  Steel, Kurt
KAHN, H S
  Sackerman, Henry
KALISCH, A
  Crescendo

KAMPF, Harold Bertram
  Kaye, Harold B
KANE, Henry
  McCall, Anthony
KANTO, Peter
  Dexter, John
  Gorman, Ginny
  Hughes, Valerina
  Hughes, Zach
  Pilgrim, Derral
  Rangely, E R
  Rangely, Olivia
  Van Heller, Marcus
KAPLAN, Jean Caryl
  Caryl, Jean
KAPP, Yvonne
  Cloud, Yvonne
KATCHAMAKOFF, Atanas
  Shannon, Monica
KATSIN, Olga
  Sagittarius
KAY, Ernest
  Ludlow, George
  Random, Alan
KAY, Frederic George
  Gee, Kenneth F
  Howard, George
KAYE, Barrington
  Kaye, Tom
KEANE, Mary Nesta
  Farrell, M J
KEATING, Lawrence Alfred
  Bassett, John Keith
KEATLEY, Sheila
  Avon, Margaret
KECK, Maud and ORBISON, Roy
  Orbison, Keck
KEDDIE, Margaret Manson
  Auntie Margaret
KEEGAN, Mary Constance
  Heathcott, Mary
  Raymond, Mary
KEELING, Jill Annette
  Shaw, Jill A

KEESING, Nancy
  King, Frank
KEEVILL, Henry John
  Allison, Clay
  Alvord, Burt
  Bonney, Bill
  Earp, Virgil
  Harding, Wes
  McLowery, Frank
  Mossman, Burt
  Reno, Mark
  Ringo, Johnny
KELLEY, Audrey and ROOS,
  William
  Roos, Kelley
KELLY, Elizabeth
  Kellier, Elizabeth
  Stevenson, Christine
KELLY, Harold Ernest
  Carson, Lance
  Glinto, Darcy
  Toler, Buck
KENNEDY, H A
  H A K
KENSDALE, W E N
  Norwood, Elliott
KENT, Arthur
  Boswell, James
  Bradwell, James
  Du Bois, M
  Granados, Paul
  Stamper, Alex
  Vane, Brett
KENYON, Fred
  Cumberland, Gerald
KERR, D
  Colt, Russ
KERR, Doris Boake
  Boake, Capel
KERR, James Lennox
  Dawlish, Peter
  Kerr, Lennox
KERSHAW, John H D
  D'Allenger, Hugh

KETTLE, Jocelyn
  Kettle, Pamela
KIEFER, Warren and
  MIDDLETON, Harry Joseph
  Kiefer, Middleton
KING, Albert
  Albion, Ken
  Bannon, Mark
  Brennan, Walt
  Brent, Catherine
  Bronson, Wade
  Cleveland, Jim
  Conrad, Paul
  Cooper, Craig
  Creedi, Joel
  Dallas, Steve
  Doan, Reece
  Driscoll, Eli
  Ford, Wallace
  Foreman, Lee
  Foster, Evan
  Gibson, Floyd
  Gifford, Matt
  Girty, Simon
  Hammond, Brad
  Harlan, Ross
  Harmon, Gil
  Hoffman, Art
  Holland, Tom
  Howell, Scott
  Hoyt, Nelson
  Kane, Mark
  Kelsey, Janice
  Kimber, Lee
  King, Ames
  King, Berta
  King, Christopher
  Mason, Carl
  Muller, Paul
  Ogden, Clint
  Owen, Ray
  Prender, Bart
  Ripley, Alvin
  Santee, Walt

Scott, Grover
Shelby, Cole
Taggart, Dean
Tyler, Ellis
Waldron, Simon
Wallace, Agnes
Wetzel, Lewis
Yarbo, Steve
KING, Francis
Cauldwell, Frank
KING, James Clifford
Fry, Pete
King, Clifford
KING, John
Boswell, John
Kildare, John
KING-HALL, Stephen
Etienne
KIRK, Richard Edmund
Church, Jeffrey
KIRKHAM, Nellie
Myatt, Nellie
KIRKUP, James
James, Andrew
Terahata, Jun
Tsuyuki Shigeru
KIRWAN, Molly
Morrow, Charlotte
KIRWAN-WARD, Bernard
Ward, Kirwan
KIRKWOOD, Joyce
Corlett, Joyce I
KITCHIN, F H
Copplestone, Bennet
KLEIN, Grace and COOPER, Mae
Klein
Farewell, Nina
KLEINHAUS, Theodore John
Littlejohn, Jon R
KNAPP, Clarence
Glutz, Ambrose
KNIGHT, Bernard
Picton, Bernard
KNIGHT, Eric
Hallas, Richard

KNIGHT, Francis Edgar
Salter, Cedric
KNIGHTS, Leslie
Leslie, Val
KNIPSCHEER, James M W
Fox, James M
KNOTT, William Cecil
Carol, Bill J
Knott, Bill
KNOWLES, Mabel Winifred
Wynne, May
KNOWLTON, Winthrop and
GOODMAN, George Jerome
Goodman, Winthrop
KNOX, Bill
Macleod, Robert
Webster, Noah
KNOX, E V
Evoe
KNUDSEN, Margrethe
Knudsen, Greta
KOESTLER, Arthur
Costler, (Dr) A
KOFFLER, Camilla
Ylla
KORNBLUTH, Cyril M and
MERRIL, Judith
Judd, Cyril
KORZENIOWSKI, Jessie
Conrad, Jessie
KORZENIOWSKI, Teodor Jozef
Konrad
Conrad, Joseph
KOVAR, Edith May
Lowe, Edith
KRONMILLER, Hildegarde
Lawrence, Hilda
KUBIS, Patricia Lou
Scott, Casey
KURNITZ, Harry
Page, Marco
KUTTNER, Henry
Padgett, Lewis
Vance, Jack

LAFFEATY, Christina
  Carstens, Netta
  Fortina, Martha
LAFFIN, John
  Dekker, Carl
  Napier, Mark
  Sabre, Dirk
LAIDLER, Graham
  Pont
LAKE, Kenneth Robert
  Boyer, Robert
  King, Arthur
  Roberts, Ken
  Soutter, Fred
LAKRITZ, Esther
  Collingswood, Frederick
  Marion, S T
LAMB, Antonia
  Hellerlamb, Toni
LAMB, Elizabeth Searle
  Mitchell, K L
LAMB, Geoffrey Frederick
  Balaam
LAMBERT, Hubert Steel
  Marle, T B
LAMBERT, Leslie Harrison
  Alan, A J
LAMBOT, Isobel Mary
  Ingham, Daniel
  Turner, Mary
LAMBURN, Richmal Crompton
  Crompton, Richmal
L'AMOUR, Louis
  Burns, Tex
LANDELLS, Anne
  Sibley, Lee
LANDELLS, Richard
  Baron, Paul
  Dryden, Keith
  Gaunt, Richard
  Lanzol, Cesare
  Pelham, Randolph
LANDON, Melville de Lancy
  Perkins, Eli

LANE, Kenneth Westmacott
  West, Keith
LANE, (Sir) Ralph Norman
  Angell
  Angell, Norman
LANGBEHN, Theo
  Lang, Theo
  Piper, Peter
LANGDON, John
  Gannold, John
LANGDON-DAVIES, John
  James, John
  Nada, John
  Stanhope, John
LANGE, Maria
  Lang, Maria
LANGLEY, Sarah
  Langley, Lee
LANGMAID, Kenneth Joseph
  Robb
  Graham, Peter
  Laing, Kenneth
LARBALESTIER, Phillip George
  Archer, G Scott
LARCOMBE, Jennifer Geraldine
  Rees, J Larcombe
LARIAR, Lawrence
  Knight, Adam
LARKINS, William
  Long, Gerry
LASKY, Jesse L
  Love, David
  Smeed, Frances
LAUGHLIN, Virginia Carla
  Clarke, John
  Laklan, Carli
LAVENDER, David
  Catlin, Ralph
LAW, Michael
  Kreuzenau, Michael
LAWLOR, Patrick
  Penn, Christopher
LAWRENCE, Dulcie
  Hamilton, Judith
  Mace, Margaret

LAWRENCE, Elizabeth
  Bradburne, E S
LAWRENCE, James Duncan
  Lancer, Jack
LAWRENCE, T E
  C D
  C J G
  J C
  Ross, J H
  Shaw, T E
LAWSON, Alfred
  Torroll, G D
LAZENBY, Norman
  Norton, Jed
LE GALLIENNE, Richard
  Logroller
LE RICHE, P J
  Kish
LEE, Austin
  Austwick, John
  Callender, Julian
LEE, Elsie
  Cromwell, Elsie
  Gordon, Jane
LEE, Henry David Cook
  Parios
LEE, Manfred and DANNAY,
  Frederic
  Queen, Ellery
  Ross, Barnaby
LEE, Maureen
  Northe, Maggie
LEE, Norman
  Armstrong, Raymond
LEE, Norman
  Corrigan, Mark
LEE HOWARD, L A
  Howard, Leigh
  Krislov, Alexander
LEEMING, Jill
  Chaney
LEE-RICHARDSON, James
  Dunne, Desmond

LEFFINGWELL, Albert
  Chambers, Dana
  Jackson, Giles
LEHMAN, Paul Evan
  Evan, Paul
LENANTON, (Lady)
  Lenanton, C
  Oman, Carola
LENT, Blair
  Small, Ernest
LEON, Henry Cecil
  Cecil, Henry
  Maxwell, Clifford
LEONARD, Lionel Frederick
  Lonsdale, Frederick
LESLIE, Cecilie
  Macadam, Eve
LESLIE, Henrietta
  Mendl, Gladys
LESLIE, Josephine A C
  Dick, R A
LESSER, Milton
  Marlowe, Stephen
L'ESTRANGE, C James and ELY,
  George Herbert
  Strang, Herbert
LEVIN, Bernard
  Battle, Felix
  Cherryman, A E
  Taper
LEVY, Newman
  Flaccus
LEWING, Anthony
  Bannerman, Mark
LEWIS, Alfred Henry
  Quin, Dan
LEWIS, Charles Bertrand
  Quad, M
LEWIS, Clifford and LEWIS,
  Judith Mary `
  Berrisford, Judith
LEWIS, Mary Christianna
  Berrisford, Mary

Brand, Christianna
Thompson, China
LEWIS, Mildred
De Witt, James
LEWIS, Roy
Lewis, J B
Springfield, David
LEY, Willy
Willey, Robert
LEYLAND, Eric
Little, Sylvia
LIDDELOW, Marjorie Joan
Law, Marjorie J
LIEBERS, Arthur
Love, Arthur
LIGHTNER, A M
Hopf, Alice L
LILLIE, Gordon W
Pawnee Bill
LILLEY, Peter and
 STANSFIELD, Anthony
Buckingham, Bruce
LINDSAY, Barbara and
 STERNE, E G
James, Josephine
LINDSAY, Jack
Preston, Richard
LINDSAY, Kathleen
Cameron, Margaret
Richmond, Mary
LINDSAY, Maurice
Brock, Gavin
LININGTON, Elizabeth
Blaisdell, Anne
Egan, Lesley
O'Neill, Egan
Shannon, Dell
LIPSCHITZ, (Rabbi) Chaim
Yerushalmi, Chaim
LIST, Ilka Katherine
Macduff, Ilka
Obolensky, Ilka

LITTLE, Constance and LITTLE,
 Gwenyth
Little, Conyth
LITTLE, D F
Wessex, Martin
LITTLE, Gwenyth and LITTLE,
 Constance
Little, Conyth
LIVERTON, Joan
Medhurst, Joan
LIVINGSTON, A D
Delano, Al
LLOYD, Richard Dafydd Vivian
Llewellyn
Llewellyn, Richard
LOADER, William
Nash, Daniel
LOBAUGH, Elma K
Lowe, Kenneth
LOBLEY, Robert
Nong
LOCKIE, Isobel
Knight, Isobel
LOCKRIDGE, Frances Louise
 and LOCKRIDGE, Richard
Richards, Francis
LOEWENGARD, Heidi H F
Albrand, Martha
Holland, Katrin
LOFTS, Norah
Curtis, Peter
LONG, Gladys
Beaton, Jane
LONG, Leonard
Long, Shirley
LONG, Lois
Lipstick
LONGRIGG, Roger Erskine
Drummond, Ivor
Erskine, Rosalind
LOOKER, Samuel Joseph
Game Cock
Pundit, Ephraim
Wade, Thomas

LOOMIS, Noel Miller
  Miller, Frank
  Water, Silas
LORD, Doreen
  Ireland, Doreen
LORD, Phillips H
  Parker, Seth
LORDE, Andre Geraldin
  Domini, Rey
LOTTICH, Kenneth
  Conrad, Kenneth
LOW, Lois
  Paxton, Lois
LOWNDES, Marie Adelaide Belloc
  Curtin, Philip
LU KUAN YU
  Luk, Charles
LUARD, William Blaine
  Luard, L
LUCAS, Beryl Llewellyn
  Llewellyn
LUCAS, E V
  E V L
  V V V
LUCEY, James D
  James, Matthew
LUM, Bettina Peter
  Lum, Peter
LUMSDEN, Jean
  Swift, Rachelle
LUNN, Hugh Kingsmill
  Kingsmill, Hugh
LUTYENS, Mary
  Wyndham, Esther
LYBURN, Eric Frederic
 St John
  Toller
LYLE-SMYTHE, Alan
  Caillou, Alan
LYND, Robert
  Y Y
LYNDS, Dennis
  Collins, Michael
LYNE, Charles
  De Castro, Lyne

LYNES, Daisy Elfreda
  Glyn-Forest, D
LYNN, Elwyn
  Augustus
LYONS, John Benignus
  Fitzwilliam, Michael
LYTTLETON, Edith Joan
  Lancaster, G B

MACALLISTER, Alister
  Brock, Lynn
  Wharton, Anthony
McCALL, Virginia
  Nielson, Virginia
McCARTHY, J L
  Callas, Theo
  Cory, Desmond
McCARTNEY, R J
  Scott, Bruce
McCONNELL, James Douglas
  Rutherford
  Rutherford, Douglas
McCONNELL, James Douglas
  Rutherford and DURBRIDGE,
  Francis
  Temple, Paul
McCORMICK, George
  Deacon, Richard
McCORQUODALE, Barbara
  Hamilton
  Cartland, Barbara
McCULLOCH, Derek
  Uncle Mac
McCUTCHAN, Philip D
  Galway, Robert Conington
  MacNeil, Duncan
  Wigg, T I G
McDERMOTT, John Richard
  Ryan, J M
McDONALD, Margaret Josephine
  McDonald, Jo
MACDONALD, Philip
  Porlock, Martin

MACDONELL, A G
   Cameron, John
   Gordon, Neil
McEVOY, Marjorie
   Bond, Gillian
   Harte, Marjorie
McFARLANE, David
   Tyson, Teilo
MACFARLANE, George Gordon
   Miller, Patrick
McGAUGHY, Dudley Dean
   Owen, Dean
McGEOGH, Andrew
   Paul, Adrian
MACGREGOR, James Murdoch
   McIntosh, J T
MACGREGOR, Miriam
   Pegden, Helen
McGUINNESS, Bernard
   McGuinness, Brian
McHARGUE, Georgess
   Chase, Alice
   Usher, Margo Scegge
MACHLIN, Milton
   Jason, William
   Roberts, McLean
McILWAIN, David
   Maine, Charles Eric
   Rayner, Richard
   Wade, Robert
McILWRAITH, Maureen Mollie
  Hunter
   Hunter, Mollie
MACINTOSH, Joan
   Blaike, Avona
McINTOSH, Kinn Hamilton
   Aird, Catherine
MACINTYRE, John
   Brandane, John
MACK, Elsie Frances
   Moore, Frances Sarah
MACK, J C O
   Beg, Callum

MACKAY, Lewis
   Matheson, Hugh
MACKAY, Minnie
   Corelli, Marie
MACKENZIE, Joan
   Finnigan, Joan
MACKEOWN, N R
   Giles, Norman
MACKESY, Leonora Dorothy
  Rivers
   Starr, Leonora
MACKIE, Albert David
  Macnib
MACKINLAY, Lelia A S
   Grey, Brenda
MACKINNON, Charles Roy
   Conte, Charles
   Donald, Vivian
   Macalpin, Rory
   Montrose, Graham
   Rose, Hilary
   Stuart, Charles
   Torr, Iain
MACKINTOSH, Elizabeth
   Daviot, Gordon
   Tey, Josephine
MACLEAN, Alistair
   Stuart, Ian
MACLEOD, Charlotte
   Hughes, Matilda
MACLEOD, Ellen
   Anderson, Ella
MACLEOD, Jean Sutherland
   Airlie, Catherine
MACLEOD, Joseph Todd
  Gordon
   Drinan, Adam

> How public, like a frog
> To tell your name the
> livelong day
> To an admiring bog.
> — Emily Dickinson

MACLEOD-SMITH, D
　Mariner, David
McMILLAN, Donald
　Stuart, John Roy
MACMILLAN, Douglas
　Cary, D M
McMILLAN, James
　Coriolanus
McMORDIE, John Andrew
　Shan
MACMULLAN, Charles W
　Kirkpatrick
　Munro, C K
McNALLY, Mary Elizabeth
　O'Brien, Deirdre
McNAMARA, Barbara Willard
　O'Conner, Elizabeth
McNAUGHT, Ann Boyce
　Gilmour, Ann
McNEILE, H C
　Sapper
MACPHERSON, Jessie
　Kennie, Jessie
MACQUARRIE, Hector
　Cameron, Hector
MACQUEEN, James William
　Edwards, James G
MACRORY, Patrick
　Greer, Patrick
MACVEAN, Phyllis
　Greaves, Gillian
　Hambledon, Phyllis
MADDISON, Angela Mary
　Banner, Angela
MAGEE, James
　Taylor, John
MAGEE, William Kirkpatrick
　Eglinton, John
MAGRAW, Beatrice
　Padeson, Mary
MAGRILL, David S
　Dalheath, David
MAGUIRE, Robert A J
　Taaffe, Robert

MAHONEY, Elizabeth
　Mara, Thalia
MAINPRIZE, Don
　Rock, Richard
MAINWARING, Daniel
　Homes, Geoffrey
MAIR, George Brown
　Macdouall, Robertson
MAIZEL, Clarice Louise
　Maizel, Leah
MALLESON, Lucy
　Gilbert, Anthony
　Meredith, Anne
MANFRED, Frederick Feikema
　Feikema, Feike
MANN, George
　Schwarz, Bruno
MANN, Violet Vivian
　Allen, Barbara
　Stuart, Alex
　Stuart, Vivian
MANNING, Adelaide Frances
　Oke and COLES, Cyril Henry
　Coles, Manning
　Gaite, Francis
MANNING, Rosemary
　Voyle, Mary
MANNOCK, Laura
　Adair, Sally
　Mannock, Jennifer
　Whetter, Laura
MANTLE, Winifred Langford
　Fellowes, Anne
　Lang, Frances
　Langford, Jane
MAREK, Kurt W
　Ceram, C W
MARLOWE, Stephen
　Less, Milton
MARQUAND, John Phillips
　Phillips, John
MARQUARD, Leopold
　Burger, John
MARQUES, Susan Lowndes
　Lowndes, Susan

56

MARRECO, Anne
  Acland, Alice
MARRISON, Leslie William
  Dowley, D M
MARSH, John
  Davis, Julia
  Elton, John
  Harley, John
  Lawrence, Irene
  Marsh, Joan
  Richmond, Grace
  Sawley, Petra
  Ware, Monica
  Woodward, Lillian
MARSHALL, Arthur Hammond
  Marshall, Archibald
MARSHALL, Evelyn
  Marsh, Jean
MARSHALL, Marjorie
  March, Stella
MARSTON, J E
  Jeffery, E Jeffery
MARTEAU, F A
  Bride, Jack
  Rameaut, Maurice
MARTENS, Anne Louise
  Kendall, Jane
MARTIN, Charles Morris
  Martin, Chuck
MARTIN, Malachi
  Serafian, Michael
MARTIN, Netta
  Ashton, Lucy
MARTIN, Patricia Miles
  Miles, Miska
MARTIN, Reginald Alec
  Dixon, Rex
  Eliott, E C
  Martin, Rex
  Martin, Robert
  Martin, Scott
MARTIN, Robert Bernard
  Bernard, Robert
MARTIN, Robert Lee
  Roberts, Lee

MARTIN, Tim
  Tim
MARTIN, Violet Florence
  Ross
  Ross, Martin
MARTINEZ-DELGADO, Luis
  Luimardel
MARTTIN, Paul
  Plaut, Martin
MARTYN, Wyndham
  Grenvil, William
MASCHWITZ, Eric
  Marvel, Holt
MASON, Arthur Charles
  Scrope, Mason
MASON, Douglas Rankine
  Rankine, John
MASON, F Van Wyck
  Coffin, Geoffrey
  Mason, Frank W
  Weaver, Word
MASON, Michael
  Blake, Cameron
MASON, Philip
  Woodruff, Philip
MASON, Sydney Charles
  Carr, Charles
  Carr, Elaine
  Hatton, Cliff
  Hayes, Clanton
  Henderson, Colt
  Holmes, Caroline
  Horn, Chester
  Langley, John
  Ledgard, Jake
  Lee, Jesse
  Lomax, Jeff
  Maddern, Stan
  Maine, Stirling
  Mann, Stanley
  Marlow, Phyllis
  Masters, Steve
  Merrick, Spencer
  Stanley, Margaret

MASTERS, Kelly
  Ball, Zachary
MATHERS, Edward Powys
  Torquemada
MATHESON, Donald H
  Harmston, Donald
MATTHEWMAN, Phyllis
  Surrey, Kathryn
MATTHEWS, Edwin J
  Saxon
MATTHEWS, Margaret Bryan
  Goodyear, Susan
MATUSON, Harvey Marshall
  Allenby, Gordon
  Matusow, Marshall
  Muldoon, Omar
  Sadballs, John
MAUGHAM, Robert Cecil
  Romer (Viscount)
  Maugham, Robin
MAVOR, Osborne Henry
  Bridie, James
MAXFIELD, Prudence
  Hill, Prudence
MAXTONE-GRAHAM, Joyce
  Struther, Jan
MAXWELL, Patricia Anne
  Trehearne, Elizabeth
MAY, John
  Duffer, Allan
MAYER, Jane and SPIEGEL,
  Clara E
  Jaynes, Clare
MAYNE, Ethel Colburn
  Huntly, Frances E
MAYNE, William J C and
  CAESAR, Richard Dynely
  James, Dynely
MAZURE, Alfred
  Cullner, Lenard
MEAD, Martha Norburn
  Norburn, Martha
MEAD, Sidney
  Moko

MEAKER, Marijane
  Packer, Vin
MEANS, Mary and SAUNDERS,
  Theodore
  Scott, Denis
MEARES, John Willoughby
  Uncut Cavendish
MEARES, Leonard F
  Grover, Marshall
  McCoy, Marshall
MEE, Arthur
  Idris
MEGAW, Arthur Stanley
  Stanley, Arthur
MEGROZ, R L
  Cumberland, Roy
  Dimsdale, C D
MEHTA, Rustam
  Hartman, Roger
  Martin, R J
MEIGS, Cornelia Lynde
  Aldon, Adair
MEINZER, Helen Abbott
  Abbott, A C
MELIDES, Nicholas
  Macguire, Nicolas
MELLETT, John Calvin
  Brooks, Jonathan
MELLING, Leonard
  Lummins
MELONEY, William
  Frenken-Meloney
  Grant, Margaret
MENZEL, Donald H
  Howard, Don
MERCER, Cecil William
  Yates, Dornford
MEREDITH, Kenneth Lincoln
  Mayo, Arnold
MERRICK, Hugh
  Meyer, H A
MERRIL, Judith and
  KORNBLUTH, Cyril M
  Judd, Cyril

MERTZ, Barbara C
   Michaels, Barbara
   Peters, Elizabeth
METHOLD, Kenneth
   Cade, Alexander
MEYER, Harold Albert
   Merrick, Hugh
MEYERS, Roy
   Lethbridge, Rex
MEYNELL, Esther H
   Moorhouse, E Hallam
MEYNELL, Laurence Walter
   Baxter, Valerie
   Eton, Robert
   Ludlow, Geoffrey
   Tring, A Stephen
MEYNELL, Shirley Ruth
   Darbyshire, Shirley
MEYNELL, Wilfred
   Oldcastle, John
MIDDLETON, Harry Joseph
  and KIEFER, Warren
   Kiefer, Middleton
MIDDLETON, Henry Clement
   Simplex, Simon
MILKOMANE, George Alexi
  Milkomanovich
   Bankoff, George
   Borodin, George
   Braddon, George
   Conway, Peter
   Redwood, Alec
   Sava, George
MILLAR, Kenneth
   Macdonald, John Ross
   Macdonald, Ross
MILLAR, Minna
   Collier, Joy
MILLAY, Edna St Vincent
   Boyd, Nancy
MILLER, J A
   Pook, Peter
MILLER, Mary
   Durack, Mary

MILLER, Warren
   Vail, Amanda
MILLER, William and WADE,
  Robert
   Masterson, Whit
   Miller, Wade
MILLER, Wright
   North, Mark
MILLETT, Nigel
   Oke, Richard
MILLIGAN, Elsie
   Burr, Elsie
MILLS, Hugh Travers
   Travers, Hugh
MILLS, Janet Melanie Ailsa
   Challoner, H K
MILLWARD, Pamela
   Midling, Perspicacity
MILNE, Charles
   Milne, Ewart
MILNER, Marion
   Field, Joanna
MILTON, Gladys Alexandra
   Carlyle, Anthony
M'ILWRAITH, Jean N
   Forsyth, Jean
MINTO, Frances
   Cowen, Frances
   Hyde, Eleanor
   Munthe, Frances
MINTO, Mary
   Macqueen, Jay
MITCHELL, Clare Mary
   Canfield, Cleve
MITCHELL, Gladys
   Hockaby, Stephen
   Torrie, Malcolm
MITCHELL, Isabel
   Plain, Josephine
MITCHELL, James
   Munro, James
MITCHELL, James Leslie
   Gibbon, Lewis Grassic
MIZNER, Elizabeth Howard
   Howard, Elizabeth

MOCKLER, Gretchen
 Travis, Gretchen
MODELL, Merriam
 Piper, Evelyn
MOGRIDGE, Stephen
 Stevens, Jill
MOHAN, Josephine Elizabeth
 Jemonte
MONGER, Ifor
 Manngian, Peter
 Richards, Peter
MONRO-HIGGS, Gertrude
 Monro, Gavin
MONTGOMERY, Robert Bruce
 Crispin, Edmund
MONTGOMERY, Leslie
 Alexander
 Doyle, Lynn
MONTGOMERY, Rutherford
 George
 Avery, Al
 Proctor, Everitt
MOORE, Harold William
 Roome, Holdar
MOORE, John
 Trotwood, John
MOORE, Mary McLeod
 Pandora
MOORHOUSE, Hilda
 Vansittart, Jane
MOORHOUSE, Sydney
 Langdale, Stanley
 Lyndale, Sydney M
MOREAU, David
 Merlin, David
MORETTI, Ugo
 Drug, Victor
 Gouttier, Maurice
 Sherman, George
MOREWOOD, Sarah L
 Hope, Noel
MORGAN, Charles
 Menander
MORGAN, Diana
 Blaine, Sara

MORGAN, Thomas Christopher
 Muir, John
MORIN, Claire
 France, Claire
MORLAND, Nigel
 Garnett, Roger
 Shepherd, Neal
MORLEY, Leslie Reginald
 William
 Hutchins, Anthony
MORRIS, David
 Hall, Martyn T
MORRIS, John
 McGaw, J W
MORRISON, Arthur
 Hewitt, Martin
MORRISON, Eula A
 Delmonico, Andrea
MORRISON, Margaret Mackie
 Cost, March
 Morrison, Peggy
MORRISON, Thomas
 Muir, Alan
MORSE, Martha
 Wilson, Martha
MORTON, A Q
 Kew, Andrew
MORTON, Guy Mainwaring
 Traill, Peter
MORTON, J B
 Beachcomber
MOSS, Robert Alfred
 Moss, Nancy
 Moss, Roberta
MOSTYN, Anita Mary
 Fielding, Ann Mary
MOTT, Edward Spencer
 Gubbins, Nathaniel
MOTTRAM, Ralph Hale
 Marjoram, J
MOUNT, Thomas Ernest
 Cody, Stone
 King, Oliver
MOUNTBATTEN, (Lord) Louis
 Marco

MOUNTFIELD, David
  Grant, Neil
MUDDOCK, Joyce Emerson
  Donovan, Dick
MUGGESON, Margaret
  Dickinson, Margaret
  Jackson, Everatt
MUIR, Marie
  Blake, Monica
  Kaye, Barbara
MUIR, Wilhelmina Johnstone
  Muir, Willa
  Scott, Agnes Neill
MULHEARN, Winifred
  Grandma
MUMFORD, A H
  Videns
MUNRO, Hector Hugh
  Saki
MUNRO, Hugh
  Jason
MURFREE, Mary Noailles
  Craddock, Charles Egbert
  Denbry, R Emmet
MURIEL, John
  Dewes, Simon
  Lindsey, John
MURPHY, John and CORLEY,
  Edwin
  Buchanan, Patrick
MURPHY, Lawrence D
  Lawrence, Steven C
MURRAY, Andrew Nicholas
  Islay, Nicholas
MURRAY, Blanche
  Murray, Geraldine
MURRAY, Joan
  Blood, Joan Wilde
MURRAY, Ruth Hilary
  Finnegan, Ruth
MURRAY, Venetia Pauline and
  BIRCH, Jack Ernest Lionel
  Flight, Francies
MURRY, John Middleton Jr
  Cowper, Richard

Murry, Colin
  Murry, Colin Middleton
MURRY, Violet
  Arden, Mary
MUSKETT, Netta Rachel
  Hill, Anne
MUSSI, Mary
  Edgar, Josephine
  Howard, Mary
MUSTO, Barry
  Simon, Robert
MYERS, Mary
  Borer, Mary Cathcart
MYSTERY WRITERS OF
  AMERICA INC: CALIFORNIA
  CHAPTER
  Durrant, Theo

NELSON, Ethel
  Nina
NERNEY, Patrick W
  Nudnick
NETTELL, Richard
  Kenneggy, Richard
NEUBAUER, William Arthur
  Arthur, William
  Garrison, Joan
  Marsh, Rebecca
  Newcomb, Norma
NEVILLE, Alison
  Candy, Edward
NEVILLE, Derek
  Salt, Jonathan
NEWLIN, Margaret
  Rudd, Margaret
NEWMAN, Bernard
  Betteridge, Don
NEWMAN, Mona A J
  Fitzgerald, Barbara
  Stewart, Jean
NEWMAN, Terence
  O'Connor, Dermot
NEWNHAM, Don
  Eden, Matthew

61

NEWTON, Dwight Bennett
　　Bennett, Dwight
NEWTON, H Chance
　　Gawain
NEWTON, William Simpson
　　Mitcham, Gilroy
　　Newton, Macdonald
NICHOLS, (Captain) G H F
　　Quex
NICHOLSON, Joan
　　Craig, Alison
　　Weir, Jonnet
NICHOLSON, Margaret Beda
　　Yorke, Margaret
NICHOLSON, Violet
　　Hope, Lawrence
NICKSON, Arthur
　　Hodson, Arthur
　　Peters, Roy
　　Saunders, John
　　Winstan, Matt
NICOL, Eric
　　Jabez
NICOLE, Christopher
　　Grange, Peter
　　York, Andrew
NILSON, Annabel
　　Nilson, Bee
NISOT, Mavis Elizabeth
　　Penmare, William
NOLAN, Cynthia
　　Reed, Cynthia
NOLAN, William F
　　Anmar, Frank
　　Cahill, Mike
　　Edwards, F E
NOONAN, Robert
　　Tressall, Robert
　　Tressell, Robert
NORGATE, Walter
　　Le Grys, Walter
NORTH, William
　　Rodd, Ralph
NORTHAM, Lois Edgett
　　Nelson, Lois

NORTHCOTT, Cecil
　　Miller, Mary
NORTON, Alice Mary
　　Norton, Andre
NORTON, Marjorie
　　Ellison, Marjorie
NORTON, Olive Marion
　　Neal, Hilary
　　Noon, T R
　　Norton, Bess
　　Norway, Kate
NORWAY, Nevil Shute
　　Shute, Nevil
NORWICH, (Viscount)
　　Norwich, John Julius
NORWOOD, Victor George
Charles
　　Banton, Coy
　　Baxter, Shane V
　　Bowie, Jim
　　Brand, Clay
　　Cody, Walt
　　Corteen, Craig
　　Corteen, Wes
　　Dangerfield, Clint
　　Destry, Vince
　　Fargo, Doone
　　McCord, Whip
　　Rand, Brett
　　Russell, Shane
　　Shane, Rhondo
　　Tressidy, Jim
NOWELL, Elizabeth Cameron
　　Clemons, Elizabeth
NUMANO, Allen
　　Corenanda, A L A
NUTT, David
　　Brand, David
NUTT, Lily Clive
　　Arden, Clive
NUTTALL, Anthony
　　Allyson, Alan
　　Bardsley, Michael
　　Curtis, Spencer

Lenton, Anthony
Tracey, Grant
Trent, Lee
Wells, Tracey
NYE, Nelson Coral
Colt, Clem
Denver, Drake C

OAKLEY, Eric Gilbert
Capon, Peter
Gregson, Paul
Scott-Morley, A
O'BRIEN, Conor Cruise
O'Donnell, Donat
O'CONNOR, Patrick Joseph
Fiacc, Padraic
O'CONNOR, Richard
Archer, Frank
Wayland, Patrick
O'CONNOR, T P
T P
O'CONNOR WIBBERLEY,
  Leonard Patrick
Holton, Leonard
O'Connor, Patrick
Webb, Christopher
Wibberley, Leonard
O'DONOGHUE, Elinor Mary
Oddie, E M
O'DONOVAN, Michael Francis
O'Connor, Frank
OGNALL, Leo H
Carmichael, Harry
Howard, Hartley
O'GRADY, John
Culotta, Nino
O'Grada, Sean
OLD, Phyllis Muriel Elizabeth
Shiel-Martin
OLD COYOTE, Elnora A
Old Coyote, Sally
Wright, Elnora A
Wright, Sally
OLDFIELD, Claude Houghton
Houghton, Claude

OLDMEADOW, Ernest James
Downman, Francis
OLIVER, Amy Roberta
Onions, Berta
Ruck, Berta
OLIVER, Doris M
Hughes, Alison
OLIVER, George
Onions, Oliver
OLSEN, Theodore Victor
Stark, Joshua
O'MALLEY, (Lady)
Bridge, Ann
O'MORE, Peggy
Bowman, Jeanne
O'NEILL, Herbert Charles
Strategicus
O'NOLAN, Brian
Knowall, George
Na Gopaleen, Myles
O'Brien, Flann
OPPENHEIM, E Phillips
Partridge, Anthony
OPPENHEIMER, Carlota
Carlota
ORBISON, Roy and KECK, Maud
Orbison, Keck
ORDE-WARD, F W
Williams, F Harald
ORGA, Irfan
Riza, Ali
ORME, Eve
Day, Irene
O'ROURKE, Frank
O'Malley, Frank
ORTON, Thora
Colson, Thora
OSBORNE, Dorothy Gladys
Arthur, Gladys
OSLER, Eric Richard
Dick, T
OSTERGAARD, Geoffrey
Gerard, Gaston
OSTLERE, Gordon Stanley
Gordon, Richard

O'Conner, Clint
Pindell, Jon
St George, Arthur
Sharp, Helen
Slaughter, Jim
Standish, Buck
Stuart, Margaret
Thompson, Buck
Thompson, Russ
Thorn, Barbara
Undine, P F
PALESTRANT, Simon
  Edward, Stephen
  Stevens, S P
  Strand, Paul E
PALMER, Cecil
  Ludlow, John
PALMER, John Leslie and
  SAUNDERS, Hilary Aidan
 St George
  Beeding, Francis
  Pilgrim, David
PALMER, Madelyn
  Peters, Geoffrey
PANOWSKI, Eileen Janet
  Thompson, Eileen
PARCELL, Norman Howe
  Nicholson, John
PARES, Marion
  Campbell, Judith
PARGETER, Edith Mary
  Peters, Ellis
PARKER, Dorothy
  Constant Reader
PARKER, Marion
  Dominic, (Sister) Mary
PARKES, Frank
  Dompo, Kwesi
PARKES, James W
  Hadham, John
PAKHILL, Forbes
  Martinez, J D
PARR, Olive Katherine
  Chase, Beatrice

PARRIS, John
  Lascelles, Alison
PARRY, Hugh J
  Cross, James
PARRY, Margaret G
  Glyn, Megan
PARSONS, Anthony
  Nicholls, Anthony
PARSONS, Charles P
  Craven Hill
PARTRIDGE, Eric
  Vigilans
PATERSON, W R
  Swift, Benjamin
PATRICK, Keats
  Karig, Walter
PATRY, M and WILLIAMS, D F
  Williams, Patry
PATTEN, Gilbert
  Standish, Burt L
PATTERSON, Henry
  Fallon, Martin
  Graham, James
  Higgins, Jack
  Marlowe, Hugh
  Patterson, Harry
PATTINSON, James
  Ryder, James
PATTINSON, Lee
  Holland, Rosemary
  Maxwell, Ann
  Miller, Ellen
PATTINSON, Nancy
  Asquith, Nan
PATTISON, Andrew Seth P
  Seth, Andrew
PAUL, Maury
  Benedict, Billy
  Knickerbocker, Cholly
  Madison, Dolly
  Stuyvesant, Polly

> My name is legion:
> for we are many
> — St Mark's Gospel 1,30

PAXTON, Lois
Low, Dorothy Mackie
PAYNE, Charles J
Snaffles
PAYNE, Donald Gordon
Cameron, Ian
Gordon, Donald
Marshall, James Vance
PAYNE, Eileen Mary
Mansell, C R
PAYNE, Pierre Stephen Robert
Young, Robert
PAYNE, Robert
Cargoe, Richard
PAYNE, Ronald Charles and
GARROD, John William
Castle, John
PAZ, Magdeleine
Marx, Magdeleine
PEARCE, Brian
Hussey, Leonard
Redman, Joseph
PEARCE, Melville Chaning
Nicodemus
PEARCE, Raymond
Maplesden, Ray
PECHEY, Archibald Thomas
Cross, Mark
Valentine
PEDLAR, Ann
Stafford, Ann
PEDRICK-HARVEY, Gale
Pedrick, Gale
PEEL, Hazel
Hayman, Hazel
Peel, Wallis
PEEPLES, Samuel Anthony
Ward, Brad
PEERS, Edgar Allison
Truscot, Bruce
PEMBER, William Leonard
Monmouth, Jack
PEMBER-DEVEREUX,
Margaret R R
Devereux, Roy

PENWARDEN, Helen
Smith, Jessica
PEPPER, Joan
Alexander, Joan
PERKINS, Kenneth
Phillips, King
PERRY, Martin
Martyn, Henry
PETERS, Arthur A
Peters, Fritz
PETERS, Robert Louis
Bridge, John
PETERSON, Corinna
Cochrane, Corinna
PETERSON, Margaret
Green, Glint
PETRIE, Rhona
Duell, Eileen-Marie
PETRONE, Jane Gertrude
Muir, Jane
PEYTON, Kathleen Wendy and
PEYTON, Michael
Peyton, K M
PHILIPS, Judson Pentecost
Pentecost, Hugh
PHILLIPS, Dennis John Andrew
Challis, Simon
Chambers, Peter
Chester, Peter
PHILLIPS, Hubert
Dogberry
PHILLIPS, Hugh
Hughes, Philip
PHILLIPS, Olga
Olga
PHILLIPS, Pauline
Van Buren, Abigail
PHILLPOTTS, Eden
Hext, Harrington
PHILPOT, Joseph H
Lafargue, Philip
PHILPOTT, Alexis Robert
Pantopuck
PHYSICK, Edward Harold
Visiak, E H

PIGGOTT, William
  Wales, Hubert
PILCHER, Rosamunde
  Fraser, Jane
PINTO, Jacqueline
  Blairman, Jacqueline
PILLEY, Phil
  Lindley, Gerard
PIPER, David Towry
  Towry, Peter
PIPER, Evelyn
  Modell, Merriam
PLACE, Marian Templeton
  White, Dale
  Whitinger, R D
PLATH, Sylvia
  Lucas, Victoria
PLATT, Edward
  Trent, Paul
PLOMER, William
  D'Arfey, William
PLUMLEY, Ernest F
  Clevedon, John
PLUMMER, Clare
  Emsley, Clare
POCOCK, Tom
  Allcot, Guy
POLAND, Dorothy E H
  Farely, Alison
  Hammond, Jane
POLLEY, Judith Anne
  Hagar, Judith
  Luellen, Valentina
PONSONBY, Doris Almon
  Rybot, Doris
POOLE, Reginald Heber
  Heber, Austin
  Heber, Reginald
  Poole, Michael
PORN, Alice
  Ali-Mar
PORTER, Barbara Conney
  Conney, Barbara
PORTER, Maurice
  Mouthpiece

PORTER, William Sydney
  Henry, O
POTTER, George William
  Withers, E L
POTTER, Heather
  Jenner, Heather
POU, Genevieve
  Holden, Genevieve
POWELL-SMITH, Vincent
  Elphinstone, Francis
  Justiciar
  Santa Maria
POWLEY, (Mrs) A A
  Gene, Marta
PRAFULLA, Das
  Subhadra-Nandan
PRATHER, Richard S
  Knight, David
  Ring, Douglas
PRATT, John
  Winton, John
PRATT, Theodore
  Brace, Timothy
PRATT, William Henry
  Karloff, Boris
PRESLAND, John
  Bendit, Gladys
PREVOST-BATTERSBY, H F
  Prevost, Francis
PRICE, Beverly Joan
  Randell, Beverly
PRICE, Florence Alice
  Warden, Florence
PRICE, Jeremie
  Lane, Marvyn
PRIESTLEY, Clive Ryland
  Ryland, Clive
PRIOR, Mollie
  Roscoe, Janet
PRITCHARD, William Thomas
  Dexter, William
PUDDEPHA, Derek
  Quill

PUECHNER, Ray
  Haddo, Oliver
  Victor, Charles B
PULLEIN-THOMPSON, Dennis
  Cannan, Denis
PULLEN, George
  Culpeper, Martin
PUNNETT, Margaret and
  PUNNETT, Ivor
  Simons, Roger
PURCELL, Victor W W S
  Buttle, Myra
PURDY, Ken
  Prentiss, Karl
PURVES, Frederick
  Lloyd, Joseph M

QUIBELL, Agatha
  Pearce, A H
QUIGLEY, Aileen
  Fabian, Ruth
  Lindley, Erica
QUIGLY, Elizabeth Pauline
  Elisabeth
QUILLER-COUCH, (Sir) Arthur
  Q

RADETZBY von RADETZ,
  (Countess)
  Harding, Bertita
RAE, Hugh Cranford
  Crawford, Robert
  Houston, R B
RAME, Marie Louise
  Ouida
RAMSKILL, Valerie
  Brooke, Carol
RANSFORD, Oliver
  Wylcotes, John
RAPHAEL, Chaim
  Davey, Jocelyn
RASH, Dora
  Wallace, Doreen
RAUBENHEIMER, George H
  Harding, George

RAVENSCROFT, John R
  Ravenscroft, Rosanne
RAYMOND, Rene
  Chase, James Hadley
  Grant, Ambrose
  Marshall, Raymond
RAYMOND, Walter
  Cobbleigh, Tom
RAYNER, Claire
  Brandon, Sheila
  Lynton, Ann
  Martin, Ruth
REACH, James
  Manning, Roy
  West, Tom
READ, Anthony
  Ferguson, Anthony
READ, James
  Bacon, Jeremy
READ, John
  Jan
REAGAN, Thomas B
  Thomas, Jim
REANEY, James
  Spoonhill
REDMAN, Ben
  Lord, Jeremy
REDMON, Lois
  Rogers, Rachel
REECE, Alys
  Wingfield, Susan
REEMAN, Douglas
  Kent, Alexander
REES, Helen
  Oliver, Jane
REES, Joan
  Avery, June
  Bedford, Ann
  Strong, Susan
REEVE-JONES, Alan
  Lunchbasket, Roger
REEVES, John Morris
  Reeves, James

REID, John
  Caliban
REILLY, Helen
  Abbey, Kieran
RENFREW, A
  Patterson, Shott
RENNIE, James Alan
  Denver, Boone
RENTOUL, T Laurence
  Gage, Gervais
RESSICH, John S M and
 DE BANZIE, Eric
  Baxter, Gregory
REYNOLDS, Helen Mary
  Greenwood Dickson
  Reynolds, Dickson
REYNOLDS, John E
  Dexter, Ross
RICCI, Lewis Anselm da Costa
  Bartimeus
RICE, Brian Keith
  Vigilans
RICE, Dorothy
  Borne, D
  Vicary, Dorothy
RICE, Joan
  Hallam, Jay
RICHARDS, James
  Cladpole, Jim
RICHARDS, Ronald C W
  Saddler, K Allen
RICHARDSON, Eileen
  Shane
RICHARDSON, Gladwell
  Blacksnake, George
  Jones, Calico
  Kent, Pete
  Kildare, Maurice
  O'Riley, Warren
  Warner, Frank
  Winslowe, John R
RICHARDSON, Mary Kathleen
  Norton, S H
RIDDOLLS, Brenda H
  English, Brenda H

RIDGE, William Pett
  Simpson, Warwick
RIGONI, Orlando Joseph
  Ames, Leslie
  Wesley, James
RIMANOCZY, A
  Eland, Charles
RISTER, Claude
  Billings, Buck
  Holt, Tex
RIVETT, Edith Caroline
  Carnac, Carol
  Lorac, E C R
ROARK, Garland
  Garland, George
ROBERTS, Eric
  Robin
ROBERTS, Irene
  Carr, Roberta
  Harle, Elizabeth
  Roberts, Ivor
  Rowland, Iris
  Shaw, Irene
ROBERTS, James
  Horton, Robert J
ROBERTS, Keith J K
  Bevan, Alistair
ROBERTS, Ursula
  Miles, Susan
ROBERTSHAW, James Denis
  Gaunt, Michael
ROBERTSON, Frank Chester
  Crane, Robert
ROBERTSON, James Robin
  Connell, John
ROBERTSON, James Logie
  Haliburton, Hugh
ROBERTSON, Keith
  Keith, Carlton
ROBERTSON, Margery Ellen
  Thorp, Ellen
  Thorp, Morwenna
ROBERTSON, Walter George
  Werrerson, Talbot

69

ROBEY, Timothy Lester
Townsend
Townsend, Timothy
ROBINS, Denise
French, Ashley
Gray, Harriet
Kane, Julia
ROBINSON, H
Madeoc
ROBINSON, Joan Gale
Thomas, Joan Gale
ROCHE, Thomas
Yes Tor
ROCHESTER, George Ernest
Gaunt, Jeffrey
RODDA, Charles
Holt, Gavin
RODDA, Charles and AMBLER, Eric
Reed, Eliot
ROE, Eric
Roe, Tig
ROE, Ivan
Savage, Richard
ROGERS, Ruth
Alexander, Ruth
ROGERSON, James
Hamilton, Roger
ROLFE, Frederick
Corvo, (Baron)
ROLLINS, Kathleen and DRESSER, Davis
Debrett, Hal
RONNS, Edward and AYRES, Paul
Aarons, Edward Sidney
ROOME, Gerald Antony
Leslie, Colin
ROOS, William and KELLEY, Audrey
Roos, Kelley
ROSCOE, John
Roscoe, Mike
ROSE, Flizabeth Jane
Elizabeth

ROSE, Graham
Graham, John
ROSE, Ian
Rose, Robert
ROSEN, Michael
Landgrave of Hesse
ROSENKRANTZ, Linda
Damiano, Laila
ROSS, Isaac
Ross, George
ROSS, William Edward Daniel
Ames, Leslie
Dana, Rosa
McCormack, Charlotte
ROSTEN, Leo C
Ross, Leonard Q
ROTH, Arthur
McGurk, Slater
ROTHWELL, Henry Talbot
Talbot, Henry
ROUSSEAU, Leon
Strydom, Len
ROWE, John Gabriel
Rowe, Alice E
Walters, T B
ROWLAND, Donald Sydney
Adams, Annette
Bassett, Jack
Baxter, Hazel
Benton, Karla
Berry, Helen
Brant, Lewis
Bray, Alison
Brayce, William
Brockley, Fenton
Bronson, Oliver
Buchanan, Chuck
Caley, Rod
Carlton, Roger
Cleve, Janita
Court, Sharon
Craig, Vera
Craile, Wesley
Dryden, John
Fenton, Freda

Field, Charles
Kroll, Burt
Langley, Helen
Lansing, Henry
Lant, Harvey
Lynn, Irene
McHugh, Stuart
Madison, Hank
Mason, Chuck
Murray, Edna
Page, Lorna
Patterson, Olive
Porter, Alvin
Random, Alex
Rimmer, W J
Rix, Donna
Rockwell, Matt
Roscoe, Charles
Scott, Norford
Scott, Valerie
Segundo, Bart
Shaul, Frank
Spurr, Clinton
Stan, Roland
Stevens, J B
Suttling, Mark
Talbot, Kay
Travers, Will
Vinson, Elaine
Walters, Rick
Webb, Neil
RUBEL, James Lyon
  Macrae, Mason
RUBINS, Harold
  Robbins, Harold
RUBENSTEIN, Stanley Jack
  Ar, Esjay
RUDNYCKYJ, Jaroslav B
  Bij-Bijchenko
RUMBOLD-GIBBS, Henry
  St John C
  Gibbs, Henry
  Harvester, Simon
  Saxon, John

RUNBECK, Margaret Lee
  McKinley, Karen
RUNDLE, Anne
  Lamont, Marianne
  Marshall, Joanne
  Sanders, Jeanne
RUSSELL, Elizabeth Mary
  (Countess)
  Elizabeth
RUSSELL, George William
  A E
RUSSELL, Shirley
  King, Stephanie
  Vernon, Marjorie
RUSSELL, Ursula D'Ivry
  D'Ivry, Ursula
RUSTERHOLTZ, Winsome Lucy
  Turvey, Winsome
RYALL, William Bolitho
  Bolitho, William
RYAN, Paul William
  Finnegan, Robert
RYDBERG, Ernie
  Brouillette, Emil
  McCary, Reed
RYDER, M L
  Lawson, Michael
RYDER, Vera
  Cook, Vera
  Mortimer, June
RYNNE, Alice
  Curtayne, Alice

SAINT, Dora Jessie
  Read, Miss
ST JOHN, Wylly Folk
  Fox, Eleanor
  Larson, Eve
  Pierce, Katherine
  Vincent, Mary Keith
  Williams, Michael
SAKLATVALA, Beram
  Marsh, Henry

SALMON, Annie Elizabeth
  Ashley, Elizabeth
  Martin, Elizabeth
SALMON, Geraldine Gordon
  Sarasin, J G
SALMON, P R
  Panlake, Richard
SALSBURY, Nate
  Ireland, Baron
SALTZMANN, Sigmund
  Salten, Felix
SAMBROT, William Anthony
  Ayes, Anthony
SAMMAN, Fern
  Powell, Fern
SAMPSON, Richard Henry
  Hull, Richard
SANDERSON, Douglas
  Brett, Martin
SANDFORD, Matthew
  Matt
SANDS, Leo G
  Craig, Lee
  Helmi, Jack
  Herman, Jack
  Meuron, Skip
SASSOON, Siegfried
  S S
  Sigma Sashûn
SATHERLEY, David and
  WHITEHAND, James
  Whitehand, Satherley
SAUNDERS, Ann Loreille
  Cox-Johnson, Ann
SAUNDERS, Hilary Aidan
  St George and PALMER, John
  Leslie
  Beeding, Francis
  Pilgrim, David
SAUNDERS, Jean
  Innes, Jean
SAUNDERS, Theodore and
  MEANS, Mary
  Scott, Denis

SAVAGE, Lee
  Stewart, Logan
SAVAGE, Mildred
  Barrie, Jane
SAWKINS, Raymond Harold
  Raine, Richard
SAYER, Nancy Margetts
  Bradfield, Nancy
SAYER, Walter William
  Quiroule, Pierre
SAYERS, James D
  James, Dan
SCHAAF, M B
  Goffstein, M B
SCHIFF, Sydney
  Hudson, Stephen
SCHISGALL, Oscar
  Hardy, Stuart
SCHOFIELD, Sylvia Anne
  Matheson, Sylvia A
  Mundy, Max
SCOBIE, Stephen Arthur Cross
  Waverley, John
SCOTT, Hilda R
  Smith, Harriet
SCOTT' Leslie
  Cole, Jackson
  Scott, Bradford
SCOTT, Mary E
  Graham, Jean
SCOTT, Peter Dale
  Greene, Adam
  Sproston, John
SCOTT, Rose Laure
  Buckley, Eunice
SCOTT, Winifred Mary
  Wynne, Pamela
SCOTT-HANSEN, Olive
  Murrell, Shirley
SCROGGIE, Marcus Graham
  Cathode Ray
SEAMAN, (Sir) Owen
  Nauticus
  O S

SEBENTHALL, Roberta
  Kruger, Paul
SEBLEY, Frances Rae
  Jeffs, Rae
SEEDO, Sonia
  Fuchs, Sonia
SELCAMM, George
  Machlis, Joseph
SELDES, Gilbert
  Johns, Foster
SELDON TRUSS, Leslie
  Selmark, George
SERAILLIER, Anne
  Rogers, Anne
SERVADIO, Gaia
  Mostyn-Owen, Gaia
SEUFFERT, Muriel
  Faulkner, Mary
  Seuffert, Muir
SHACKLETON, Edith
  Heald, Edith
SHAMBROOK, Rona
  Randall, Rona
SHANN, Renée
  Gaye, Carol
SHAPPIRO, Herbert Arthur
  Arthur, Burt
  Herbert, Arthur
SHARP, (Sir) Henry
  Ainsworth, Oliver
SHAW, George Bernard
  Corno di Bassetto
  G B S
SHAW, Howard
  Howard, Colin
SHAW, Jane
  Gillespie, Jane
SHEA, Patrick
  Laughlin, P S
SHELDON, Peter
  Gaddes, Peter
SHELLABARGER, Samuel
  Esteven, John
  Loring, Peter

SHEPPARD, John Hamilton
  George
  Creek, Nathan
SHERIDAN, H B
  Sherry, Gordon
SHIEL, M P and TRACY, Louis
  Holmes, Gordon
SHIPMAN, Natalie
  Arthur, Phyllis
SHIRREFFS, Gordon D
  Donalds, Gordon
  Gordon, Stewart
  Maclean, Art
SILVETTE, Herbert
  Dogbolt, Barnaby
SIM, Katherine Phyllis
  Nuraini
SIMMONDS, Michael Charles
  Essex, Frank
  Simmonds, Mike
SIMMONS, J S A
  Cromie, Stanley
  Montgomery, Derek
SIMONS, Katherine Drayton
  Mayrant
  Mayrant, Drayton
SIMPSON, Bertram L
  Weale, B Putnam
SIMPSON, Evan John
  John, Evan
SIMPSON, John Frederick
  Norman Hampson
  Hampson, John
SIMPSON, Keith
  Bailey, Guy
SIMSON, Eric Andrew
  Kirk, Laurence
SKIDELSKY, Simon Jasha
  Simon, S J
SLANEY, George Wilson
  Woden, George
SLATER, Ernest
  Gwynne, Paul
SLAUGHTER, Frank Gill
  Terry, C V

SLAVITT, David
   Sutton, Henry
SLOGGETT, Nellie
   Cornwall, Nellie
SMITH, Charles H
   Arp, Bill
SMITH, Dorothy Gladys
   Anthony, C L
   Smith, Dodie
SMITH, Edgar
   Mason, Michael
SMITH, Edward Ernest
   Lindall, Edward
SMITH, Edward Percy
   Percy, Edward
SMITH, Ernest Bramah
   Bramah, Ernest
SMITH, Frederick E
   Farrell, David
SMITH, H Everard
   Everard, Henry
SMITH, Helen Zenna
   Price, Evadne
SMITH, June Johns
   Johns, June
SMITH, Lillian M
   Warner, Leigh
SMITH, Lily
   Wanderer
SMITH, Marjorie Seymour
   Fearn, Elena
SMITH, Mary
   Drewery, Mary
SMITH, Norman Edward Mace
   Sheraton, Neil
   Shore, Norman
SMITH, R C
   Charles, Robert
   Leader, Charles
SMITH, Robert
   Chattan, Robert
SMITH, Sidney Wallace
   Brodie, Gordon
SMITHELLS, Doreen
   Boscawen, Linda

SMITHERS, Muriel
   Redmayne, Barbara
SMITHIES, Muriel
   Howe, Muriel
SMITTER, Eliott-Burton
   Hadley, Leila
SNODGRASS, W D
   Gardons, S S
   McConnell, Will
   Prutkov, Kozma
SNOW, Donald Clifford
   Fall, Thomas
SNOW, Charles Horace
   Averill, H C
   Ballew, Charles
   Hardy, Russ
   Lee, Ranger
   Marshall, Gary
   Smith, Wade
   Wills, Chester
SNOW, Helen Foster
   Wales, Nym
SOLOMON, Samuel
   Moolson, Melusa
SOMERVILLE, Edith Oenone
   Graham, Viva
   Herring, Geilles
   Somerville
SOUTER, Helen Greig
   Aunt Kate
SOUTHERN, Terry
   Kenton, Maxwell
SOUTHWOLD, Stephen
   Bell, Neil
SPECK, Gerald Eugene
   Kepps, Gerald
   Science Investigator
   Stone, Eugene
SPENCE, William
   Bowden, Jim
   Ford, Kirk
   Rogers, Floyd
   Spence, Duncan

SPIEGEL, Clara E and MAYER,
  Jane
  Jaynes, Clare
SPINELLI, Grace
  Spinelli, Marcos
SPOONER, Peter Alan
  Mellor, Michael
  Peters, Alan
  Rennie, Jack
  Underwood, Keith
SPRATLING, Walter Norman
  Sparlin, W
SPRIGG, Christopher St John
  Caudwell, Christopher
SPROULE, Howard
  Sproule, Wesley
SQUIBBS, H W Q
  Quirk
STACEY, P M de Cosqueville
  De Cosqueville, Pierre
  Shelton, Michael
STAMP, Roger
  Mingston, R Gresham
STANIER, Maida
  Culex
STANLEY, Nora Kathleen Begbie
  Stange, Nora K
STANNARD, Eliza Vaughan
  Winter, John Strange
STANSFIELD, Anthony and
  LILLEY, Peter
  Buckingham, Bruce
STANTON-HOPE, W E
  Hope, Stanton
STAPLES, Reginald Thomas
  Brewster, Robin
STARKEY, James Sullivan
  O'Sullivan, Seumas
STARR, Richard
  Essex, Richard
STEEGMULLER, Francis
  Keith, David
  Steel, Byron
STEELE, Patricia M V
  Joudry, Patricia

STEFFENS, Arthur Joseph
  Hardy, Arthur S
STEIN, Aaron Marc
  Bagby, George
  Stone, Hampton
STEIN, Gertrude
  Toklas, Alice B
STEPHEN, Joyce Alice
  Thomas, J Bissell
STEPHENS, Donald Ryder
  Sinderby, Donald
STEPHENS, Eve
  Anthony, Evelyn
STERN, Philip Van Doren
  Storme, Peter
STERNE, E G and LINDSAY,
  Barbara
  James, Josephine
STEVENS, Frances Moyer
  Hale, Christopher
STEVENSON, James Patrick
  Radyr, Tomos
STEWART, Alfred Walter
  Connington, J J
STEWART, John Innes
  Mackintosh
  Innes, Michael
STEWART, Kenneth Livingston
  Livingston, Kenneth
STICKLAND, Louise Annie
  Beatrice
  Somers, J L
STICKLAND, M E
  Stand, Marguerite
STITT, James M
  Brunswick, James
STOCKS, Mary and others
  Heptagon
STODDARD, William Osborn
  Forrest, (Colonel) Cris
STODDART, Jane T
  Lorna
STOKER, Alan
  Evans, Alan

STOKES, Francis William
 Everton, Francis
STONE, Grace Zaring
 Vance, Ethel
STONE, Irving
 Tennenbaum, Irving
STONEBRAKER, Florence
 Stuart, Florence
STONEHAM, Charles Thurley
 Thurley, Norgrove
STORY, Rosamond Mary
 Jeskins, Richard
 Lee, Charles H
 Lindsay, Josephine
 Tracy, Catherine
 Woods, Ross
STOUTENBURG, Adrien
 Kendall, Lace
STRACHAN, Gladys Elizabeth
 Bill
STRATEMEYER, Edward
 Bonehill, Ralph
 Winfield, Allen
 Winfield, Arthur M
STREATFEILD, Noel
 Scarlett, Susan
STREET, Cecil John Charles
 Rhode, John
STRONG, Charles Stanley
 Stanley, Chuck
 Stoddard, Charles
STUART-HEATON, Peter
 Heaton, Peter
STUBBS, Harry Clement
 Clement, Hal
STUBBS, Jean
 Darby, Emma
 March, Emma
STUDDERT, Annie
 Rixon, Annie
STURE-VASA, Mary
 O'Hara, Mary
STURT, George
 Bourne, George

STYLES, Showell
 Carr, Glyn
SUDDABY, William Donald
 Griff, Alan
SULLIVAN, Edward Alan
 Murray, Sinclair
SUMMERS, Hollis
 Hollis, Jim
SUMMERTON, Margaret
 Roffman, Jan
SUTTON, Margaret
 Sutton, Rachel B
SUTTON, Phyllis Mary
 Riches, Phyllis
SWAN, Annie S
 Lyall, David
 Orchard, Evelyn
SWARD, Robert S
 Dr Soft
SWATRIDGE, Irene M M
 Chandos, Fay
 Lance, Leslie
 Mossop, Irene
 Storm, Virginia
 Tempest, Jan
SWEET, John
 Kim
SWETENHAM, Violet Hilda
 Drummond, Violet Hilda
SWINNERTON, Frank
 Pure, Simon
SYMINGTON, David
 Halliday, James
SYMONDS, E M
 Paston, George
SYMONS, Dorothy G
 Groves, Georgina

TABORI, Paul
 Stafford, Peter
 Stevens, Christopher
TAIT, Euphemia Margaret
 Ironside, John
TAIT, George B
 Barclay, Alan

TAMES, Richard Lawrence
   Lawrence, James
TANNER, Edward Everett
   Dennis, Patrick
   Rowans, Virginia
TATHAM, Laura
   Martin, John
   Phipps, Margaret
TATTERSALL, Muriel Joyce
   Wand, Elizabeth
TAYLOR, Constance Lindsay
   Cullingford, Guy
TAYLOR, Deems
   Smeed
TAYLOR, Phoebe Atwood
   Tilton, Alice
TAYLOR, Stephana Vere
   Benson, S Vere
TEAGUE, John Jessop
   Gerard, Morice
TEGNER, Henry
   Northumbrian Gentleman
   Ruffle
TWILHET, Darwin le Ora
   Fisher, Cyrus T
TELLER, Neville
   Owen, Edmund
TENNYSON, Margaret
   Forrest, Carol
TETTMAR, Betty Eileen
   Spence, Betty E
THIMBLETHORPE, June
   Thorpe, Sylvia
THOM, William Albert Strang
   Morrison, J Strang
THOMAS, Ernest Lewys
   Vaughan, Richard
THOMAS, John Oram
   Oram, John
THOMAS, Ross
   Bleeck, Oliver
THOMAS, Stanley A C
   Wyandotte, Steve
THOMPSON, A M
   Dangle

THOMPSON, Antony Allert
   Alban, Antony
THOMPSON, Arthur Leonard
  Bell
   Clifford, Francis
THOMPSON, George Selden
   Selden, George
THOMPSON, Phyllis
   Morgan, Phyllis
   Rose, Phyllis
THOMSON, Christine Campbell
   Alexander, Dair
THOMSON, Daisy
   Roe, M S
   Thomson, Jon H
THORNE, Isabel Mary
   Villiers, Elizabeth
THORNETT, Ernest Basil
  Charles
   Penny, Rupert
THORP, Joseph
   T
THORPE, John
   Campbell, Duncan
   Centaur
   Scott, Douglas
THORPE-CLARK, Mavis
   Latham, Mavis
TIERNEY, John
   James, Brian
TILLETT, Dorothy Stockbridge
   Strange, John Stephen
TILLEY, E D
   Tilley, Gene
TOMLIN, Eric
   Stuart, Frederick

> What song the Syrens sang,
> or what name Achilles
> assumed,
> though puzzling questions,
> are not beyond all
> conjecture.
> — Sir Thomas Browne

TOMLINSON, Joshua Leonard
   Linson
TONKIN, C B
   Pledger, P J
TORDAY, Ursula
   Allardyce, Paula
   Blackstock, Charity
   Keppel, Charlotte
TOWNSEND, Joan
   Pomfret, Joan
TRACY, Louis and SHIEL, M P
   Holmes, Gordon
TRALINS, S Robert
   O'Shea, Sean
TRENT, Ann
   Carlton, Ann
   Crosse, Elaine
   Desana, Dorothy
   Sernicoli, Davide
TREWIN, J C
   J C T
TRIMBLE, Chloe Maria
   Gartner, Chloe
TRIMBLE, Louis
   Brock, Stuart
TRIMMER, Eric
   Jameson, Eric
TRIPP, Miles Barton
   Brett, John Michael
TROUBETZKOI, (Princess)
   Rives, Amelia
TROWBRIDGE, John Townsend
   Creyton, Paul
TRUMAN, Marcus George
   Beckett, Mark
TUCK, John Erskine
   Erskine, John T
TUCKER, Agnes
   Carruth, Agnes K
TUCKER, James
   Craig, David
TULLETT, Denis John
   Dee, John
   Melmoth
   Sutton, John

TUNLEY, Roul
   Boyd, Edward
TURNER, John Victor
   Hume, David
TURNER, Lida Larrimore
   Larrimore, Lida
TUTE, Warren
   Warren, Andrew

UHR, Elizabeth
   Stern, Elizabeth
ULLYETT, Kenneth
   Bentley, W J
UNDERWOOD, Mavis Eileen
   Kilpatrick, Sarah
UNETT' John
   Preston, James
UNWIN, David Storr
   Severn, David
UPWARD, Edward Falaise
   Chalmers, Allen
UREN, Malcolm
   Malcolm, John
   Matelot
URIS, Auren
   Auren, Paul
URQUHART, Macgregor
   Hart, Max
USHER, Frank Hugh
   Franklin, Charles
   Lester, Frank
USHER, John Gray
   Gray, Christopher

VAHEY, John George Haslette
   Mowbray, John
VAN ESSEN, W
   Serjeant, Richard
VAN ZELLER, Claud H
   Brother Choleric
   Venning, Hugh
VANN, Gerald
   Oke, Simon
VAUGHAN, Owen
   Rhoscomyl, Owen

VEITCH, Thomas
  Kentigern, John
VERNON, Kathleen Rose
  Dixon, Lesley
  Vernon, Kay
VERWER, Johanne
  Johanson, Elizabeth
  Verwer, Hans
VESEY, Ernest Blakeman
  Lewis, Ernest
VIDAL, Gore
  Box, Edgar
VILLIERS, David Hugh
  Buckingham, David
VINING, Elizabeth Gray
  Gray, Elizabeth Janet
VIVIAN, Evelyn C H
  Cannell, Charles
VOELKER, John Donaldson
  Traver, Robert
VULLIAMY, Colwyn Edward
  Rolls, Anthony
  Teg, Twm

WACE, M A
  Golden Gorse
WADDELL, Martin
  Sefton, Catherine
WADDELL, Samuel
  Mayne, Rutherford
WADDINGTON, Miriam
  Merritt, E B
WADE, Arthur Sarsfield
  Rohmer, Sax
WADE, Robert and MILLER,
  William
  Masterson, White
  Miller, Wade
WADE, Rosalind
  Carr, Catharine
WAGENKNECHT, Edward Charles
  Forrest, Julian
WAGNER, Margaret Dale
  Wagner, Peggy

WAINWRIGHT, Gordon Ray
  Gordon, Ray
WALDO, Edward Hamilton
  Sturgeon, Theodore
WALKER, Edith
  Trafford, Jean
  Walker, Jean Brown
WALKER, Emily Kathleen
  Ash, Pauline
  Barry, Eileen
  Devon, Sara
  Foster, Delia
  Lawson, Christine
  Lester, Jane
  Mayne, Cora
  Murray, Jill
  Tilbury, Quenna
  Treves, Kathleen
  Vincent, Heather
  Vincent, Honor
  Winchester, Kay
WALKER, John
  Thirlmere, Rowland
WALKER, Kenneth Macfarlane
  Macfarlane, Kenneth
WALKER, Peter Norman
  Coram, Christopher
  Ferris, Tom
  Manton, Paul
WALKER, Rowland
  Kenworthy, Hugh
WALKER, Stella Archer
  Archer-Batten, S
WALKER, W Sylvester
  Coo-ee
WALL, John W
  Sarban
WALLACE, Henry
  Uncle Henry
WALLER, Leslie
  Cody, C S
WALMSLEY, Arnold
  Roland, Nicholas
WALSH, James Morgan
  Hill, H Haverstock

WALTER, Dorothy Blake
    Blake, Katherine
    Blake, Kay
    Ross, Katherine
    Walter, Katherine
    Walter, Kay
WALTON, John and BRIGHOUSE,
  Harold
    Conway, Olive
WALZ, Audrey
    Bonnamy, Francis
WARD, Robert Spencer
    King, Evan
WARE, Eugene Fitch
    Ironquill
WARRINER, Thurman
    Kersey, John
    Troy, Simon
WATERHOUSE, Keith and
  DEGHY, Guy
    Froy, Herald
    Gibb, Lee
WATFORD, Joel
    Essex, John
WATKINS-PITCHFORD, Denys
  James
    B B
WATNEY, Bernard
    Dolley, Marcus J
WATSON, Elliot Grant
    Lovegood, John
WATSON, Jack Charles
  Wauchope
    Chrystie, Edward M
WATSON, Jane Werner
    Werner, Jane
WATSON, Julia
    De Vere, Jane
    Hamilton, Julia
WATSON, R A
    Cromarty, Deas
WATT, Alexander Peter Fordham
    Fraser, Peter
WATT, Esme
    Jeans, Angela

WATTS, Edgar John Palmer
    Palmer, John
WATTS, Peter Christopher
    Chisholm, Matt
    James, Cy
    Owen, Tom
WAUGH, Hillary Baldwin
    Taylor, H Baldwin
WAY, Elizabeth Fenwick
    Fenwick, Elizabeth
WAYE, Ellen
    Jose, Ellen J
WEALE, Anne
    Blake, Andrea
WEBB, Godfrey, E C
    England, Norman
    Godfrey, Charles
WEBB, Jack
    Grady, Tex
WEBB, Richard Wilson and
  WHEELER, Hugh Callingham
    Patrick, Q
    Quentin, Patrick
    Stagge, Jonathan
WEBB, Robert Forrest and
  ELIADES, David
    Forrest, David
WEBB, Ruth Enid
    Morris, Ruth
WEBBE, Gale Dudley
    Cole, Stephen
WEBSTER, Alica Jane
  Chandler
    Webster, Jean
WEBSTER, Owen
    Pilgrim, Adam
WEES, Frances Shelley
    Shelley, Frances
WEI, Rex
    Williams, Rex
WEIGHTMAN, Archibald John
    Stuart, Alan
WEINER, Margery
    Lake, Sarah

WEINSTEIN, Nathan Wallenstein
  West, Nathaniel
WEIR, Rosemary
  Bell, Catherine
  Green, R
WELCH, Colin
  Simple, Peter
WELDON, A E
  Macnamara, Brinsley
WELLS, Helen
  Lewis, Francine
WERNER, Elsa Jane
  Bedford, Annie North
  Nast, Elsa Ruth
WERTENBAKER, Lael Tucker
  Tucker, Lael
WEST, Betty Bowen
  Bowen, Betty
WEST, Gertrude
  West, Trudy
WEST, Morris
  East, Michael
  Morris, Julian
WEST-WATSON, Keith
  Campbell
  Campbell, Keith
WESTHEIMER, David
  Smith, Z Z
WESTLAKE, Donald Edwin
  Coe, Tucker
  Stark, Richard
WESTMARLAND, Ethel Louisa
  Courtney, Christine
  Elliott, Ellen
WHARMBY, Margot
  Winn, Alison
WHARTON, Michael
  Simple, Peter
WHEAR, Rachel
  Low, Rachel
WHEELER, Hugh Callingham and
  WEBB, Richard Wilson
  Patrick, Q
  Quentin, Patrick
  Stagge, Jonathan

WHELAN, Jerome Bernard
  Brien, R N
WHELPTON, Eric
  Lyte, Richard
WHITBY, Anthony Charles
  Lesser, Anthony
WHITE, Alan
  Fraser, James
WHITE, Celia
  Tustin, Elizabeth
WHITE, Pauline Arnold
  Arnold, Pauline
WHITE, Stanhope
  Bana, Dan
  Sabiad
WHITE, William Anthony P
  Boucher, Anthony
  Holmes, H H
WHITEHAND, James and
  SATHERLEY, David
  Whitehand, Satherley
WHITEMAN, William Meredith
  Turner, C John
WHITFIELD, John
  Pilio, Gerone
WHITFORD, Joan
  Ford, Barry
  Oldham, Hugh R
WHITSON, John Harvey
  Sims, (Lieut) A K
WHITTEN, Wilfred
  John o' London
WHITTET, George Sorley
  Kerr, John O'Connell
  Monkland, George
WHITTINGTON, Harry
  Harrison, Whit
  Holland, Kel
  Myers, Harriet Kathryn
  Philips, Steve
  Stuart, Clay
  Wells, Hondo
  White, Harry
  Whitney, Hallam

WILSON, John Anthony Burgess
    Burgess, Anthony
    Kell, Joseph
    Wilson, John Burgess
WILSON, Robert McNair
    Wynne, Anthony
WILSON, William and GRANT,
  Donald
    Ness, K T
WIMHURST, Cecil Gordon Eugene
    Brent, Nigel
WINCHELL, Prentice
    Dean, Spencer
    Sterling, Stewart
WINDER, Mavis Areta
    Areta, Mavis
    Winder, Mavis
    Wynder, Mabis Areta
WINKWORTH, Derek W
    5029
WINTER, Bevis
    Cagney, Peter
    Hill, Bennet
WINTERS, Bayla
    Winters, Bernice
WINTERTON, Paul
    Bax, Roger
    Garve, Andrew
WINTRINGHAM, Tom
    Gracchus
WISE, Arthur
    McArthur, John
WITCOMBE, Rick
    Marker, Clare
WOHL, Ludwig von
    De Wohl, Louis
WOLFF, William
    Martindale, Spencer
WONG, Elizabeth
    Chi Lien
WOOD, James
    Macleod, Finlay
    Stuart, Gordon
WOOD, Lilian Catherine
    Cymry Bach

WOOD, Patricia E W
    Ross, Patricia
WOOD, Samuel Andrew
    Temple, Robin
WOOD, Violet
    Wood, Quality
WOODCOCK, E Page
    Uncle Reg
WOODFORD, Irene-Cecile
    Barrie, Jane
    Goff, Madeleine
    Lee, Veronica
    Woodford, Cecile
WOODRICH, Mary Neville
    Neville, Mary
WOODS, Olwen
    Woods, Jonah
WOOLLEY, Catherine
    Thayer, Jane
WOOLRICH, Cornell
    Hopley, George
    Irish, William
WOOLSEY, Sarah Chauncey
    Coolidge, Susan
WORBOYS, Anne Eyre
    Eyre, Annette
WORDINGHAM, James A
    Dare, Michael
WORNER, Philip A I
    Incledon, Philip
    Sylvester, Philip
WORNUM, Miriam
    Dennis, Eve
WORTHINGTON-STUART,
  Brian Arthur
    Meredith, Peter
    Stuart, Brian
WRIGHT, Elinor
    Lyon, Elinor
WRIGHT, George T
    Wright, Ted
WRIGHT, John
    Wright, Wade
WRIGHT, Marjory Beatrice
    Pilgrim

WRIGHT, Mary
  Bawn, Mary
WURMBRAND, Richard
  Moses, Ruben
WRIGHT, R L Gerard
  Bristowe, Edwin
WRIGHT, Sydney Fowler
  Fowler, Sydney
WRIGHT, Willard Huntington
  Van Dine, S S
WYLLIE, James McLeod
  Barras Seer
WYND, Oswald
  Black, Gavin
WYNDHAM LEWIS, D B
  Shy, Timothy
WYNNE-TYSON, Esme
  De Morny, Peter

YARDUMIAN, Miryam
  Miryam
YATES, Alan Geoffrey
  Brown, Carter
YELLOT, Barbara Leslie
  Jordan, Barbara Leslie

YORKE, Henry Vincent
  Green, Henry
YOUNG, Janet Randall
  Randall, Janet
  Young, Jan
YOUNG, Phyllis Brett
  Young, Kendal
YOUNGER, Elizabeth
  Hely, Elizabeth
YOUNGER, William Anthony
  Mole, William

ZILLIACUS, Konni
  Covenanter
  Vigilantes
  Williams, Roth
ZIM, Sonia
  Bleeker, Sonia
ZIMMER, Maude Files
  Baird, Maude F
  Fileman, Nan
ZUBER, Mary E L
  Rowlands, Lesley

PSEUDONYMS AND PEN-NAMES

A A
  Willis, A A
A A B
  Baumann, Arthur A
A BACHELOR OF ARTS
  Bentley, Phyllis
A E
  Russell, George William
A H
  Hawkins, (Sir) Anthony Hope
A H G
  Girdleston, A H
A P H
  Herbert, (Sir) Alan P
AARONS, Edward Sidney
  Ayres, Paul and Ronns,
    Edward
ABBEY, Kieran
  Reilly, Helen
ABBOT, Anthony
  Oursler, Fulton
ABBOTT, A C
  Meinzer, Helen Abbott
ABERCROMBIE, Patricia Barnes
  Barnes, Patricia
ACLAND, Alice
  Marreco, Anne
ADAIR, Cecil
  Green, Evelyn Everett
ADAIR, Hazel
  Addis, Hazel Iris
ADAIR, Sally
  Mannock, Laura
ADAMS, Andy
  Harkins, Peter
ADAMS, Annette
  Rowland, Donald Sydney
ADAMS, Bart
  Bingley, David Ernest
ADELER, Max
  Clark, Charles Heber
AGARD, H E
  Evans, Hilary Agard
AINSWORTH, Harriet
  Cadell, Elizabeth

AINSWORTH, Oliver
  Sharp, (Sir) Henry
AINSWORTH, Patricia
  Bigg, Patricia Nina
AINSWORTH, Ruth
  Gilbert, Ruth
AINSWORTHY, Roy
  Paine, Lauran Bosworth
AIRD, Catherine
  McIntosh, Kinn Hamilton
AIRLIE, Catherine
  Macleod, Jean Sutherland
ALAN, A J
  Lambert, Leslie Harrison
ALAN, Jane
  Chisholm, Lilian
ALAN, Marjorie
  Bumpus, Doris Marjorie
ALBAN, Antony
  Thompson, Antony Allert
ALBERT, Ned
  Braun, Wilbur
ALBION, Ken
  King, Albert
ALBRAND, Martha
  Loewengard, Heidi H F
ALDON, Adair
  Meigs, Cornelia Lynde
ALEXANDER, Dair
  Thomson, Christine Campbell
ALEXANDER, Joan
  Pepper, Joan
ALEXANDER, L G
  Ftyaras, Louis George
ALEXANDER, Martin
  Daventry, Leonard John

> Wherefore is it that thou
> dost ask after my name?
> — Book of Genesis, 32, 29

ALEXANDER, Ruth
  Rogers, Ruth
ALGOL
  Bretherton, C H
ALI-MAR
  Porn, Alice
ALIEN
  Baker, Louisa Alice
ALIKI
  Brandenberg, Alyce Christina
ALIUNAS
  Baronas, Aloyzas
ALLABEN, Anne E
  Farrell, Anne Elizabeth
ALLAN, Luke
  Amy, William Lacey
ALLARDYCE, Paula
  Torday, Ursula
ALLCOT, Guy
  Pocock, Tom
ALLEN, Barbara
  Mann, Violet Vivian
ALLEN, Betsy
  Headley, Elizabeth
ALLEN, Clay
  Paine, Lauran Bosworth
ALLEN, Eric
  Allen-Ballard, Eric
ALLEN, F M
  Downey, Edmund
ALLEN, Ronald
  Ayckbourne, Alan
ALLEN, Steve
  Allen, Stephen Valentine
ALLENBY, Gordon
  Matusow, Harvey Mitchell
ALLERTON, Mark
  Cameron, William Ernest
ALLERTON, Mary
  Govan, Mary Christine
ALLISON, Clay
  Keevill, Henry John
ALLYSON, Alan
  Nuttall, Anthony

ALMONTE, Rosa
  Paine, Lauran Bosworth
ALPHA OF THE PLOUGH
  Gardiner, Alfred George
ALVORD, Burt
  Keevill, Henry John
AMBERLEY, Richard
  Bourquin, Paul
AMBERLEY, Simon
  Hoar, Peter
AMES, Felicia
  Burden, Jean
AMES, Jennifer
  Greig, Maysie
AMES, Leslie
  Rigoni, Orlando Joseph
AMES, Leslie
  Ross, William Edward Daniel
AMIS, Breton
  Best, Rayleigh Breton Amis
AMOR, Amos
  Harrell, Irene Burk
AMPHIBIAN
  Aston, (Sir) George
AMPLEGIRTH, Anthony
  Dent, Anthony
ANAUTA
  Blackmore, Anauta
ANDERS, Rex
  Barrett, Geoffrey John
ANDERSON, Ella
  Macleod, Ellen
ANDERSON, Rachel
  Bradby, Rachel
ANDOM, R
  Barrett, Alfred Walter
ANDREWS, A A
  Paine, Lauran Bosworth
ANDREWS, Lucilla
  Crichton, Lucilla Matthew
ANGELL, Norman
  Lane, (Sir) Ralph Norman
  Angell
ANMAR, Frank
  Nolan, William F

ANSTEY, F
　Guthrie, Thomas Anstey
ANSTRUTHER, James
　Graham, James Maxtone
ANTHONY, C L
　Smith, Dorothy Gladys
ANTHONY, Evelyn
　Stevens, Eve
ANTHONY, John
　Beckett, Ronald Brymer
ANTHONY, Piers
　Jacob, Piers Anthony
AP EVANS, Humphrey
　Drummond, Humphrey
AR, Esjay
　Rubinstein, Stanley Jack
ARCHER, Frank
　O'Connor, Richard
ARCHER, G Scott
　Larbalestier, Phillip George
ARCHER, Owen
　Greenwood, Augustus George
ARCHER-BATTEN, S
　Walker, Stella Archer
ARCHESTRATUS
　Driver, Christopher
ARDEN, Clive
　Nutt, Lily Clive
ARDEN, Mary
　Murry, Violet
ARETA, Mavis
　Winder, Mavis Areta
ARGUS, M K
　Eisenstadt-Jeleznov, Mikhail
ARIEL
　Arden, Adrian
ARION
　Chesterton, G K
ARMOUR, John
　Paine, Lauran Bosworth
ARMSTRONG, Anthony
　Willis, George Anthony
　　Armstrong
ARMSTRONG, Raymond
　Lee, Norman
ARMSTRONG, Sybil
　Edmondson, Sybil

ARMSTRONG, Warren
　Bennett, William E
ARNOLD, Pauline
　White, Pauline Arnold
ARNOLD, Wilcox
　Aitken, Andrew
ARP, Bill
　Smith, Charles H
ARTHUR, Burt
　Shappiro, Herbert Arthur
ARTHUR, Elisabeth
　Irish, Betty M
ARTHUR, Gladys
　Osborne, Dorothy Gladys
ARTHUR, Phyllis
　Shipman, Natalie
ARTHUR, William
　Neubauer, William Arthur
ASCHE, Oscar
　Heiss, John Stanger
ASH, Fenton
　Atkins, Frank A
ASH, Pauline
　Walker, Emily Kathleen
ASHE, Elizabeth
　Hyde, Lavender Beryl
ASHE, Gordon
　Creasey, John
ASHE, Susan
　Best, Carol Anne
ASHFORD, Jeffrey
　Jeffries, Roderic Graeme
ASHLEY, Elizabeth
　Salmon, Annie Elizabeth
ASHTON, Lucy
　Martin, Netta
ASKHAM, Francis
　Greenwood, Julia E C
ASQUITH, Nan
　Pattinson, Nancy
ASSIAC
　Fraenkel, Heinrich
AUBREY, Frank
　Atkins, Frank A

87

AUCHTERLONIE, Dorothy
    Green, Dorothy
AUGUSTUS
    Lynn, Elwyn
AULD, Philip
    Burns, Bernard
AUNT DAISY
    Basham, Daisy
AUNT KATE
    Souter, Helen Greig
AUNT MAYSIE
    Jeffrey-Smith, May
AUNTIE MARGARET
    Keddie, Margaret Manson
AUREN, Paul
    Uris, Auren
AUSTIN, Brett
    Floren, Lee
AUSTIN, Frank
    Faust, Frederick
AUSTWICK, John
    Lee, Austin
AVERILL, H C
    Snow, Charles Horace
AVERY, Al
    Montgomery, Rutherford
    George
AVERY, June
    Rees, Joan
AVERY, Richard
    Cooper, Edmund
AVON, Margaret
    Keatley, Sheila
AWDRY, R C
    Charles, Richard
AYE, John
    Atkinson, John
AYES, Anthony
    Sambrot, William Anthony

B B
    Watkins-Pitchford, Denys
    James
BAB
    Gilbert, William Schwenck

BACK-BACK
    Brown, Kay
BACON, Jeremy
    Read, James
BAGBY, George
    Stein, Aaron Marc
BAGNOLD, Enid
    Jones, (Lady) Roderick
BAILEY, Guy
    Simpson, Keith
BAIRD, Maude F
    Zimmer, Maude Files
BALAAM
    Lamb, Geoffrey Frederick
BALBUS
    Huxley, Julian Sorell
BALDRY, Enid
    Citovich, Enid
BALDWIN, Bates
    Jennings, John
BALL, Zachary
    Masters, Kelly
BALLARD, P D
    Ballard, Willis Todhunter
BALLARD, Todhunter
    Ballard, Willis Todhunter
BALLENTINE, John
    Da Cruz, Daniel
BALLEW, Charles
    Snow, Charles Horace
BALLINGER, W A
    Baker, William Howard
BAMFYLDE, Walter
    Bevan, Tom
BANA, Dan
    White, Stanhope
BANCROFT, John
    Jenkins, Alan Charles
BANKOFF, George
    Milkomane, George Alexis
    Milkomanovich
BANNATYNE, Jack
    Gaston, William J
BANNER, Angela
    Maddison, Angela Mary

BANNERMAN, Mark
  Lewing, Anthony
BANNON, Mark
  King, Albert
BANNON, Peter
  Durst, Paul
BANTON, Coy
  Norwood, Victor George
    Charles
BARAKA, Imamu Amiri
  Jones, Le Roi
BARBELLION, W N P
  Cummings, Bruce Frederick
BARBER, Antonia
  Anthony, Barbara
BARCLAY, Alan
  Tait, George B
BARCLAY, Ann
  Greig, Maysie
BARCYNSKA, Hélène (Countess)
  Evans, Marguerite Florence
BARDSLEY, Michael
  Nuttall, Anthony
BARKER, Jack
  Barker, Michael
BARLING, Charles
  Barrington, Pamela
BARLING, Muriel Vere
  Barrington, Pamela
BARLING, Pamela
  Barrington, Pamela
BARNARD, Nancy
  Hale, Sylvia
BARNWELL, J O
  Caruso, Joseph
BARON, Paul
  Landells, Richard
BARR, Elisabeth
  Edward, Irene
BARRAS SEER
  Wyllie, James McLeod
BARRATT, Robert
  Beeton, D R
BARRIE, Hester
  Hector, Barbara

BARRIE, Jane
  Savage, Mildred
BARRIE, Jane
  Woodford, Irene Cecile
BARRING, Ludwig
  Schreiber, Hermann O L
BARRINGTON, E
  Beck, Eliza Louisa Moresby
BARRY, Ann
  Byers, Amy
BARRY, Charles
  Bryson, Charles
BARRY, Eileen
  Walker, Emily Kathleen
BARRY, Jocelyn
  Bowden, Jean
BARTIMEUS
  Ricci, Lewis Anselm da Costa
BARTLETT, Kathleen
  Paine, Lauran Bosworth
BARTON, Jack
  Chadwick, Joseph
BASSERMANN, Lujo
  Schreiber, Hermann O L
BASSETT, Jack
  Rowland, Donald Sydney
BASSETT, John Keith
  Keating, Lawrence Alfred
BATCHELOR, Reg
  Paine, Lauran Bosworth
BATTLE, Felix
  Levin, Bernard
BAWN, Mary
  Wright, Mary
BAX, Roger
  Winterton, Paul
BAXTER, George Owen
  Faust, Frederick
BAXTER, Gillian
  Hirst, Gillian
BAXTER, Gregory
  Ressich, John S M and
    De Banzie, Eric
BAXTER, Hazel
  Rowland, Donald Sydney

BAXTER, John
  Hunt, E Howard
BAXTER, Olive
  Eastwood, Helen
BAXTER, Shane V
  Norwood, Victor George
  Charles
BAXTER, Valerie
  Maynell, Laurence Walter
BAYLISS, Timothy
  Baybars, Taner
BEACHCOMBER
  Morton, J B
BEAR, Bullen
  Donnelly, Augustine
BEAR, I D
  Douglass, Percival Ian
BEATON, George
  Brenan, Edward Fitzgerald
BEATON, Jane
  Long, Gladys
BEATTY, Baden
  Casson, Frederick
BECK, Christopher
  Bridges, Thomas Charles
BECK, Harry
  Paine, Lauran Bosworth
BECK, Lily Adams
  Beck, Eliza Louisa Moresby
BECKET, Lavinia
  Course, Pamela
BECKETT, Mark
  Truman, Marcus George
BECKWITH, Lillian
  Comber, Lillian
BEDFORD, Ann
  Rees, Joan
BEDFORD, Annie North
  Werner, Elsa Jane
BEDFORD, Kenneth
  Paine, Lauran Bosworth
BEE
  Boshell, Gordon
BEECH, Margaret
  Barclay, Vera C

BEEDING, Francis
  Saunders, Hilary Aidan
  St George and Palmer,
  John Leslie
BEG, Callum
  Mack, J C O
BELL, Catherine
  Weir, Rosemary
BELL, John
  Johnson, Victor
BELL, Josephine
  Ball, Doris Bell
BELL, Nancy
  Irish, Betty M
BELL, Neil
  Southwold, Stephen
BELLMAN, Walter
  Barrett, Hugh Gilchrist
BELVEDERE, Lee
  Grayland, Valerie M
BENARY-ISBERT, Margot
  Benary, Margot
BENDER, Jay
  Deindorfer, Robert G
BENDIT, Gladys
  Presland, John
BENEDICT, Billy
  Paul, Maury
BENNETT, Dwight
  Newton, Dwight Bennett
BENNETT, H O
  Hardison, O B
BENNEY, Mark
  Degras, Henry Ernest
BENSON, Adam
  Bingley, David Ernest
BENSON, S Vere
  Taylor, Stephana Vere
BENTINCK, Ray
  Best, Rayleigh Breton Amis
BENTLEY, James
  Hanley, James
BENTLEY, W J
  Ullyett, Kenneth

90

BENTON, Karla
  Rowland, Donald Sydney
BENTON, Will
  Paine, Lauran Bosworth
BERG, Ila
  Garber, Nellia B
BERGER, Helen
  Bamberger, Helen R
BERKELEY, Anthony
  Cox, A B
BERKLEY, Tom
  Geen, Clifford
BERNARD, Robert
  Martin, Robert Bernard
BERNE, Leo
  Davies, Leslie Purnell
BERNECK, Ludwig
  Schreiber, Hermann O L
BERRINGTON, John
  Brownjohn, Alan
BERRISFORD, Judith
  Lewis, Clifford and Lewis,
    Judith Mary
BERRISFORD, Mary
  Lewis, Mary Christianna
BERRY, Erick
  Best, Allena
BERRY, Helen
  Rowland, Donald Sydney
BERTRAM, Arthur
  Ibbott, Arthur Pearson
BETHUNE, Mary
  Clopet, Liliane M C
BETTERIDGE, Don
  Newman, Bernard
BETTINA
  Ehrlich, Bettina
BEVAN, Alistair
  Roberts, Keith J K
BICKERDYKE, John
  Cooke, C H
BIJ-BIJCHENKO, B
  Rudnyckyj, Jaroslav B
BILL
  Strachan, Gladys Elizabeth

BILLINGS, Buck
  Rister, Claude
BIRD, Lilian
  Barradell-Smith, Walter
BIRD, Richard
  Barradell-Smith, Walter
BIRKENHEAD, Edward
  Birkenhead, Elijah
BIRMINGHAM, George A
  Hannay, James Owen
BIZET, George
  Bisset-Smith, G T
BLACK, Gavin
  Wynd, Oswald
BLACK, Jett
  Black, Oliver
BLACK, Kitty
  Black, Dorothy
BLACK, Lionel
  Barker, Dudley
BLACK, Mansell
  Dudley-Smith, Trevor
BLACK, Veronica
  Black, Maureen
BLACKBURN, Martin
  Allfree, P S
BLACKER, Hereth
  Chalke, Herbert
BLACKLIN, Malcolm
  Chambers, Aidan
BLACKSNAKE, George
  Richardson, Gladwell
BLACKSTOCK, Charity
  Torday, Ursula
BLACKWELL, John
  Collings, Edwin
BLAIKE, Avona
  Macintosh, Joan
BLAINE, Jeff
  Barrett, Geoffrey John
BLAINE, Sara
  Morgan, Diana
BLAIR
  Blair-Fish, Wallace Wilfred

91

BLAIRMAN, Jacqueline
Pinto, Jacqueline
BLAISDELL, Anne
Linington, Elizabeth
BLAKE
Adam, Ronald
BLAKE, Andrea
Weale, Anne
BLAKE, Cameron
Mason, Michael
BLAKE, Katherine
Walter, Dorothy Blake
BLAKE, Kay
Walter, Dorothy Blake
BLAKE, Monica
Muir, Marie
BLAKE, Nicholas
Day Lewis, Cecil
BLAKE, Robert
Davies, Leslie Purnell
BLAKE, Vanessa
Brown, May
BLAKE, William
Blech, William James
BLAKE, William James
Blech, William James
BLAUTH, Christopher
Blauth-Muszkowski, Peter
BLEECK, Oliver
Thomas, Ross
BLEEKER, Sonia
Zin, Sonia
BLINDERS, Belinda
Coke, Desmond
BLISS, Adam
Burkhardt, Eve and
Burkhardt, Robert Ferdinand
BLIXEN, Karen
Blixen-Finecke, Karen
Christence (Baroness)
BLOOD, Joan Wilde
Murray, Joan
BLOOMFIELD, Robert
Edgley, Leslie

BLUNDELL, Peter
Butterworth, Frank Nestle
BLYTH, John
Hibbs, John
BOAKE, Capel
Kerr, Doris Boake
BOAS, Marie
Hall, Marie
BODEN, Hilda
Bodenham, Hilda
BOGLE, Charles
Dukenfield, William Claude
BOILEAU, Marie
Hardy, Jane
BOLD, Ralph
Griffiths, Charles
BOLITHO, Ray D
Blair, Dorothy
BOLITHO, William
Ryall, William Bolitho
BOLSTER, Evelyn
Bolster, (Sister) M Angela
BOLT, Ben
Binns, Ottwell
BOLT, Lee
Faust, Frederick
BON VIVEUR
Cradock, Phyllis Nan Sortain
and Cradock, John
BOND, Gillian
McEvoy, Marjorie
BONEHILL, Ralph
Stratemeyer, Edward
BONETT, Emery
Carter, Felicity Winifred
BONETT, John
Coulson, John
BONNAMY, Francis
Walz, Audrey
BONNER, Parker
Ballard, Willis Todhunter
BONNEY, Bill
Keevill, Henry John
BOON, August
Breton-Smith, Clare

BORDEN, Leo
  Borden, Deal
BORER, Mary Cathcart
  Myers, Mary Cathcart
BORG, Jack
  Borg, Philip Anthony John
BORNE, D
  Rice, Dorothy
BORODIN, George
  Milkomane, George Alexis
    Milkomanovich
BORTH, Willan G
  Bosworth, Willan George
BOSCAWEN, Linda
  Smithells, Doreen
BOSCO, Jack
  Holliday, Joseph
BOSWELL, James
  Kent, Arthur
BOSWELL, John
  King, John
BOSWORTH, Frank
  Paine, Lauran Bosworth
BOUCHER, Anthony
  White, William Anthony P
BOURNE, George
  Sturt, George
BOURNE, John
  John, Owen
BOURNE, Peter
  Jeffries, Graham Montague
BOVEE, Ruth
  Paine, Lauran Bosworth
BOWDEN, Jim
  Spence, William
BOWEN, Betty
  West, Betty Bowen
BOWEN, Marjorie
  Campbell, Gabrielle
    Margaret Vere
BOWIE, Jim
  Norwood, Victor George
    Charles
BOWIE, Sam
  Ballard, Willis Todhunter

BOWMAN, Jeanne
  O'More, Peggy
BOWOOD, Richard
  Daniell, Albert Scott
BOX, Edgar
  Vidal, Gore
BOY
  Fowkes, Aubrey
BOYD, Edward
  Tunley, Roul
BOYD, Nancy
  Millay, Edna St Vincent
BOYD, Prudence
  Gibbs, Norah
BOYER, Robert
  Lake, Kenneth Robert
BRACE, Timothy
  Pratt, Theodore
BRACKEN, Steve
  Farris, John Lee
BRACKETT, Leigh
  Hamilton, Leigh Brackett
BRADBURNE, E S
  Lawrence, Elizabeth
BRADDEN, George
  Milkomane, George Alexis
    Milkomanovich
BRADEN, Walter
  Finney, Jack
BRADFIELD, Nancy
  Sayer, Nancy Margetts
BRADFORD, Will
  Paine, Lauran Bosworth
BRADLEY, Concho
  Paine, Lauran Bosworth
BRADLEY, Shelland
  Birt, Francis Bradley
BRADWELL, James
  Kent, Arthur
BRAHMS, Caryl
  Abrahams, Doris Caroline
BRAMAH, Ernest
  Smith, Ernest Bramah
BRAMWELL, James
  Byrom, James

93

BRAND, Christianna
  Lewis, Mary Christianna
BRAND, Clay
  Norwood, Victor George
  Charles
BRAND, David
  Nutt, David
BRAND, Max
  Faust, Frederick
BRAND, Mona
  Fox, Mona Alexis
BRANDANE, John
  Macintyre, John
BRANDON, Bruce
  Braun, Wilbur
BRANDON, Joe
  Davis, Robert Prunier
BRANDON, Sheila
  Rayner, Claire
BRANT, Lewis
  Rowland, Donald Sydney
BRAY, Alison
  Rowland, Donald Sydney
BRAYCE, William
  Rowland, Donald Sydney
BRENAN, Gerald
  Brenan, Edward Fitzgerald
BRENNAN, Walt
  King, Albert
BRENNAN, Will
  Paine, Lauran Bosworth
BRENNING, L H
  Hunter, Alfred John
BRENT, (of Bin Bin)
  Franklin, Stella Maria Sarah
  Miles
BRENT, Calvin
  Hornby, John W
BRENT, Catherine
  King, Albert
BRENT, Nigel
  Wimhurst, Cecil Gordon
  Eugene
BREOLA, Tjalmar
  De Jong, David Cornel

BRESTER, Benjamin
  Folsom, Franklin Brewster
BRETT, John Michael
  Tripp, Miles Barton
BRETT, Martin
  Sanderson, Douglas
BRETT, Michael
  Brett, Leslie Frederick
BRETT, Rosalind
  Blair, Kathryn
BREWER, Mike
  Guinness, Maurice
BREWSTER, Robin
  Staples, Reginald Thomas
BRIDE, Jack
  Marteau, F A
BRIDGE, Ann
  O'Malley, (Lady)
BRIDGE, John
  Peter, Robert Louis
BRIDGEMAN, Richard
  Davies, Leslie Purnell
BRIDGER, Adam
  Bingley, David Ernest
BRIDGES, Victor
  De Freyne, George
BRIDGWATER, Donald
  Henderson, Donald Landels
BRIDIE, James
  Mavor, Osborne Henry
BRIEN, R N
  Whelan, Jerome Bernard
BRINSMEAD, H F
  Brinsmead, Hesba
BRIONY, Henry
  Ellis, Oliver
BRISTOWE, Edwin
  Wright, R L Gerrard
BROCK, Gavin
  Lindsay, Maurice
BROCK, Lynn
  Macallister, Alister
BROCK, Stuart
  Trimble, Louis

94

BROCKLEY, Fenton
  Rowland, Donald Sydney
BRODIE, Gordon
  Smith, Sidney Wallace
BROGAN, James
  Hodder-Williams, Christopher
BRONSON, Oliver
  Rowland, Donald Sydney
BRONSON, Wade
  King, Albert
BROOK, Esther
  Huggett, Berthe
BROOK, Peter
  Chovil, Alfred Harold
BROOKE, Carol
  Ramskill, Valerie
BROOKER, Clark
  Fowler, Kenneth
BROOKS, Jonathan
  Mellett, John Calvin
BROOME, Adam
  James, Godfrey Warden
BROOME, Dora
  Wild, Dora Mary
BROTHER CHOLERIC
  Van Zeller, Claud H
BROTHER GRAHAM
  Jeffrey, Graham
BROUILLETTE, Emil
  Rydberg, Ernie
BROWN, Carter
  Yates, Alan Geoffrey
BROWN, Mandy
  Brown, May
BROWN, Marel
  Brown, Margaret Elizabeth
    Snow
BROWNE, Courtney
  Courtney-Browne, Reginald D S
BROWNING, John
  Brown, John
BRUCE, Charles
  Francis, Arthur Bruce Charles
BRUCE, Leo
  Croft-Cooke, Rupert

BRUNSWICK, James
  Stitt, James M
BRYAN, John
  Delves-Broughton, Josephine
BRYANS, Robin
  Bryans, Robert Harbinson
BRYHER
  Ellerman, Annie Winifred
BUCHANAN, Chuck
  Rowland, Donald Sydney
BUCHANAN, Patrick
  Corley, Edwin and Murphy,
    John
BUCKINGHAM, Bruce
  Lilley, Peter and Stansfield,
    Anthony
BUCKINGHAM, David
  Villiers, David Hugh
BUCKLEY, Eunice
  Scott, Rose Laure
BUCKMASTER, Henrietta
  Henkle, Henrietta
BUCKROSE, J E
  Jameson, Annie Edith
BUDD, Jackson
  Budd, William John
BULLEN BEAR
  Donnelly, Augustine
BULLINGHAM, Ann
  Jones, A Miles
BURCHELL, Mary
  Cook, Ida
BURFIELD, Eva
  Ebbett, Eve
BURFORD, Eleanor
  Hibbert, Eleanor Alice Burford
BURGEON, G A L
  Barfield, Arthur Owen
BURGER, John
  Marquand, Leopold
BURGESS, Anthony
  Wilson, John Anthony
    Burgess
BURKE, Edmund
  Boggs, Winifred

95

BURKE, Fielding
  Dargan, Olive
BURKE, Jonathan
  Burke, John Frederick
BURKE, Shifty
  Benton, Peggie
BURNS, Bobby
  Burns, Vincent
BURNS, Mary
  Hare, Walter B
BURNS, Sheila
  Bloom, Ursula
BURNS, Tex
  L'Amour, Louis
BURR, Elsie
  Milligan, Elsie
BURROUGHS, Margaret
  Feldman, Eugene P R
BURROWAY, Janet
  Eysselinck, Janet Gay
BURTON, Conrad
  Edmundson, Joseph
BUTLER, Joan
  Alexander, Robert William
BUTLER, Richard
  Butler, Arthur Ronald
BUTLER, Walter C
  Faust, Frederick
BUTTLE, Myra
  Purcell, Victor W W S
BYRNE, Donn
  Donn-Byrne, Brian Oswald

C D
  Lawrence, T E
C J G
  Lawrence, T E
C O
  Collinson Owen, H
CABBY WITH CAMERA
  Green, Maxwell
CABLE, Boyd
  Ewart, Ernest Andrew
CABOCHON, Francis
  Allan, Philip Bertram Murray

CADE, Alexander
  Methold, Kenneth
CADWALLADER
  Clemens, Paul
CAGNEY, Peter
  Winter, Bevis
CAHILL, Mike
  Nolan, William F
CAILLOU, Alan
  Lyle-Smythe, Alan
CAILLOUX, Pousse
  Bethell, Leonard Arthur
CALDECOTT, Veronica
  Cohen, Victor
CALDWELL, Elinor
  Breton-Smith, Clare
CALEHAS
  Garvin, J L
CALEY, Rod
  Rowland, Donald Sydney
CALHOUN, Mary
  Wilkins, Mary Louise
CALIBAN
  Reid, John
CALLAHAN, John
  Chadwick, Joseph
CALLAS, Theo
  McCarthy, J L
CALLENDER, Julian
  Lee, Austin
CALLISTHENES
  Costa, Gabriel
CALLUM, Michael
  Greaves, Michael
CALLUM BEG
  Mack, J C O
CALVIN, Henry
  Hanley, Clifford
CAM
  Campbell, Barbara Mary
CAMBRIDGE, Elizabeth
  Hodges, Barbara
CAMDEN, Richard
  Beeston, L J

CAMERON, D Y
  Cook, Dorothy Mary
CAMERON, Hector
  Macquarrie, Hector
CAMERON, Ian
  Payne, Donald Gordon
CAMERON, John
  Macdonell, A G
CAMERON, Margaret
  Lindsay, Kathleen
CAMPBELL, Berkeley
  Duddington, Charles Lionel
CAMPBELL, Bruce
  Epstein, Samuel
CAMPBELL, Colin
  Christie, Douglas
CAMPBELL, Duncan
  Thorpe, John
CAMPBELL, Judith
  Pares, Marion
CAMPBELL, Keith
  West-Watson, Keith Campbell
CAMPION, Sarah
  Alpers, Mary Rose
CANAWAY, Bill
  Canaway, W H
CANDY, Edward
  Neville, Alison
CANFIELD, Cleve
  Mitchell, Clare May
CANFIELD, Dorothy
  Fisher, Dorothea F C
CANNAN, Denis
  Pullein-Thompson, Dennis
CANNELL, Charles
  Vivian, Evelyn C H
CANNON, Elliott
  Elliott-Cannon, Arthur Elliott
CANUCK, Abe
  Bingley, David Ernest
CANUSI, Jose
  Barker, S Omar
CAPE, Judith
  Page, P K

CAPON, Peter
  Oakley, Eric Gilbert
CAPSTAN
  Hardinge, Rex
CAREY, James
  Carew-Slater, Harold James
CARFAX, Catherine
  Fairburn, Eleanor
CARGOE, Richard
  Payne, Robert
CARLETON, Janet
  Adam Smith, Janet Buchanan
CARLOTA
  Oppenheimer, Carlota
CARLTON, Ann
  Trent, Ann
CARLTON, Roger
  Rowland, Donald Sydney
CARLYLE, Anthony
  Milton, Gladys Alexander
CARMAN, Dulce
  Drummond, Edith
CARMICHAEL, Harry
  Ognall, Leo Horace
CARMICHAEL, Philip
  Harrison, Philip
CARNAC, Carol
  Rivett, Edith Caroline
CARNEGIE, Sacha
  Carnegie, Raymond Alexander
CAROL, Bill J
  Knott, William Cecil
CARP, Augustus
  Bashford, (Sir) Henry Howarth
CARR, Catherine
  Wade, Rosalind
CARR, Charles
  Mason, Sydney Charles
CARR, Elaine
  Mason, Sydney Charles

> A self-made man may
> prefer a self-made name.
> — Judge Learned Hand

97

CARR, Glyn
Styles, Showell
CARR, Philippa
Hibbert, Eleanor Alice Burford
CARR, Roberta
Roberts, Irene
CARREL, Mark
Paine, Lauran Bosworth
CARRICK, Edward
Craig, Edward Anthony
CARRICK, John
Crosbie, Hugh Provan
CARRINGTON, Michael
Williams, Meurig
CARRINGTON, V
Hughes, Valerie Anne
CARROLL, Martin
Carr, Margaret
CARRUTH, Agnes K
Tucker, Agnes
CARSON, Anthony
Brooke, Peter
CARSON, Lance
Kelly, Harold Ernest
CARSTAIRS, Kathleen
Jacobs, Thomas Curtis Hicks
CARSTAIRS, Rod
Dalton, Gilbert
CARSTENS, Netta
Laffeaty, Christina
CARTER, Bruce
Hough, Richard A
CARTER, Diana
Copper, Dorothy
CARTER, John L
Carter, Compton Irving
CARTER, Nevada
Paine, Lauran Bosworth
CARTER, Nick
Avallone, Michael Angelo Jr
CARTER, Nick
Carter, Bryan
CARTLAND, Barbara
McCorquodale, Barbara
Hamilton

CARVER, Dave
Bingley, David Ernest
CARY, Arthur
Cary, Joyce
CARY, D M
Macmillan, Douglas
CARYL, Jean
Kaplan, Jean Caryl
CASE, Justin
Gleadow, Rupert
CASEY, Mart
Casey, Michael T and
Casey, Rosemary
CASEY, T
Cordes, Theodor K
CASSADY, Claude
Paine, Lauran Bosworth
CASSANDRA
Connor, (Sir) William
CASSELLS, John
Duncan, William Murdoch
CASSIUS
Foot, Michael
CASTLE, Douglas
Brown, John Ridley
CASTLE, John
Payne, Ronald Charles and
Garrod, John William
CATHODE RAY
Scroggie, Marcus Graham
CATLIN, Ralph
Lavender, David
CATO
Foot, Michael; Howard, Peter
and Owen, Frank
CATTO, Max
Catto, Maxwell Jeffrey
CAUDWELL, Christopher
Sprigg, Christopher St John
CAULDWELL, Frank
King, Francis
CAUSEWAY, Jane
Cork, Barry
CAVANNA, Betty
Harrison, Elizabeth C

CAVENDISH, Peter
  Horler, Sydney
CECIL, Henry
  Leon, Henry Cecil
CELTICUS
  Bevan, Aneurin
CENSOR
  Bunce, Oliver Bell
CENTAUR
  Thorpe, John
CERAM, C W
  Marek, Kurt W
CHABER, M E
  Crossen, Kendell Foster
CHACE, Isobel
  Hunter, Elizabeth
CHALLIS, George
  Faust, Frederick
CHALLIS, Simon
  Phillips, Dennis John Andrew
CHALMERS, Allen
  Upward, Edward Falaisie
CHALLONER, H K
  Mills, Janet Melanie Ailsa
CHALON, Jon
  Chaloner, John Seymour
CHAMBERS, Dana
  Leffingwell, Albert
CHAMBERS, Peter
  Phillips, Dennis John Andrew
CHANAIDH, Fear
  Campbell, John Lorne
CHANCE, Jonathan
  Chance, John Newton
CHANDOS, Fay
  Swatridge, Irene M M
CHANEY
  Leeming, Jill
CHANNEL, A R
  Catherall, Arthur
CHAPMAN, Mariston
  Chapman, Mary I and Chapman,
    John Stanton
CHARLES, Frederick
  Ashford, F C

CHARLES, Robert
  Smith, R C
CHARQUES, Dorothy
  Emms, Dorothy
CHASE, Alice
  McHargue, Georgess
CHASE, Beatrice
  Parr, Olive Katherine
CHASE, James Hadley
  Raymond, Rene
CHATHAM, Larry
  Bingley, David Ernest
CHATTAN, Robert
  Smith, Robert
CHEETHAM, Hal
  Cheetham, James
CHEIRO
  Hamon, Louis (Count)
CHELTON, John
  Durst, Paul
CHERRYMAN, A E
  Levin, Bernard
CHESHAM, Henry
  Bingley, David Ernest
CHESTER, Peter
  Phillips, Dennis John Andrew
CHI LIEN
  Wong, Elizabeth
CHISHOLM, Matt
  Watts, Peter Christopher
CHRISTIAN, Jill
  Dilcock, Noreen
CHRYSTIE, Edward M
  Watson, Jack Charles Wauchope
CHU FENG
  Blofeld, John
CHURCH, Jeffrey
  Kirk, Richard Edmund
CLADPOLE, Jim
  Richards, James
CLAIRE
  Andrews, Claire and
    Andrews, Keith
CLAPP, Patricia
  Cone, P C L

CLARE, Elizabeth
  Cook, Dorothy Mary
CLARE, Helen
  Blair, Pauline Hunter
CLARE, Marguerite
  Heppell, Mary
CLARK, Mary Lou
  Clark, Maria
CLARKE, John
  Laughlin, Virginia Carli
CLARKE, Merle
  Gessner, Lynne
CLARKE, Pauline
  Blair, Pauline Hunter
CLARKE, Richard
  Paine, Lauran Bosworth
CLARKE, Robert
  Paine, Lauran Bosworth
CLAUDE
  Forde, Claude Marie
CLAUGHTON-JAMES, James
  Bentley, James W B
CLAY, Bertha M
  Braeme, Charlotte Monica
CLAY, Weston
  Ford, T W
CLAYMORE, Tod
  Clevely, Hugh Desmond
CLEMENT, Hal
  Stubbs, Harry Clement
CLEMENTIA
  Feehan, (Sister) Mary Edward
CLEMENTS, E H
  Hunter, Eileen
CLEMONS, Elizabeth
  Nowell, Elizabeth Cameron
CLERIHEW, E
  Bentley, Edmund Clerihew
CLEVE, Janita
  Rowland, Donald Sydney
CLEVEDON, John
  Plumley, Ernest F
CLEVELAND, Jim
  King, Albert

CLIFFORD, Francis
  Thompson, Arthur Leonard
  Bell
CLIFFORD, John
  Bayliss, John Clifford
CLIFFORD, Martin
  Hamilton, Charles Harold
  St John
CLINTON, Jeff
  Bickham, Jack M
CLIVE, Clifford
  Home-Gall, Edward Reginald
CLOUD, Yvonne
  Kapp, Yvonne
CLYDE, Craig
  Gossman, Oliver
COBBLEIGH, Tom
  Raymond, Walter
COCHRAN, Jeff
  Durst, Paul
COCHRANE, Corinna
  Peterson, Corinna
COCKIN, Joan
  Burbridge, Edith Joan
CODY, A R
  Joscelyn, Archie Lynn
CODY, Al
  Joscelyn, Archie Lynn
CODY, C S
  Waller, Leslie
CODY, Stetson
  Gribble, Leonard Reginald
CODY, Stone
  Mount, Thomas Ernest
CODY, Walt
  Norwood, Victor George
  Charles
COE, Tucker
  Westlake, Donald Edwin
COFFIN, Geoffrey
  Mason, F Van Wyck
COLBERE, Hope
  Coolbear, Marian H
COLE, Jackson
  Scott, Leslie

COLE, Richard
    Barrett, Geoffrey John
COLE, Stephen
    Webbe, Gale Dudley
COLEMAN, Lonnie
    Coleman, William Lawrence
COLES, Manning
    Manning, Adelaide Frances Oke
    and Coles, Cyril Henry
COLLIER, Douglas
    Fellowes-Gordon, Ian
COLLIER, Joy
    Millar, Minna
COLLINGS, Jillie
    Collings, I J
COLLINGSWOOD, Frederick
    Lakritz, Esther
COLLINS, D
    Bulleid, H A V
COLLINS, Geoffrey
    Jeffries, Greg
COLLINS, Hunt
    Hunter, Evan
COLLINS, Joan
    Collins, Mildred
COLLINS, Michael
    Lynds, Dennis
COLLINSON, Peter
    Hammett, Dashiell
COLLYER, Doric
    Fellows, Dorothy Alice
COLMAN, George
    Glassco, John
COLSON, Thora
    Orton, Thora
COLT, Clem
    Nye, Nelson Coral
COLT, Russ
    Kerr, D
COLTMAN, Will
    Bingley, David Ernest
COLTON, A J
    Hook, Alfred Samuel
COMPERE, Mickie
    Davidson, Margaret

COMPTON, Guy
    Compton, D G
COMYNS, Barbara
    Carr, Barbara Irene Veronica
    Comyns
CONDON, Patricia
    Gooden, P E
CONDRAY, Bruno
    Humphrys, Leslie George
CONISTON, Ed
    Bingley, David Ernest
CONNELL, John
    Robertson, James Robin
CONNEY, Barbara
    Porter, Barbara Conney
CONNINGTON, J J
    Stewart, Alfred Walter
CONNOR, Ralph
    Gordon, Charles William
CONQUEST, Owen
    Hamilton, Charles Harold
    St John
CONRAD, Jack
    Conrad, Isaac
CONRAD, Jessie
    Korzeniowski, Jessie
CONRAD, Joseph
    Korzeniowski, Teodor Józef
    Konrad
CONRAD, Kenneth
    Lottich, Kenneth
CONRAD, Paul
    King, Albert
CONROY, Jim
    Chadwick, Joseph
CONROY, Robert
    Goldston, Robert
CONSTANT READER
    Parker, Dorothy
CONTE, Charles
    Mackinnon, Charles Roy
CONWAY, Celine
    Blair, Kathryn
CONWAY, Hugh
    Fargus, Frederick John

CONWAY, Keith
Hetherington, Keith James
CONWAY, Laura
Ansle, Dorothy Phoebe
CONWAY, Olive
Walton, John and Brighouse,
Harold
CONWAY, Peter
Milkomane, George Alexis
Milkomanovich
CONWAY, Troy
Avallone, Michael Angelo Jr
COO-EE
Walker, W Sylvester
COOK, Vera
Ryder, Vera
COOK, Will
Cook, William Everett
COOKE, M E
Creasey, John
COOKE, Margaret
Creasey, John
COOKRIDGE, John Michael
Holroyd, Ethel Mary
COOLIDGE, Susan
Woolsey, Sarah Chauncey
COOPER, Craig
King, Albert
COOPER, Henry St John
Creasey, John
COOPER, William
Hoff, Harry Summerfield
COPPLESTONE, Bennet
Kitchin, F H
CORAM, Christopher
Walker, Peter Norman
CORD, Barry
Germano, Peter
CORDELL, Alexander
Graber, George Alexander
CORELLI, Marie
Mackay, Minnie
CORENANDA, A L A
Numano, Allen

CORIOLANUS
McMillan, James
CORLETT, Joyce I
Kirkwood, Joyce
CORNO DI BASSETTO
Shaw, George Bernard
CORNWALL, Nellie
Sloggett, Nellie
CORONET
James, Charles
CORRIGAN, Mark
Lee, Norman
CORTEEN, Craig
Norwood, Victor George
Charles
CORTEEN, Wes
Norwood, Victor George
Charles
CORVO, (Baron)
Rolfe, Frederick
CORY, Caroline
Freeman, Kathleen
CORY, Desmond
McCarthy, J L
COST, March
Morrison, Margaret Mackie
COSTLER, (Dr) A
Koestler, Arthur
COTTERELL, Brian
Dingle, A E
COULSDON, John
Hincks, Cyril Malcolm
COURT, Sharon
Rowland, Donald Sydney
COURTLAND, Roberta
Dern, Erolie Pearl
COURTNEY, Christine
Westmarland, Ethel Louisa
COVENANTER
Zilliacus, Konni
COWAN, Alan
Gilchrist, Alan
COWEN, Frances
Minto, Frances

COWPER, Richard
   Murray, John Middleton Jr
COX, Edith
   Goaman, Muriel
COX, Jack
   Cox, John
COX, Lewis
   Cox, Euphrasia Emeline
COX-JOHNSON, Ann
   Saunders, Ann Loreille
CRAD, Joseph
   Ansell, Edward Clarence
   Trelawney
CRADDOCK, Charles Egbert
   Murfree, Mary Noailles
CRADOCK, Fanny
   Cradock, Phyllis Nan Sortain
CRAIG, A A
   Anderson, Poul
CRAIG, Alison
   Nicholson, Joan
CRAIG, David
   Tucker, James
CRAIG, Jennifer
   Brambleby, Ailsa
CRAIG, John Eland
   Chipperfield, Joseph
CRAIG, Lee
   Sands, Leo G
CRAIG, Vera
   Rowland, Donald Sydney
CRAIGIE, David
   Craigie, Dorothy
CRAILE, Wesley
   Rowland, Donald Sydney
CRANE, Henry
   Douglass, Percival Ian
CRANE, Robert
   Robertson, Frank Chester
CRANSTON, Edward
   Fairchild, William
CRAVEN HILL
   Parsons, Charles P

CRAWFORD, Anthony
   Hugill, John Anthony
   Crawford
CRAWFORD, Robert
   Rae, Hugh Cranford
CRECY, Jeanne
   Creasey, Jeanne
CREEDI, Joel
   King, Albert
CREEK, Nathan
   Sheppard, John Hamilton
   George
CRESCENDO
   Kalisch, A
CRESTON, Dormer
   Baynes, Dorothy Julia
CREYTON, Paul
   Trowbridge, John Townsend
CRIBLECOBLIS, Otis
   Dukenfield, William Claude
CRISPIE
   Crisp, S E
CRISPIN, Edmund
   Montgomery, Robert Bruce
CRISTY, R J
   De Cristoforo, R J
CROMARTY, Deas
   Watson, R A
CROMIE, Stanley
   Simmons, J S A
CROMPTON, Richmal
   Lamburn, Richmal Crompton
CROMWELL, Elsie
   Lee, Elsie
CRONHEIM, F G
   Godfrey, Frederick M
CRONIN, Michael
   Cronin, Brendan Leo
CROSBIE, Provan
   Crosbie, Hugh Provan
CROSS, Brenda
   Colloms, Brenda
CROSS, James
   Parry, Hugh J

CROSS, Mark
　　Pechey, Archibald Thomas
CROSS, Nancy
　　Baker, Anne
CROSS, T T
　　Da Cruz, Daniel
CROSSE, Elaine
　　Trent, Ann
CROSSE, Victoria
　　Griffin, Vivian Cory
CRUMPET, Peter
　　Buckley, Fergus Reid
CRUNDEN, Reginald
　　Cleaver, Hylton Reginald
CULEX
　　Stanier, Maida
CULLINGFORD, Guy
　　Taylor, Constance Lindsay
CULLNER, Lenard
　　Mazure, Alfred
CULOTTA, Nino
　　O'Grady, John
CULPEPER, Martin
　　Pullen, George
CUMBERLAND, Gerald
　　Kenyon, Fred
CUMBERLAND, Roy
　　Mégroz, R L
CUNNINGHAM, E V
　　Fast, Howard
CUNNINGHAM, Ray
　　Arthur, Frances Browne
CURLING, Audrey
　　Clark, Marie Catherine Audrey
CURRY, Avon
　　Bowden, Jean
CURTAYNE, Alice
　　Rynne, Alice
CURTIN, Philip
　　Lowndes, Marie Adelaide
　　Belloc
CURTIS, Peter
　　Lofts, Norah
CURTIS, Spencer
　　Nuttall, Anthony

CURTIS, Tom
　　Jacobs, Thomas Curtis Hicks
CURZON, Virginia
　　Hawton, Hector
CUSTER, Clint
　　Paine, Lauran Bosworth
CYMRY BACH
　　Wood, Lilian Catherine
CYNICUS
　　Anderson, Martin

DAEDALUS
　　Cordes, Theodor K
DAINTON, Courtney
　　Dainton, William
DALE, Edwin
　　Home-Gall, Edward Reginald
DALE, Frances
　　Cradock, Phyllis Nan Sortain
DALE, Jack
　　Holliday, Joseph
DALEY, Bill
　　Appleman, John Alan
DALHEATH
　　Magrill, David
DALL, Ian
　　Higgins, Charles
DALLAS, John
　　Duncan, William Murdoch
DALLAS, Steve
　　King, Albert
D'ALLENGER, Hugh
　　Kershaw, John H D
DALTON, Clive
　　Clark, Frederick Stephen
DALTON, Priscilla
　　Avallone, Michael Angelo Jr
D'AMBROSIO, Raymond
　　Brosia, D M
DAMIANO, Laila
　　Rosenkrantz, Linda
DAN BANA
　　White, Stanhope
DANA, Amber
　　Paine, Lauran Bosworth

DANA, Richard
  Paine, Lauran Bosworth
DANA, Rosa
  Ross, William Edward Daniel
DANE, Clemence
  Ashton, Winifred
DANE, Mark
  Avallone, Michael Angelo Jr
DANFORTH, Paul M
  Allen, John E
DANGERFIELD, Clint
  Norwood, Victor George
    Charles
DANGERFIELD, Harlan
  Padgett, Ron
DANGLE
  Thompson, A M
DANIELL, David Scott
  Daniell, Albert Scott
DANIELS, John S
  Overholser, Wayne D
DANVERS, Jack
  Casseleyr, Camille
DARBY, Catherine
  Black, Maureen
DARBY, Emma
  Stubbs, Jean
DARBY, J N
  Govan, Mary Christine
DARBYSHIRE, Shirley
  Meynell, Shirley Ruth
DARE, Alan
  Goodchild, George
DARE, Michael
  Wordingham, James A
DARE, Simon
  Huxtable, Marjorie
D'ARFEY, William
  Plomer, William
DARLINGTON, Con
  Best, Carol Anne
DATALLER, Roger
  Eaglestone, Arthur Archibald
DAVEY, Jocelyn
  Raphael, Chaim

DAVIDSON, Mickie
  Davidson, Margaret
DAVIES, Louise
  Golding, Louise
DAVIES, Lucian
  Beeston, L J
DAVIOT, Gordon
  Mackintosh, Elizabeth
DAVIS, Audrey
  Paine, Lauran Bosworth
DAVIS, Gordon
  Hunt, E Howard
DAVIS, Julia
  Marsh, John
DAVIS, Rosemary L
  Davis, Lily May and
    Davis, Rosemary
DAVIS, Stratford
  Bolton, Miriam
DAWLISH, Peter
  Kerr, James Lennox
DAWSON, Jane
  Critchlow, Dorothy
DAWSON, Michael
  Boyle, John Howard Jackson
DAWSON, Oliver
  Coxall, Jack Arthur
DAWSON, Peter
  Faust, Frederick
DAWSON, Peter
  Glidden, Jonathan H
DAY, Adrian
  Harvey, Peter Noel
DAY, Harvey
  Cleary, C V H
DAY, Irene
  Orme, Eve
DAY, Lionel
  Black, Ladbroke Lionel Day
DAYLE, Malcolm
  Hincks, Cyril Malcolm
DE CASTRO, Lyne
  Lyne, Charles
DE COSQUEVILLE, Pierre
  Stacey, P M de Cosqueville

DE CULWEN, Dorothea
  Hines, Dorothea
DE FACCI, Liane
  De Bellet, Liane
DE LACY, Louise
  Hickey, Madelyn E
DE LAUBE
  Cardena, Clement
DE LIMA, Sigrid
  Greene, Sigrid
DE MORNY, Peter
  Wynne-Tyson, Esme
DE PRE, Jean-Anne
  Avallone, Michael Angelo Jr
DE SALIGNAC, Charles
  Hasson, James
DE VERE, Jane
  Watson, Julia
DE WITT, James
  Lewis, Mildred
DE WOHL, Louis
  Wohl, Ludwig von
DEACON, Richard
  McCormick, George
DEAN, Lyn
  Garret, Winifred Selina
DEAN, Spencer
  Winchell, Prentice
DEANE, Norman
  Creasey, John
DEBRETT, Hal
  Dresser, Davis and Rollins,
    Kathleen
DEE, John
  Tullett, Denis John
DEHAN, Richard
  Graves, Clotilda Inez Mary
DEKKER, Carl
  Laffin, John
DELAFIELD, E M
  De la Pasture, Edmée
    Elizabeth Monica
DELANEY, Denis
  Green, Peter

DELANO, Al
  Livingston, A D
DELL, Belinda
  Bowden, Jane
DELMONICO, Andrea
  Morrison, Eula A
DELTA
  Hazlewood, Rex
DELVING, Michael
  Williams, Jay
DEMAREST, Doug
  Barker, Will
DEMPSTER, Guy
  Heming, Dempster E
DENBIE, Roger
  Brodie, Julian Paul and
    Green, Alan Baer
DENBRY, R Emmet
  Murfree, Mary Noailles
DENDER, Jay
  Deindorfer, Robert G
DENHAM, Peter
  Jones, P D
DENNING, Patricia
  Willis, Corinne
DENNIS, Eve
  Wornum, Mirian
DENNIS, Patrick
  Tanner, Edward Everett
DENNISON, Dorothy
  Golden, Dorothy
DENOVAN, Saunders
  Harvey, William
DENVER, Boone
  Rennie, James Alan
DENVER, Drake C
  Nye, Nelson Coral
DENVER, Lee
  Gribble, Leonard Reginald
DERBY, Mark
  Wilcox, Harry
DERMOTT, Stephen
  Bradbury, Parnell
DERN, Peggy
  Dern, Erolie Pearl

DERVENTIO
  Hughes, Walter Dudley
DESANA, Dorothy
  Trent, Ann
DESPARD, Leslie
  Howitt, John Leslie Despard
DESTRY, Vince
  Norwood, Victor George
    Charles
DEVEREUX, Roy
  Pember-Devereux, Margaret R R
DEVON, Sara
  Walker, Emily Kathleen
DEWES, Simon
  Muriel, John
DEXTER, John
  Kanto, Peter
DEXTER, Martin
  Faust, Frederick
DEXTER, Ross
  Reynolds, John E
DEXTER, William
  Pritchard, William Thomas
DICK, Alexandra
  Dick-Erikson, Cicely Sibyl
    Alexandra
DICK, R A
  Leslie, Josephine A C
DICK, T
  Osler, Eric Richard
DICKENS, Irene
  Copper, Dorothy
DICKINSON, Margaret
  Muggeson, Margaret
DICKSON, Carr
  Carr, John Dickson
DICKSON, Carter
  Carr, John Dickson
DICKSON, Frank C
  Danson, Frank Corse
DIETRICH, Robert
  Hunt, E Howard
DIGGES, Jeremiah
  Berger, Josef

DIMSDALE, C D
  Mégroz, R L
DINESEN, Isak
  Blixen-Finecke, Karen
    Christence (Baroness)
DIPLOMAT
  Carter, John Franklin
DITTON, James
  Clark, Douglas
DIVINE, David
  Divine, Arthur Durham
D'IVRY, Ursula
  Russell, Ursula d'Ivry
DIX, Dorothy
  Gilmer, Elizabeth Meriwether
DIXON, Lesley
  Vernon, Kathleen Rose
DIXON, Rex
  Martin, Reginald Alec
DOAN, Reece
  King, Albert
DR A
  Asimov, Isaac
DR SEUSS
  Geisel, Theodor Seuss
DR SOFT
  Sward, Robert S
DOGBERRY
  Phillips, Hubert
DOGBOLT, Barnaby
  Silvette, Herbert
DOLBERG, Alexander
  Burg, David
DOLLEY, Marcus J
  Watney, Bernard
DOMINI, Rey
  Lorde, Andre Geraldin
DOMINIC, (Sister) Mary
  Parker, Marion
DOMPO, Kwesi
  Parkes, Frank
DONALD, Vivian
  Mackinnon, Charles Roy
DONALDS, Gordon
  Shirreffs, Gordon D

DONNE, Jack
  Bloom, Jack Don
DONOVAN, Dick
  Muddock, Joyce Emerson
DORMAN, Luke
  Bingley, David Ernest
DOUGLAS, Albert
  Armstrong, Douglas
DOUGLAS, D
  Wilkes-Hunter, Richard
DOUGLAS, Ellen
  Williamson, Ellen Douglas
DOUGLAS, George
  Brown, George Douglas
DOUGLAS, George
  Fisher, Douglas George
DOUGLAS, Noel
  Chetham-Strode, Warren
DOUGLAS, O
  Buchan, Anna
DOUGLAS, Shane
  Wilkes-Hunter, Richard
DOWER, Penn
  Jacobs, Thomas Curtis Hicks
DOWLEY, D M
  Marrison, Leslie William
DOWNES, Quentin
  Harrison, Michael
DOWNMAN, Francis
  Oldmeadow, Ernest James
DOYLE, Lynn
  Montgomery, Leslie Alexander
DRACO, F
  David, Julia
DRAKE, Joan
  Davies, Joan Howard
DRAX, Peter
  Addis, E E
DREWERY, Mary
  Smith, Mary
DREXLER, J F
  Paine, Lauran Bosworth
DRINAN, Adam
  Macleod, Joseph Todd Gordon

DRISCOLL, Eli
  King, Albert
DRUG, Victor
  Moretti, Ugo
DRUMMOND, Anthony
  Hunter, Alfred John
DRUMMOND, Ivor
  Longrigg, Roger
DRUMMOND, John
  Chance, John Newton
DRUMMOND, Violet Hilda
  Swetenham, Violet Hilda
DRURY, C M
  Abrahall, Clare Hoskyns
DRYDEN, John
  Rowland, Donald Sydney
DRYDEN, Kathryn
  Landells, Richard
DU BOIS, M
  Kent, Arthur
DU VAUL, Virginia
  Coffman, Virginia
DUCHESNE, Antoinette
  Paine, Lauran Bosworth
DUELL, Eileen-Marie
  Petrie, Rhone
DUFFER, Allan
  May, John
DUFFIELD, Anne
  Duffield, Dorothy Dean
DUKE, Margaret
  Dunk, Margaret
DUNCAN, A H
  Cleary, C V H
DUNCAN, Alex
  Duke, Madelaine
DUNCAN, Jane
  Cameron, Elizabeth Jane
DUNNE, Desmond
  Lee-Richardson, James
DURACK, Mary
  Miller, Mary
DURHAM, John
  Paine, Lauran Bosworth

DURIE, Lynn
  Christie, Douglas
DURRANT, Theo
  Mystery Writers of America
    Inc; California Chapter
DYKES, Jack
  Owen, Jack
DYMOKE, Juliet
  De Schanschieff, Juliet Dymoke

E H
  Hiscock, Eric
E H A
  Aitken, E H
E V L
  Lucas, E V
EAGLESFIELD, Francis
  Guirdham, Arthur
EARLE, Olive L
  Daughtrey, Olive Lydia
EARP, Virgil
  Keevill, Henry John
EAST, Michael
  West, Morris
EAST, Roger
  Burford, Roger d'Este
EASTERTIDE
  Blagbrough, Harriet
EASTLUND, Madelyn
  Hickey, Madelyn E
EDEN, Matthew
  Newnham, Don
EDEN, Rob
  Burkhardt, Eve and Burkhardt,
    Robert Ferdinand
EDGAR, Icarus Walter
  Bishop, Stanley
EDGAR, Josephine
  Mussi, Mary
EDMONDS, Charles
  Carrington, Charles
EDWARD, Stephen
  Palestrant, Simon
EDWARDS, Charman
  Edwards, Frederick Anthony

EDWARDS, F E
  Nolan, William F
EDWARDS, June
  Bhatia, June
EDWARDS, James G
  Macqueen, James William
EDWARDS, Laurence
  Edwards, Florence
EDWARDS, Leonard
  Wild, Reginald
EDWARDS, Olwen
  Owen, Dilys
EDWARDS, Samuel
  Gerson, Noel Bertram
EGAN, Lesley
  Linington, Elizabeth
EGERTON, Denise
  Duggan, Denise Valerie
EGLINTON, John
  Magee, William Kirkpatrick
EGOMET
  Fowler, Henry Watson
ELAND, Charles
  Rimanoczy, A
ELDERSHAW, M Barnard
  Barnard, Marjorie Faith and
    Eldershaw, Flora Sydney
ELIOTT, E C
  Martin, Reginald Alec
ELISABETH
  Quigly, Elizabeth Pauline
ELIZABETH
  Rose, Elizabeth Jane
ELIZABETH
  Russell, Elizabeth Mary
    (Countess)
ELLIOTT, Ellen
  Westmarland, Ethel Louisa

My own Ernest! I felt
from the start that you
could have no other name.
— Oscar Wilde

109

ELLISON, Marjorie
  Norton, Marjorie
ELPHINSTONE, Francia
  Powell-Smith, Vincent
ELRON
  Hubbard, L Ron
ELSNA, Hebe
  Ansle, Dorothy Phoebe
ELTON, John
  Marsh, John
ELWART, Joan Potter
  Elwart, Joan Frances
EMSLEY, Clare
  Plummer, Clare
ENGLAND, Edith M
  Anders, Edith Mary
ENGLAND, Jane
  Jervis, Vera Murdock Stuart
ENGLAND, Norman
  Webb, Godfrey E C
ENGLISH, Brenda H
  Riddolls, Brenda H
ENQUIRING LAYMAN
  Grierson, Walter
ENRIGHT, Elizabeth
  Gillham, Elizabeth Wright
    Enright
EPHESIAN
  Bechoffer Roberts, C E
ERIC, Kenneth
  Henley, Art
ERMINE, Will
  Drago, Harry Sinclair
ERNEST, Paul
  Focke, E P W
ERSKINE, John T
  Tuck, John Erskine
ERSKINE, Rosalind
  Longrigg, Roger Erskine
ERSKINE-GRAY
  Cordes, Theodor K
ESSEX, Frank
  Simmonds, Michael Charles
ESSEX, Jon
  Watford, Joel

ESSEX, Mary
  Bloom, Ursula
ESSEX, Richard
  Starr, Richard
ESTERBROOK, Tom
  Hubbard, L Ron
ESTEVEN, John
  Shellabarger, Samuel
ESTORIL, Jean
  Allan, Mabel Esther
ETIENNE
  King-Hall, Stephen
ETON, Robert
  Maynell, Laurence Walter
EVAN, Evin
  Faust, Frederick
EVAN, Paul
  Lehman, Paul Evan
EVANS, Alan
  Stoker, Alan
EVANS, Cherry
  Drummond, Cherry
EVANS, Evan
  Faust, Frederick
EVANS, John
  Brown, Howard
EVANS, Margiad
  Williams, Peggy Eileen
    Arabella
EVANS, Morgan
  Davies, Leslie Purnell
EVERARD, Henry
  Smith, H Everard
EVERETT, Wade
  Cook, William Everett
EVERTON, Francis
  Stokes, Francis William
EVOE
  Knox, E V
EYRE, Annette
  Worboys, Anne Eyre

F P A
  Adams, Franklin Pierce

110

FABIAN, Ruth
  Quigley, Aileen
FABIAN, Warner
  Adams, Samuel Hopkins
FABRIZIUS, Peter
  Fabry, Joseph B
FAGYAS, Maria
  Bush-Fekete, Marie Ilona
FAID, Mary
  Dunn, Mary
FAIR, A A
  Gardner, Erle Stanley
FAIRWAY, Sidney
  Daukes, Sidney Herbert
FALK, Elsa
  Escherich, Elsa Antonie
FALL, Thomas
  Snow, Donald Clifford
FALLON, George
  Bingley, David Ernest
FALLON, Martin
  Patterson, Henry
FANSHAWE, Caroline
  Cust, Barbara Kate
FARELY, Alison
  Poland, Dorothy E H
FAREWELL, Nina
  Klein, Grace and Cooper,
  Mae Klein
FARGO, Doone
  Norwood, Victor George
  Charles
FARR, C
  Wilkes-Hunter, Richard
FARRELL, David
  Smith, Frederick E
FARRELL, M J
  Keane, Mary Nesta
FARRER, E Maxwell
  Williams, Edward John
FAULKNER, Mary
  Seuffert, Muriel
FAWCETT, C
  Cookson, Catherine

FAWKES, Guy
  Benchley, Robert
FEARN, Elena
  Smith, Marjorie Seymour
FEARN, Roberta
  Hutchinson, Barbara Beatrice
FECAMPS, Elise
  Creasey, John
FECHER, Constance
  Heaven, Constance
FEIKEMA, Feike
  Manfred, Frederick Feikema
FELLOWES, Anne
  Mantle, Winifred Langford
FEMORA
  Brodey, Jim
FENNER, Carol
  Williams, Carol Elizabeth
FENTON, Freda
  Rowland, Donald Sydney
FENWICK, Elizabeth
  Way, Elizabeth Fenwick
FENWICK, Peter
  Holmes, Peter
FERGUSON, Anthony
  Read, Anthony
FERN, Edwin
  Cryer, Neville
FERNWAY, Peggy
  Braun, Wilbur
FERRAND, Georgina
  Castle, Brenda
FERRARS, E X
  Brown, Morna Doris
FERRARS, Elizabeth
  Brown, Morna Doris
FERRIS, Tom
  Walker, Peter Norman
FETHERSTON, Patrick
  Fetherstonhaugh, Patrick
  William Edward
FETTSMAN, Ann
  Hoffman, Anita
FEW, Betty
  Few, Eunice Beatty

FIAGG, Padraic
O'Connor, Patrick Joseph
FICKLING, G G
Fickling, Forrest E and Fickling,
Gloria
FIDLER, Kathleen
Goldie, Kathleen Annie
FIELD, Charles
Rowland, Donald Sydney
FIELD, Joanna
Milner, Marion
FIELDING, A
Feilding, Dorothy
FIELDING, Ann Mary
Mostyn, Anita Mary
FIELDING, Gabriel
Barnsley, Alan
FIELDING, Xan
Fielding, Alexander
FIELDS, W C
Dukenfield, William Claude
FILEMAN, Nan
Zimmer, Maude Files
FINCH, John
Cooper, John
FINCH, Matthew
Fink, Merton
FINCH, Merton
Fink, Merton
FINDLATER, Richard
Bain, K B F
FINDLEY, Ferguson
Frey, Charles Weiser
FINNEGAN, Robert
Ryan, Paul William
FINNEGAN, Ruth
Murray, Ruth Hilary
FINNIGAN, Joan
Mackenzie, Joan
FISHER, Clay
Allen, Henry
FISHER, Cyrus T
Teilhet, Darwin le Ora
FISHER, Margot
Paine, Lauran Bosworth

FITT, Mary
Freeman, Kathleen
FITZALAN, Roger
Dudley-Smith, Trevor
FITZGERALD, Barbara
Newman, Mona A J
FITZGERALD, Errol
Clarke, (Lady)
FITZWILLIAM, Michael
Lyons, John Benignus
5029
Winkworth, Derek W
FLACCUS
Levy, Newman
FLAMANK, E
Harper, Edith
FLECK, Betty
Paine, Lauran Bosworth
FLEMING, George
Fletcher, Constance
FLEMING, Harry
Bird, William Henry Fleming
FLEMMING, Cardine
Grieveson, Mildred
FLEMMING, Sarah
Gilderdale, Michael
FLETCHER, Adam
Flexner, Stuart
FLETCHER, John
Fletcher, Harry L Verne
FLIGHT, Francies
Birch, Jack Ernest Lionel and
Murray, Venetia Pauline
FLYING OFFICER X
Bates, H E
FLYNT, Josiah
Willard, Josiah Flynt
FOLEY, Helen
Fowler, Helen
FOLEY, Rae
Denniston, Elinore
FOLEY, Scott
Dareff, Hal
FORD, Barry
Whitford, Joan

FORD, Elbur
   Hibbert, Eleanor Alice Burford
FORD, Ford Madox
   Hueffer, Ford Madox
FORD, Kirk
   Spence, William
FORD, Langridge
   Coleman-Cooke, John C
FORD, Leslie
   Brown, Zenith
FORD, Norrey
   Dilcock, Noreen
FORD, Wallace
   King, Albert
FORDE, Nicholas
   Elliott-Cannon, Arthur Elliott
FOREMAN, Lee
   King, Albert
FORREST, Carol
   Tennyson, Margaret
FORREST, (Colonel) Cris
   Stoddard, William Osborn
FORREST, David
   Denholm, David
FORREST, David
   Eliades, David and Webb,
     Robert Forrest
FORREST, Julian
   Wagenknecht, Edward
FORRESTER, Mary
   Humphries, Elsie Mary
FORSYTH, Jean
   M'Ilwraith, Jean N
FORSYTH, R A
   Johnston, Robert Thomson
FORSYTHE, Robert
   Crichton, Kyle
FORTINA, Martha
   Laffeaty, Christina
FORTUNE, Dion
   Firth, Violet Mary
FOSSE, Alfred
   Jelly, Oliver
FOSTER, Delia
   Walker, Emily Kathleen

FOSTER, Evan
   King, Albert
FOSTER, George
   Haswell, C J D
FOWLER, Sydney
   Wright, Sydney Fowler
FOX, Eleanor
   St John, Wylly Folk
FOX, James M
   Knipscheer, James M W
FOX, Petronella
   Balogh, Penelope
FOX, Sebastian
   Bullett, Gerald
FRANCE, Claire
   Morin, Claire
FRANCE, Evangeline
   France-Hayhurst, Evangeline
FRANCHON, Lisa
   Floren, Lee
FRANCIS, C D E
   Howarth, Patrick John
    Fielding
FRANCIS, Victor
   Hammond, Lawrence
FRANKLIN, Charles
   Usher, Frank Hugh
FRANKLIN, Eugene
   Bandy, Eugene Franklin Jr
FRANKLIN, Jay
   Carter, John Franklin
FRANKLIN, Max
   Deming, Richard
FRASER, Alex
   Brinton, Henry
FRASER, James
   White, Alan
FRASER, Jane
   Pilcher, Rosamunde
FRASER, Jefferson
   Wilding, Philip
FRASER, Peter
   Coles, Phoebe Catherine
FRASER, Peter
   Watt, Alexander Peter Fordham

FRAZER, Martin
    Clarke, Percy A
FRAZER, Robert Caine
    Creasey, John
FRAZER, Shamus
    Frazer, James Ian Arbuthnot
FRECKLES
    Dietz, Howard
FREDERICKS, Frank
    Franck, Frederick S
FREDERICS, Jocko
    Frede, Richard
FREMLIN, Celia
    Goller, Celia Margaret
FRENCH, Ashley
    Robins, Denise
FRENCH, Ellen Jean
    English, Jean Ellen
FRENCH, Fergus
    Friedlander, Peter
FRENCH, Paul
    Asimov, Isaac
FRENKEN-MELONEY
    Meloney, William
FRESHFIELD, Mark
    Field, M J
FRICK, C H
    Irwin, Constance
FRIEND, Oscar Jerome
    Jerome, Owen Fox
FROME, David
    Brown, Zenith
FROST, Frederick
    Faust, Frederick
FROST, Joni
    Paine, Lauran Bosworth
FROY, Herald
    Deghy, Guy and
        Waterhouse, Keith
FRY, Jane
    Drew, Jane B
FRY, Pete
    King, James Clifford
FUCHS, Sonia
    Seedo, Sonia

FULLER, Ed
    Fuller, Harold Edgar
FULMAN, Al
    Fuller, Harold Edgar
FYVEL, T R
    Feiwel, Raphael Joseph

G B S
    George Bernard Shaw
G K C
    Chesterton, G K
GADDES, Peter
    Sheldon, Peter
GADDIS, Peggy
    Dern, Erolie Pearl
GAGE, Gervais
    Rentoul, T Laurence
GAITE, Francis
    Coles, Cyril Henry and
        Manning, Adelaide Frances
        Oke
GALE, John
    Gase, Richard
GALE, Newton
    Guinness, Maurice
GALWAY, Robert Coningham
    McCutchan, Philip D
GAME COCK
    Looker, Samuel Joseph
GANNOLD, John
    Langdon, John
GANPAT
    Gompertz, Martin Louis Alan
GARDNER, Nancy Bruff
    Bruff, Nancy
GARDONS, S S
    Snodgrass, W D
GARFORD, James
    Blackburn, James Garford
GARLAND, George
    Roark, Garland
GARLAND, Lisette
    Gibbs, Norah
GARLAND, Madge
    Ashton, (Lady)

GARNETT, Roger
   Morland, Nigel
GARRATT, Teddie
   Garratt, Alfred
GARRISON, Joan
   Neubauer, William Arthur
GARTH, Cecil
   Carlton, Grace
GARTNER, Chloe
   Trimble, Chloe Maria
GARVE, Andrew
   Winterton, Paul
GASKELL, Jane
   Denvil, Jane Gaskell
GAUNT, Jeffrey
   Rochester, George Ernest
GAUNT, Michael
   Robertshaw, James Denis
GAUNT, Richard
   Landells, Richard
GAVIN, Amanda
   Fry, Clodagh Micaela Gibson
GAWAIN
   Newton, H Chance
GAWSWORTH, John
   Fytton Armstrong, T I
GAY, Amelia
   Hogarth, Grace
GAYE, Carol
   Shann, Renée
GEACH, Christine
   Wilson, Christine
GEE, Kenneth F
   Kay, Frederick George
GEE, Osman
   Hincks, Cyril Malcolm
GEERLINK, Will
   Hofdorp, Pim
GEISEL, Eva
   Bornemann, Eva
GELLERT, Roger
   Holmstrom, John Eric
GEMINI
   Goodwin, Geoffrey

GENE, Marta
   Powley, (Mrs) A A
GENET
   Flanner, Janet
GEORGE, Jonathan
   Burke, John Frederick
GEORGE, Vicky
   Collings, I J
GERAINT, George
   Evans, George
GERARD, Gaston
   Ostergaard, Geoffrey
GERARD, Morice
   Teague, John Jessop
GIBB, Lee
   Deghy, Guy and Waterhouse,
    Keith
GIBBON, Lewis Grassic
   Mitchell, James Leslie
GIBBS, Henry
   Rumbold-Gibbs, Henry
    St John C
GIBBS, Lewis
   Cove, Joseph Walter
GIBBS, Mary Ann
   Bidwell, Marjory Elizabeth
    Sarah
GIBSON, Floyd
   King, Albert
GIFFARD, Ann
   Greenhill, Elizabeth Ann
GIFFIN, Frank
   Carter, Ernest
GIFFORD, Matt
   King, Albert
GILBERT, Anthony
   Malleson, Lucy
GILBERT, John
   Harrison, John Gilbert
GILBERT, Nan
   Gilbertson, Mildred
GILCHRIST, John
   Gardner, Jerome
GILDEN, K B
   Gilden, Katya and Gilden, Bert

GILES, Norman
  Mackeown, N R
GILL, Hugh
  Hugill, Robert
GILL, Patrick
  Creasey, John
GILMAN, Robert Cham
  Coppel, Alfred
GILLESPIE, Jane
  Shaw, Jane
GILMOUR, Ann
  McNaught, Ann Boyce
GIRTY, Simon
  King, Albert
GLENDENNING, Donn
  Paine, Lauran Bosworth
GLENN, James
  Paine, Lauran Bosworth
GLINTO, Darcy
  Kelly, Harold Ernest
GLUTZ, Ambrose
  Knapp, Clarence
GLYN, Anthony
  Davson, (Sir) Geoffrey Leo
    Simon
GLYN, Megan
  Parry, Margaret G
GLYN-FOREST, D
  Lynes, Daisy Elfreda
GOAMAN, Muriel
  Cox, Edith Muriel
GODDEN, Rumer
  Haynes Dixon, Margaret
    Rumer
GODEY, John
  Freedgood, Morton
GODFREY, Charles
  Webb, Godfrey, E C
GOFF, Madeleine
  Woodford, Irene-Cecile
GOFFSTEIN, M B
  Schaaf, M B
GOLDEN GORSE
  Wace, M A

GOODMAN, Winthrop
  Goodman, George Jerome and
    Knowlton, Winthrop
GOODWIN, John
  Gowing, Sidney Floyd
GOODYEAR, Susan
  Matthews, Margaret Bryan
GORDON, Angela
  Paine, Lauran Bosworth
GORDON, Donald
  Payne, Donald Gordon
GORDON, Glenda
  Beadle, Gwyneth Gordon
GORDON, Ian
  Fellowes-Gordon, Ian
GORDON, Jane
  Lee, Elsie
GORDON, Keith
  Bailey, Gordon
GORDON, Lew
  Baldwin, Gordon C
GORDON, Neil
  Macdonell, A G
GORDON, Ray
  Wainwright, Gordon Ray
GORDON, Rex
  Hough, Stanley Bennett
GORDON, Richard
  Ostlere, Gordon Stanley
GORDON, Stewart
  Shirreffs, Gordon D
GORDON, William Murray
  Graydon, William Murray
GORE, William
  Gordon, Jan
GORHAM, Michael
  Folsom, Franklin Brewster
GORMAN, Beth
  Paine, Lauran Bosworth
GORMAN, Ginny
  Kanto, Peter
GOUGH, Irene
  Hall, Irene
GOULD, Alan
  Canning, Victor

GOUTTIER, Maurice
  Moretti, Ugo
GRACCHUS
  Wintringham, Tom
GRACE, Joseph
  Hornby, John W
GRADY, Tex
  Webb, Jack
GRAEME, Bruce
  Jeffries, Graham Montague
GRAEME, David
  Jeffries, Graham Montague
GRAEME, Roderic
  Jeffries, Roderic Graeme
GRAHAM, (Brother)
  Jeffery, Graham
GRAHAM, James
  Patterson, Henry
GRAHAM, Jean
  Scott, Mary E
GRAHAM, John
  Rose, Graham
GRAHAM, Neill
  Duncan, William Murdoch
GRAHAM, Peter
  Langmaid, Kenneth Joseph
  Robb
GRAHAM, Ramona
  Cook, Ramona Graham
GRAHAM, Scott
  Black, Hazleton
GRAHAM, Viva
  Somerville, Edith Oenone
GRAMMATICUS
  Blaiklock, Edward
GRANADOS, Paul
  Kent, Arthur
GRANDMA
  Mulhearn, Winifred
GRANGE, Ellerton
  Fraser-Harris, D
GRANGE, Peter
  Nicole, Christopher
GRANT, Ambrose
  Raymond, Rene

GRANT, Carol
  Copper, Dorothy
GRANT, Douglas
  Ostrander, Isabel Egerton
GRANT, Eve
  Gray, K E
GRANT, Kay
  Grant, Hilda Kay
GRANT, Landon
  Gribble, Leonard Reginald
GRANT, Margaret
  Meloney, William
GRANT, Neil
  Mountfield, David
GRANT, Richard
  Clarke, J Calvitt
GRAVELEY, George
  Edwards, George Graveley
GRAY, Adrian
  Wilkes-Hunter, Richard
GRAY, Berkeley
  Brooks, Edwy Searles
GRAY, Christopher
  Usher, John Gray
GRAY, Elizabeth Janet
  Vining, Elizabeth
GRAY, Harriet
  Robins, Denise
GRAY, Jane
  Evans, Constance May
GRAYSON, David
  Baker, Ray Stannard
GRAYSON, Richard
  Grindal, Richard
GREAVES, Gillian
  Macvean, Phyllis
GREEN, Charles M
  Gardner, Erle Stanley
GREEN, Glint
  Peterson, Margaret
GREEN, Henry
  Yorke, Henry Vincent
GREEN, Linda
  Copper, Dorothy

GREEN, O O
  Durgnat, Raymond
GREEN, R
  Weir, Rosemary
GREENE, Adam
  Scott, Peter Dale
GREENE, Robert
  Deindorfer, Robert G
GREER, Patrick
  Macrory, Patrick
GREGSON, Paul
  Oakley, Eric Gilbert
GRENVIL, William
  Martyn, Wyndham
GREX, Leo
  Gribble, Leonard Reginald
GREY, Brenda
  Mackinlay, Lelia A S
GREY, Harry
  Golberg, Harry
GREY, Louis
  Gribble, Leonard Reginald
GREY, Rowland
  Brown, L Rowland
GREYSTONE, Alexander A
  Goodavage, Joseph F
GRIER, Sydney C
  Gregg, Hilda
GRIFF, Alan
  Suddaby, William Donald
GRIFFITH, Jack
  Griffiths, Jack
GROUPE, Darryl R
  Bunch, David R
GROVER, Marshall
  Meares, Leonard F
GROVES, Georgina
  Symons, Dorothy G
GUBBINS, Nathaniel
  Mott, Edward Spencer
GUILDFORD, John
  Hunter, Bluebell Matilda
GUINNESS, Owen
  Williams, Guy
GULICK, Bill
  Gulick, Grover C

GUN BUSTER
  Austin, John and Austin,
    Richard
GUNN, Victor
  Brooks, Edwy Searles
GUTHRIE, John
  Brodie, John
GWYNNE, Arthur
  Evans, Gwynfil Arthur
GWYNNE, Paul
  Slater, Ernest
GYE, Hal
  Gye, Harold Frederick Neville

H A K
  Kennedy, H A
HAAS, Carola
  Catalani, Victoria
HACKSTON, James
  Gye, Harold Frederick Neville
HADDO, Oliver
  Puechner, Ray
HADDOW, Leigh
  Best, Rayleigh Breton Amis
HADHAM, John
  Parkes, James W
HADLEY, Leila
  Smitter, Eliott-Burton
HAGAR, Judith
  Polley, Judith Anne
HAGGARD, William
  Clayton, Richard H M
HALE, Christopher
  Stevens, Frances Moyer
HALE, Hope
  Davis, Hale Hope
HALES, Joyce
  Coombs, Joyce
HALIBURTON, Hugh
  Robertson, James Logie
HALL, Adam
  Dudley-Smith, Trevor
HALL, Claudia
  Floren, Lee

118

HALL, Martyn T
  Morris, David
HALL, Patrick
  Hall, Frederick
HALL, Rupert
  Home-Gall, Edward Reginald
HALLAM, Jay
  Rice, Joan
HALLARD, Peter
  Catherall, Arthur
HALLAS, Richard
  Knight, Eric
HALLIDAY, Brett
  Dresser, Davis
HALLIDAY, Dorothy
  Dunnett, Dorothy
HALLIDAY, James
  Symington, David
HALLIDAY, Michael
  Creasey, John
HAMBLEDON, Phyllis
  Macvean, Phyllis
HAMILTON, Judith
  Lawrence, Dulcie
HAMILTON, Julia
  Watson, Julia
HAMILTON, Kay
  De Leeuw, Cateau W
HAMILTON, Max
  Hamilton, Cecily
HAMILTON, Michael
  Chetham-Strode, Warren
HAMILTON, Paul
  Dennis-Jones, Harold
HAMILTON, Roger
  Rogerson, James
HAMILTON, William
  Canaway, W H
HAMILTON-WILKES, Monty
  Hamilton-Wilkes, Edwin
HAMMOND, Brad
  King, Albert
HAMMOND, Jane
  Poland, Dorothy E H

HAMMOND, Ralph
  Hammond-Innes, Ralph
HAMPSON, John
  Simpson, John Frederick
  Norman Hampson
HAN SUYIN
  Comber, Elizabeth
HANCOCK, Robert
  Howell, Douglas Nayler
HANNAFORD, Justin
  Fitz-Gerald, S J A
HARBINSON, Robert
  Bryans, Robert Harbinson
HARDING, Bertita
  Radetzby von Radetz, (Countess)
HARDING, George
  Raubenheimer, George H
HARDING, Matt
  Floren, Lee
HARDING, Richard
  Boulton, A Harding
HARDING, Wes
  Keevill, Henry John
HARDWICK, Sylvia
  Doherty, Ivy Ruby
HARDY, Arthur S
  Steffens, Arthur Joseph
HARDY, Bobbie
  Hardy, Marjorie
HARDY, Russ
  Snow, Charles Horace
HARDY, Stuart
  Schisgall, Oscar
HARE, Cyril
  Clark, Alfred Alexander Gordon
HARE, Robert
  Hutchinson, Robert Hare
HARGIS, Pauline
  Dillard, Polly Hargis
HARGIS, Polly
  Dillard, Polly Hargis
HARLAN, Ross
  King, Albert

HARLE, Elizabeth
  Roberts, Irene
HARLEY, John
  Marsh, John
HARMON, Gil
  King, Albert
HARMSTON, Donald
  Matheson, Donald H
HARRIS, Macdonald
  Heiney, Donald William
HARRIS, Peter
  Harris, William
HARRISON, Whit
  Whittington, Harry
HART, Francis
  Paine, Lauran Bosworth
HART, Max
  Urquhart, Macgregor
HART, R W
  Ferneyhough, Roger Edmund
HART, Susanne
  Harthoorn, Susanne
HARTE, Marjorie
  McEvoy, Marjorie
HARTFORD, Via
  Donson, Cyril
HARTMAN, Roger
  Mehta, Rustam
HARVESTER, Simon
  Rumbold-Gibbs, Henry
    St John C
HARVEY, Rachel
  Bloom, Ursula
HARVEY, Ross
  Hook, H Clarke
HASSAN i SABBAH
  Butler, Bill
HASWELL, Jock
  Haswell, C J D
HATTON, Cliff
  Mason, Sydney Charles
HAWKES, John
  Burne, Clendennin Talbot
HAWKEYE
  Carlisle, R H

HAWKINS, John
  Hagan, Stelia F
HAY, Catherine
  Hughes, Ivy
HAY, Frances
  Dick-Erikson, Cicely Sibyl
    Alexandra
HAY, Ian
  Beith, John Hay
HAY, John
  Dalrymple-Hay, Barbara
    and Dalrymple-Hay, John
HAYDEN, John
  Paine, Lauran Bosworth
HAYES, Clanton
  Mason, Sydney Charles
HAYMAN, Hazel
  Peel, Hazel
HAYNES, Dorothy K
  Gray, Dorothy K
HAYNES, John Robert
  Wilding, Philip
HAZARD, Laurence
  Barr, Patricia
HEAD, Matthew
  Canaday, John
HEADLEY, Elizabeth
  Harrison, Elizabeth C
HEALD, Edith
  Shackleton, Edith
HEARD, Gerald
  Heard, Henry Fitzgerald
HEATH, Veronica
  Blackett, Veronica
HEATHCOTT, Mary
  Keegan, Mary Constance
HEATON, Peter
  Stuart-Heaton, Peter
HEBDEN, Mark
  Harris, John
HEBER, Austin
  Poole, Reginald Heber
HEBER, Reginald
  Poole, Reginald Heber

HELLERLAMB, Toni
  Lamb, Antonia
HELMI, Jack
  Sands, Leo G
HELVICK, James
  Cockburn, Claud
HELY, Elizabeth
  Younger, Elizabeth
HENDERSON, Colt
  Mason, Sydney Charles
HENDERSON, Sylvia
  Ashton-Warner, Sylvia
HENRIQUES, Veronica
  Gosling, Veronica
HENRY, O
  Porter, William Sydney
HENRY, Will
  Allen, Henry
HEPPELL, Blanche
  Heppell, Mary
HEPPLE, Anne
  Dickinson, Anne Hepple
HEPTAGON
  Charlton, Joan; Falk,
    Katherine; Falk, Millicent;
    Fox, Winifred; Gill, Winifred;
    Jennings, Hilda and Stocks,
    Mary
HERBERT, Arthur
  Shappiro, Herbert Arthur
HEREFORD, John
  Fletcher, Harry L Verne
HERITAGE, A J
  Addis, Hazel Iris
HERITAGE, Martin
  Horler, Sydney
HERMAN, Jack
  Sands, Leo G
HERMES
  Canaway, W H
HERNE, Eric
  Garvey, Eric William
HERRING, Geilles
  Somerville, Edith Oenone

HERRIOT, James
  Wight, J A
HESSING, Dennis
  Dennis-Jones, Harold
HEWETT, Anita
  Duke, Anita
HEWITT, Martin
  Morrison, Arthur
HEXT, Harrington
  Phillpotts, Eden
HICKEY, Lyn
  Hickey, Madelyn E
HICKOK, Will
  Harrison, Chester William
HICKS, Eleanor
  Coerr, Eleanor Beatrice
HIGGINBOTHAM, Anne T
  Higginbotham, Anne D
HIGGINS, Jack
  Patterson, Henry
HIGSON, P J W
  Willoughby-Higson, Philip John
HILL, Anne
  Muskett, Netta Rachel
HILL, Bennet
  Winter, Bevis
HILL, Craven
  Parsons, Charles P
HILL, H Haverstock
  Walsh, James Morgan
HILL, Prudence
  Maxfield, Prudence
HILLIARD, Jan
  Grant, Hilda Kay
HILLMAN, Martin
  Hill, Douglas
HINDE, Thomas
  Chitty, (Sir) Thomas Willes
HOBSON, Polly
  Evans, Julia
HOCKABY, Stephen
  Mitchell, Gladys
HODGE, Merton
  Hodge, Horace Emerton

HODSON, Arthur
  Nickson, Arthur
HOFFMAN, Art
  King, Albert
HOFFMAN, Louise
  Fitzgerald, Beryl
HOFMEYER, Hans
  Fleischer, Anthony
HOGARTH, Charles
  Creasey, John
HOGARTH, John
  Finnin, Mary
HOGBIN, Ian
  Hogbin, Herbert
HOLCOMBE, Arnold
  Golsworthy, Arnold
HOLDEN, Genevieve
  Pou, Genevieve
HOLLAND, Clive
  Hankinson, Charles J
HOLLAND, Elizabeth
  Baxter, Elizabeth
HOLLAND, Katrin
  Loewengard, Heidi H F
HOLLAND, Kel
  Whittington, Harry
HOLLAND, Rosemary
  Pattinson, Lee
HOLLAND, Tom
  King, Albert
HOLLIS, Jim
  Summers, Hollis
HOLMES, (Captain) Howard
  Harbaugh, Thomas Chalmers
HOLMES, Caroline
  Mason, Sydney Charles
HOLMES, Gordon
  Shiel, M P and Tracy, Louis
HOLMES, Grant
  Fox, James
HOLMES, Rick
  Hardwick, Richard
HOLT, E Carleton
  Guigo, Ernest Philip

HOLMES, H H
  White, William Anthony P
HOLT, Gavin
  Rodda, Charles
HOLT, Helen
  Paine, Lauran Bosworth
HOLT, Tex
  Rister, Claude
HOLT, Victoria
  Hibbert, Eleanor Alice Burford
HOLTON, Leonard
  O'Connor Wibberley, Leonard
  Patrick
HOME, Michael
  Bush, Christopher
HOME-GALL, Reginald
  Home-Gall, Edward Reginald
HOME GUARD
  Ingamells, F G
HOMES, Geoffrey
  Mainwaring, Daniel
HONEYCUTT, Richard
  Hardwick, Richard
HONEYMAN, Brenda
  Clarke, Brenda
HOOLEY, Teresa
  Butler, Teresa Mary
HOPE, Andrew
  Hern, Anthony
HOPE, Anthony
  Hawkins, (Sir) Anthony Hope
HOPE, Brian
  Creasey, John
HOPE, Edward
  Coffey, Edward Hope
HOPE, Lawrence
  Nicholson, Violet
HOPE, Margaret
  Wicksteed, Margaret Hope
HOPE, Noel
  Morewood, Sarah L
HOPE, Stanton
  Stanton-Hope, W E
HOPF, Alice L
  Lightner, A M

HOPLEY, George
  Woolrich, Cornell
HORN, Chester
  Mason, Sydney Charles
HORSLEY, David
  Bingley, David Ernest
HORTON, Robert J
  Roberts, James
HOUGH, Don
  Huff, Darrell
HOUGHTON, Claude
  Oldfield, Claude Houghton
HOUGHTON, Elizabeth
  Gilzean, Elizabeth
HOUSTON, R B
  Rae, Hugh Cranford
HOUSTON, Will
  Paine, Lauran Bosworth
HOWARD, Colin
  Shaw, Howard
HOWARD, Don
  Menzel, Donald H
HOWARD, Elizabeth
  Mizner, Elizabeth Howard
HOWARD, Elizabeth
  Paine, Lauran Bosworth
HOWARD, George
  Kay, Frederic George
HOWARD, Hartley
  Ognall, Leo Horace
HOWARD, Helen
  Jacobs, Thomas Curtis Hicks
HOWARD, John M
  Hincks, Cyril Malcolm
HOWARD, Keble
  Bell, John Keble
HOWARD, Leigh
  Lee Howard, L A
HOWARD, Mary
  Mussi, Mary
HOWARD, Troy
  Paine, Lauran Bosworth
HOWE, Muriel
  Smithies, Muriel

HOWELL, Scott
  King, Albert
HOYT, Nelson
  King, Albert
HUDSON, Jeffery
  Crichton, Michael
HUDSON, Stephen
  Schiff, Sydney
HUGGINS, Ruth Mabel
  Arthur, Ruth M
HUGHES, Alison
  Oliver, Doris M
HUGHES, Brenda
  Colloms, Brenda
HUGHES, Colin
  Creasey, John
HUGHES, Matilda
  Macleod, Charlotte
HUGHES, Philip
  Phillips, Hugh
HUGHES, Terence
  Best, Rayleigh Breton Amis
HUGHES, Valerina
  Kanto, Peter
HUGHES, Zach
  Kanto, Peter
HULL, H Braxton
  Jacobs, Helen Hull
HULL, Richard
  Sampson, Richard Henry
HUMANA, Charles
  Jacobs, Charles
HUME, David
  Turner, John Victor
HUME, Frances
  Buckland-Wright, Mary
HUMPHRYS, Geoffrey
  Humphrys, Leslie George
HUNT, Charlotte
  Hodges, Doris Marjorie
HUNT, Diana
  Hunt-Bode, Gisele
HUNT, Dorothy
  Fellows, Dorothy Alice

HUNT, John
    Paine, Lauran Bosworth
HUNT, Kyle
    Creasey, John
HUNTER, Alison
    Blair, Norma Hunter
HUNTER, Jean
    Hunter, Alfred John
HUNTER, John
    Ballard, Willis Todhunter
HUNTER, John
    Hunter, Alfred John
HUNTER, John
    Hunter, Christine
HUNTER, Mollie
    McIlwraith, Maureen Mollie
    Hunter
HUNTLY, Frances E
    Mayne, Ethel Colburn
HUNTON, Mary
    Gilzean, Elizabeth Houghton
HURGERFORD, Pixie
    Brinsmead, Hesba
HUSSEY, Leonard
    Pearce, Brian
HUSSINGTREE, Martin
    Baldwin, Oliver
HUTCHINS, Anthony
    Morley, Leslie Reginald
    William
HUTCHINSON, Anne
    Burnett, Hallie
HUTCHINSON, Patricia
    Fullbrook, Gladys
HYDE, Eleanor
    Minto, Frances

I B
    Brown, Ivor
IDRIS
    Mee, Arthur
IGNOTUS
    Fuller, James Franklin
ILES, Francis
    Cox, A B

INCLEDON, Philip
    Worner, Philip A I
INGERSOL, Jared
    Paine, Lauran Bosworth
INGHAM, Daniel
    Lambot, Isobel Mary
INNES, Hammond
    Hammond-Innes, Ralph
INNES, Jean
    Saunders, Jean
INNES, Michael
    Stewart, John Innes
    Mackintosh
IRELAND, Baron
    Salsbury, Nate
IRELAND, Doreen
    Lord, Doreen
IRELAND, Noelle
    Gibbs, Norah
IRISH, William
    Woolrich, Cornell
IRONQUILL
    Ware, Eugene Fitch
IRONSIDE, John
    Tait, Euphemia Margaret
IRVING, Robert
    Adler, Irving
ISLAY, Nicholas
    Murray, Andrew Nicholas

J C
    Lawrence, T E
J C T
    Trewin, J C
JABEZ
    Nicol, Eric
JACKS, Oliver
    Gandley, Kenneth Royce
JACKSON, Everatt
    Muggeson, Margaret
JACKSON, Giles
    Leffingwell, Albert
JACKSON, Neville
    Glaskin, G M

JACKSTAFF
  Bennett, J J
JACOB, Herbert Mathias
  Davies, D Jacob
JACOT, Bernard
  Jacot de Bolnod, B L
JAMES, Andrew
  Kirkup, James
JAMES, Brian
  Tierney, John
JAMES, Cy
  Watts, Peter Christopher
JAMES, Dan
  Sayers, James D
JAMES, Dynely
  Mayne, William J C and Caesar,
    Richard Dynely
JAMES, John
  Langdon-Davies, John
JAMES, Josephine
  Lindsay, Barbara and
    Sterne, E G
JAMES, Matthew
  Lucey, James D
JAMES, Vincent
  Gribben, James
JAMESON, Eric
  Trimmer, Eric
JAN
  Read, John
JANES, Kathleen F
  Jamieson, Kathleen Florence
JASON
  Munro, Hugh
JASON, Wm
  Machlin, Milton
JAY
  Jennings, E C
JAY, Joan
  Davies, Edith
JAY, Simon
  Alexander, Colin James
JAYNES, Clare
  Spiegel, Clara E and Mayer,
    Jane

JEANS, Angela
  Watt, Esme
JEEVES, Mahatma Kane
  Dukenfield, William Claude
JEFFERIS, Jeff
  Curry, Thomas Albert
JEFFERSON, Ian
  Davies, Leslie Purnell
JEFFERSON, Sarah
  Farjeon, Eve
JEFFERY, E Jeffery
  Marston, J E
JEFFRIES, Jeff
  Boatfield, Jeffrey
JEROME, Owen Fox
  Friend, Oscar Jerome
JESKINS, Richard
  Story, Rosamond Mary
JINGLE
  Golsworthy, Arnold
JOCELYN, Richard
  Clutterbuck, Richard
JODY, J M
  Edmundson, Joseph
JOHANSON, Elizabeth
  Verwer, Johanne
JOHN, Evan
  Simpson, Evan John
JOHN O'LONDON
  Whitten, Wilfred
JOHN O' THE NORTH
  Browne, Harry T
JOHNS, Avery
  Cousins, Margaret
JOHNS, Foster
  Seldes, Gilbert
JOHNS, Hilary
  Barraud, E M
JOHNS, June
  Smith, June Johns
JOHNSON, A E
  Johnson, Annabel J and
    Johnson, Edgar R
JOHNSON, Lee
  Johnson, Lilian Beatrice

125

JOLLY, Susan
  Edwards, Florence
JONES, Bobi
  Jones, Robert Maynard
JONES, Bradshaw
  Bradshaw-Jones, Malcolm
  Henry
JONES, Calico
  Richardson, Gladwell
JONES, Clara
  Baldwin, Dorothy
JONES, Joanna
  Burke, John Frederick
JONES, Webb
  Henley, Art
JONS, Hal
  Jones, Harry Austin
JORDAN, Barbara Leslie
  Yellot, Barbara Leslie
JORDAN, Nell
  Barker, E M
JOSE, Ellen J
  Waye, Ellen
JOUDRY, Patricia
  Steele, Patricia M V
JOYCE, Thomas
  Cary, Joyce
JOYSTICK
  Holden, J R
JUDD, Cyril
  Merril, Judith and Kornbluth,
  Cyril M
JUNIOR SUB
  Beith, John Hay
JUSTICIAR
  Powell-Smith, Vincent

KANE, Jim
  Germano, Peter
KANE, Julia
  Robins, Denise
KANE, Mark
  King, Albert
KARAGEORGE, Michael
  Anderson, Poul

KARIG, Walter
  Patrick, Keats
KARLOFF, Boris
  Pratt, William Henry
KAVAN, Anna
  Edmonds, Helen
KAY, Wallace
  Arter, Wallace E
KAYE, Barbara
  Muir, Marie
KAYE, Evelyn
  Evans, Kathleen
KAYE, Harold Bertram
  Kampf, Harold Bertram
KAYE, Mary Margaret
  Hamilton, Mary Margaret Kaye
KAYE, Tom
  Kaye, Barrington
KEENE, James
  Cook, William Everett
KEESING, Nancy
  Hertzberg, Nancy
KEITH, Carlton
  Robertson, Keith
KEITH, Claire
  Andrews, Claire and Andrews,
  Keith
KEITH, David
  Steegmuller, Francis
KEITH, James
  Hetherington, Keith James
KELL, Joseph
  Wilson, John Anthony Burgess
KELLEY, Ray
  Paine, Lauran Bosworth
KELLIER, Elizabeth
  Kelly, Elizabeth
KELLOW, Kathleen
  Hibbert, Eleanor Alice Burford
KELLWAY, Mary D
  Hillyard, Mary Dorothea
KELSEY, Janice
  King, Albert
KELWAY, Christine
  Gwinn, Christine M

KENDALL, Jane
  Martens, Anne Louise
KENDALL, Lace
  Stoutenburg, Adrien
KENDRAKE, Carleton
  Gardner, Erle Stanley
KENEU
  Hazlewood, Rex
KENNEDY, Diana
  Duggleby, Jean Colbeck
KENNEDY, Elliott
  Godfrey, Lionel Robert
  Holcombe
KENNEDY, Milward
  Burge, Milward Rodon
  Kennedy
KENNEDY, R C
  Cortez-Columbus, Robert
  Cimabue
KENNEGGY, Richard
  Nettell, Richard
KENNIE, Jessie
  Macpherson, Jessie
KENNY, Charles J
  Gardner, Erle Stanley
KENT, Alexander
  Reeman, Douglas
KENT, Pete
  Richardson, Gladwell
KENT, Simon
  Catto, Maxwell Jeffrey
KENTIGERN, John
  Veitch, Thomas
KENTON, Maxwell
  Southern, Terry
KENWORTHY, Hugh
  Walker, Rowland
KENYON, Larry
  Engel, Lyle Kenyon
KEPPEL, Charlotte
  Torday, Ursula
KEPPS, Gerald E
  Speck, Gerald Eugene
KERBY, Susan Alice
  Burton, Alice Elizabeth

KERR, Carole
  Carr, Margaret
KERR, John O'Connell
  Whitter, George Sorley
KERR, Lennox
  Kerr, James Lennox
KERSEY, John
  Warriner, Thurman
KETCHUM, Jack
  Paine, Lauran Bosworth
KETTLE, Pamela
  Kettle, Jocelyn
KEVERNE, Richard
  Hosken, Clifford James
  Wheeler
KEW, Andrew
  Morton, A Q
KIDD, Russell
  Donson, Cyril
KIEFER, Middleton
  Middleton, Harry and Kiefer,
  Warren
KILBOURN, Matt
  Barrett, Geoffrey John
KILDARE, John
  King, John
KILDARE, Maurice
  Richardson, Gladwell
KILGORE, John
  Paine, Lauran Bosworth
KILPATRICK, Sarah
  Underwood, Mavis Eileen
KIM
  Sweet, John

> Bingo had told him that I
> was the author of a lot of
> mushy novels by Rosie M
> Banks, you know. Said that
> I had written them, and
> that Rosie's name on the
> title-page was my what
> d'you call it.
> — P G Wodehouse

KIMBER, Lee
King, Albert
KINDLER, Asta
Hicken, Una
KING, Ames
King, Albert
KING, Arthur
Lake, Kenneth Robert
KING, Berta
King, Albert
KING, Charles
Avenell, Donne
KING, Christopher
King, Albert
KING, Clifford
King, James Clifford
KING, Evan
Ward, Robert Spencer
KING, Frank
Keesing, Nancy
KING, Oliver
Mount, Thomas Ernest
KING, Paul
Drackett, Phil
KING, Richard
Huskinson, Richard King
KING, Sampson
Bennett, Arnold
KING, Stella
Glenton, Stella Lennox
KING, Stephanie
Russell, Shirley
KING, W Scott
Greenland, W K
KINGSLEY, Laura
Bennett, Dorothy
KINGSMILL, Hugh
Lunn, Hugh Kingsmill
KINGSTON, Syd
Bingley, David Ernest
KINNOCH, R G B
Barclay, George
KINSEY-JONES, Brian
Ball, Brian N

KIRBY, Kate
Elgin, Betty
KIRK, Laurence
Simson, Eric Andrew
KISH
Le Riche, P J
KLAXON
Bower, John Graham
KLOSE, Norma Cline
Cline, Norma
KNICKERBOCKER, Cholly
Paul, Maury
KNIGHT, Adam
Lariar, Lawrence
KNIGHT, David
Prather, Richard
KNIGHT, Gareth
Wilby, Basil
KNIGHT, Isobel
Lockie, Isobel
KNIGHT, Mallory T
Hurwood, Bernhardt J
KNOTT, Bill
Knott, William Cecil
KNOWALL, George
O'Nolan, Brian
KNUDSEN, Greta
Knudsen, Margrethe
KREUZENAU, Michael
Law, Michael
KRISLOV, Alexander
Lee Howard, L A
KROLL, Burt
Rowland, Donald Sydney
KRUGER, Paul
Sebenthall, Roberta
KYD, Thomas
Harbage, Alfred
KYLE, Elizabeth
Dunlop, Agnes M R
LA FAYETTE, Rene
Hubbard, L Ron
LAFARGUE, Philip
Philpot, Joseph H

LAING, Kenneth
    Langmaid, Kenneth Joseph
        Robb
LAKE, Sarah
    Weiner, Margery
LAKER, Rosalind
    Øvstedal, Barbara
LAKLAN, Carli
    Laughlin, Virginia Carli
LAMONT, Marianne
    Rundle, Anne
LAMONT, N B
    Barnitt, Nedda Lemmon
LAMPLUGH, Lois
    Davis, Lois Carlile
LAMPTON, Austen
    Dent, Anthony
LANCASTER, G B
    Lyttleton, Edith Joan
LANCASTER, Vicky
    Ansle, Dorothy Phoebe
LANCE, Leslie
    Swatridge, Irene M M
LANCER, Jack
    Lawrence, James Duncan
LANDER, Dane
    Clarke, Percy A
LANDELS, D H
    Henderson, Donald Landels
LANDELS, Stephanie
    Henderson, Donald Landels
LANDGRAVE OF HESSE
    Rosen, Michael
LANDIS, John
    Bell, Gerard
LANDON, Louise
    Hauck, Louise Platt
LANE, Elizabeth
    Farmers, Eileen
LANE, Jane
    Dakers, Elaine
LANE, Marvyn
    Price, Jeremie

LANE, Mary D
    Delaney, Mary Murray
LANG, Frances
    Mantle, Winifred Langford
LANG, Grace
    Floren, Lee
LANG, Theo
    Langbehn, Theo
LANG, Maria
    Lange, Maria
LANGDALE, Stanley
    Moorhouse, Sydney
LANGE, John
    Crichton, Michael
LANGFORD, Jane
    Mantle, Winifred Langford
LANGLEY, Helen
    Rowland, Donald Sydney
LANGLEY, John
    Mason, Sydney Charles
LANGLEY, Lee
    Langley, Sarah
LANIN, E B
    Dillon, E J
LANSING, Henry
    Rowland, Donald Sydney
LANT, Harvey
    Rowland, Donald Sydney
LANZOL, Cesare
    Landells, Richard
LARRIMORE, Lida
    Turner, Lida Larrimore
LARSON, Eve
    St John, Wylly Folk
LASCELLES, Alison
    Parris, John
LATHAM, Mavis
    Thorpe-Clark, Mavis
LAUDER, George Dick
    Dick-Lauder, (Sir) George
LAUGHLIN, P S
    Shea, Patrick
LAUNAY, André
    De Launay, André Joseph

LAUNAY, Droo
  De Launay, André Joseph
LAURA
  Hunter, Eileen
LAW, Marjorie J
  Liddelow, Marjorie Joan
LAWRENCE, Hilda
  Kronmiller, Hildegarde
LAWRENCE, Irene
  Marsh, John
LAWRENCE, James
  Tames, Richard Lawrence
LAWRENCE, Steven C
  Murphy, Lawrence D
LAWSON, Christine
  Walker, Emily Kathleen
LAWSON, Michael
  Ryder, M L
LAWTON, Dennis
  Faust, Frederick
LE BRETON, Thomas
  Ford, T Murray
LE CARRE, John
  Cornwell, David John Moore
LE GRAND
  Henderson, Le Grand
LE GRYS, Walter
  Norgate, Walter
LEADER, Charles
  Smith, R C
LEDGARD, Jake
  Mason, Sydney Charles
LEE, Andrew
  Auchincloss, Louis
LEE, Charles H
  Story, Rosamond Mary
LEE, David
  Garnett, David S
LEE, Gypsy Rose
  Hovick, Rose Louise
LEE, Jesse
  Mason, Sydney Charles
LEE, Ranger
  Snow, Charles Horace
LEE, Rowena
  Bartlett, Marie

LEE, Vernon
  Paget, Violet
LEE, Veronica
  Woodford, Irene-Cecile
LEE, William
  Burroughs, William
LEES, Hannah
  Fetter, Elizabeth Head
LEES, Marguerite
  Baumann, Margaret
LEIGH, Olivia
  Clamp, Helen M E
LEIGH, Ursula
  Gwynn, Ursula Grace
LEIGHTON, Lee
  Overholser, Wayne D
LEINSTER, Murray
  Jenkins, William Fitzgerald
LENANTON, C
  Lenanton, (Lady)
LENTON, Anthony
  Nuttall, Anthony
LEONA
  Button, Margaret
LEONARD, Charles L
  Heberden, Mary Violet
LEONID
  Bosworth, William George
LESIEG, Theo
  Geisel, Theodor Seuss
LESLIE, Colin
  Roome, Gerald Antony
LESLIE, Doris
  Fergusson-Hannay, (Lady)
LESLIE, Val
  Knights, Leslie
LESS, Milton
  Marlowe, Stephen
LESSER, Anthony
  Whitby, Anthony Charles
LESTER, Frank
  Usher, Frank Hugh
LESTER, Jane
  Walker, Emily Kathleen

LESTER-RANDS, A
  Judd, Frederick
LETHBRIDGE, Olive
  Banbury, Olive Lethbridge
LETHBRIDGE, Rex
  Meyers, Roy
LEWIS, Ernest
  Vesey, Ernest Blakeman
LEWIS, Francine
  Wells, Helen
LEWIS, J B
  Lewis, Roy
LEWIS, Mervyn
  Frewer, Glyn
LIGGETT, Hunter
  Paine, Lauran Bosworth
LINDALL, Edward
  Smith, Edward Ernest
LINDLEY, Erica
  Quigley, Aileen
LINDLEY, Gerard
  Pilley, Phil
LINDSAY, H
  Hudson, H Lindsay
LINDSAY, Josephine
  Story, Rosamond Mary
LINDSAY, Lee
  Barre, Jean
LINDSEY, John
  Muriel, John
LINESMAN
  Grant, M H
LINSON
  Tomlinson, Joshua Leonard
LIPSTICK
  Long, Lois
LISLE, Mary
  Cornish, Doris Mary
LITTLE, Conyth
  Little, Gwenyth and Little,
  Constance
LITTLE, Sylvia
  Leyland, Eric
LITTLEJOHN, Jon R
  Kleinhaus, Theodore John

LIVINGSTON, Kenneth
  Stewart, Kenneth Livingston
LIVINGSTONE, Margaret
  Flynn, Mary
LLEWELLYN
  Lucas, Beryl Llewellyn
LLEWELLYN, Richard
  Lloyd, Richard Dafydd Vivian
  Llewellyn
LLOYD, John
  Cooper, John
LLOYD, Joseph M
  Purves, Frederick
LLOYD, Willson
  Dennison, Enid
LOGAN, Agnes
  Adams, Agnes
LOGROLLER
  Le Gallienne, Richard
LOMAX, Bliss
  Drago, Harry Sinclair
LOMAX, Jeff
  Mason, Sydney Charles
LONG, Gerry
  Larkins, William
LONG, Shirley
  Long, Leonard
LONGBAUGH, Harry
  Goldman, William
LONGFIELD, Jo
  Howard, Felicity
LONSDALE, Frederick
  Leonard, Lionel Frederick
LORAC, E C R
  Rivett, Edith Caroline
LORD, Jeremy
  Redman, Ben
LORING, Peter
  Shellabarger, Samuel
LORNA
  Stoddart, Jane T
LORNE, Charles
  Brand, Charles Neville
LORRAINE, Anne
  Chisholm, Lilian

LOVE, Arthur
  Liebers, Arthur
LOVE, David
  Lasky, Jesse L
LOVEGOOD, John
  Watson, Elliot Grant
LOW, Dorothy Mackie
  Paxton, Lois
LOW, Rachel
  Whear, Rachel
LOWE, Edith
  Kovar, Edith May
LOWE, Kenneth
  Lobaugh, Elma K
LOWING, Anne
  Wilson, Christine
LOWNDES, Susan
  Marques, Susan Lowndes
LUARD, L
  Luard, William Blaine
LUCAS, J K
  Paine, Lauran Bosworth
LUCAS, Victoria
  Plath, Sylvia
LUDLOW, George
  Kay, Ernest
LUDLOW, Geoffrey
  Meynell, Laurence Walter
LUELLEN, Valentina
  Polley, Judith Anne
LUIMARDEL
  Martinez-Delgado, Luis
LUK, Charles
  Lu Kuan Yu
LUM, Peter
  Lum, Bettina Peter
LUMMINS
  Melling, Leonard
LUNCHBASKET, Roger
  Reeve-Jones, Alan
LUNN, Peter
  Crowe, (Lady)
LUSKA, Sidney
  Harland, Henry

LYALL, David
  Swan, Annie S
LYMINGTON, John
  Chance, John Newton
LYNCH, Eric
  Bingley, David Ernest
LYNDALE, Sydney M
  Moorhouse, Sydney
LYNDON, Barrie
  Edgar, Alfred
LYNN, Margaret
  Battye, Gladys
LYNN, Stephen
  Bradbury, Parnell
LYNTON, Ann
  Rayner, Claire
LYON, Buck
  Paine, Lauran Bosworth
LYON, Elinor
  Wright, Elinor
LYON, Jessica
  De Leeuw, Cateau W
LYTE, Richard
  Whelpton, Eric
LYTTON, Jane
  Clarke, Percy A

M B
  Faust, Frederick
MACADAM, Eve
  Leslie, Cecilia
MACALPIN, Rory
  Mackinnon, Charles Roy
McARTHUR, John
  Wise, Arthur
McBAIN, Ed
  Hunter, Evan
McCABE, Cameron
  Borneman, Ernest
McCABE, Rory
  Greenwood, T E
McCALL, Anthony
  Kane, Henry
McCALL, Isabel
  Boyd, Elizabeth Orr

McCARTHY, Shaun
  Cory, Desmond
McCARY, Reed
  Rydberg, Ernie
McCLEAN, Kathleen
  Hale, Kathleen
McCONNELL, Will
  Snodgrass, W D
McCORD, Whip
  Norwood, Victor George
    Charles
McCORMACK, Charlotte
  Ross, William Edward Daniel
McCORMICK, Theodora
  Du Bois, Theodora
McCOY, Malachy
  Caulfield, Max
McCOY, Marshall
  Meares, Leonard F
MACDIARMID, Hugh
  Grieve, Christopher Murray
MACDONALD, Anson
  Heinlein, Robert A
MACDONALD, Jo
  Macdonald, Margaret Josephine
MACDONALD, John Ross
  Millar, Kenneth
MACDONALD, Ross
  Millar, Kenneth
MACDOUALL, Robertson
  Mair, George Brown
MACDOWELL, Frederics
  Frede, Richard
MACDUFF, Ilka
  List, Ilka Katherine
MACE, Margaret
  Lawrence, Dulcie
MACEY, Carn
  Barrett, Geoffrey John
MACFARLANE, Kenneth
  Walker, Kenneth Macfarlane
MACFARLANE, Stephen
  Cross, John Keir
McGAVIN, Moyra
  Crichton, Eleanor

McGAW, J M
  Morris, John
McGILL, Ian
  Allegro, John Marco
McGUINNESS, Brian
  McGuinness, Bernard
MACGUIRE, Nicolas
  Melides, Nicholas
McGURK, Slater
  Roth, Arthur
MACHLIS, Joseph
  Selcamm, George
McHUGH, Stuart
  Rowland, Donald Sydney
McINTOSH, Ann T
  Higginbotham, Anne D
McINTOSH, J T
  Macgregor, James Murdoch
McKENZIE, Paige
  Blood, Marje
MACKIN, Anita
  Donson, Cyril
McKINLEY, Karen
  Runbeck, Margaret Lee
MACLEAN, Art
  Shirreffs, Gordon D
MACLEAN, Barry
  Chosack, Cyril
MACLEAN, Christina
  Casement, Christina
MACLEOD, Finlay
  Wood, James
MACLEOD, Robert
  Knox, Bill
MACLEODHAS, Sorche
  Alger, Leclaire Gowans
McLOWERY, Frank
  Keevill, Henry John
McMASTER, Alison
  Baker, Marjorie
MACNAMARA, Brinsley
  Weldon, A E
MACNEIL, Duncan
  McCutchan, Philip D

McNEILL, Janet
  Alexander, Janet
MACNIB
  Mackie, Albert David
MACQUEEN, Jay
  Minto, Mary
MACRAE, Mason
  Rubel, James Lyon
MACTYRE, Paul
  Adam, Robin
MADDERN, Stan
  Mason, Sydney Charles
MADEOC
  Robinson, H
MADGETT, Naomi Long
  Andrews, Naomi Cornelia
MADISON, Dolly
  Paul, Maury
MADISON, Hank
  Rowland, Donald Sydney
MAGILL, Marcus
  Hill, Brian
MAGNUS, Gerald
  Bowman, Gerald
MAGRISKA, Hélène (Countess)
  Brockies, Enid Florence
MAINE, Charles Eric
  McIlwain, David
MAINE, Stirling
  Mason, Sydney Charles
MAINSAIL
  Duff, Douglas Valder
MAIZEL, Leah
  Maizel, Clarice Louise
MALCOLM, Charles
  Hincks, Cyril Malcolm
MALCOLM, John
  Uren, Malcolm
MALLERY, Amos
  Gelb, Norman
MALLOCH, Peter
  Duncan, William Murdoch
MALLORY, Jay
  Carey, Joyce
MALLOWEN, Agatha Christie
  Christie, (Dame) Agatha

MANDEVILLE, D E
  Coates, Anthony
MANN, Abel
  Creasey, John
MANN, Deborah
  Bloom, Ursula
MANN, Patricia
  Earnshaw, Patricia
MANN, Stanley
  Mason, Sydney Charles
MANNERS, Julia
  Greenaway, Gladys
MANNGIAN, Peter
  Monger, Ifor
MANNING, David
  Faust, Frederick
MANNING, Marsha
  Grimstead, Hettie
MANNING, Roy
  Reach, James
MANNOCK, Jennifer
  Mannock, Laura
MANOR, Jason
  Hall, Oakley Maxwell
MANSBRIDGE, Pamela
  Course, Pamela
MANSELL, C R
  Payne, Eileen Mary
MANSFIELD, Katherine
  Beauchamp, Kathleen
  Mansfield
MANTON, Jo
  Gittings, Jo
MANTON, Paul
  Walker, Peter Norman
MANTON, Peter
  Creasey, John
MANVILLE, George
  Fenn, George Manville
MAO
  Addis, Hazel Iris
MAPLESDEN, Ray
  Pearce, Raymond
MARA, Thalia
  Mahoney, Elizabeth

MARCH, Emma
  Stubbs, Jean
MARCH, Hilary
  Green, Lalage Isobel
MARCH, Stella
  Marshall, Marjorie
MARCH, William
  Campbell, William Edward
    March
MARCHANT, C
  Cookson, Catherine
MARCO
  Mountbatten, (Lord) Louis
MARCUS AURELIUS
  Padley, Walter
MARDLE, Jonathan
  Fowler, Eric
MARGERISON, David
  Davies, David Margerison
MARIN, A C
  Coppel, Alfred
MARIN, Alfred
  Coppel, Alfred
MARINER, David
  Macleod-Smith, D
MARION, S T
  Lakritz, Esther
MARJORAM, J
  Mottram, Ralph Hale
MARK, Edwina
  Fadiman, Edwin J
MARK, Matthew
  Babcock, Frederic
MARKER, Clare
  Witcombe, Rick
MARKHAM, Robert
  Amis, Kingsley
MARLE, T B
  Lambert, Hubert Steel
MARLIN, Roy
  Ashmore, Basil
MARLOW, Joyce
  Connor, Joyce Mary
MARLOW, Louis
  Wilkinson, Louis Umfreville

MARLOW, Phyllis
  Mason, Sydney Charles
MARLOWE, Hugh
  Patterson, Henry
MARLOWE, Piers
  Gribble, Leonard Reginald
MARLOWE, Stephen
  Lesser, Milton
MARR, Nancy J
  Johnson, Nancy Marr
MARRIC, J J
  Creasey, John
MARSDEN, James
  Creasey, John
MARSH, Henry
  Saklatvala, Beram
MARSH, Jean
  Marshall, Evelyn
MARSH, Joan
  Marsh, John
MARSH, Rebecca
  Neubauer, William Arthur
MARSHALL, Archibald
  Marshall, Arthur Hammond
MARSHALL, Beverley
  Holroyd, Ethel Mary
MARSHALL, Gary
  Snow, Charles Horace
MARSHALL, James Vance
  Payne, Donald Gordon
MARSHALL, Joanne
  Rundle, Anne
MARSHALL, Lloyd
  Wilding, Philip
MARSHALL, Lovat
  Duncan, William Murdoch

A man that should call
everything by its right
name, would hardly pass
the streets without being
knocked down as a
common enemy.
— Marquis of Halifax

135

MARSHALL, Raymond
  Raymond, Rene
MARSTEN, Richard
  Hunter, Evan
MARTELL, James
  Bingley, David Ernest
MARTIN, Ann
  Best, Carol Ann
MARTIN, Bruce
  Paine, Lauran Bosworth
MARTIN, Christopher
  Hoyt, Edwin Palmer Jr
MARTIN, Chuck
  Martin, Charles Morris
MARTIN, John
  Tatham, Laura
MARTIN, Nancy
  Salmon, Annie Elizabeth
MARTIN, Peter
  Chaundler, Christine
MARTIN, R J
  Mehta, Rustam
MARTIN, Rex
  Martin, Reginald Alec
MARTIN, Richard
  Creasey, John
MARTIN, Robert
  Martin, Reginald Alec
MARTIN, Ruth
  Rayner, Claire
MARTIN, Scott
  Martin, Reginald Alec
MARTIN, Tom
  Paine, Lauran Bosworth
MARTINDALE, Spencer
  Wolff, William
MARTINEZ, J D
  Parkhill, Forbes
MARTON, Francesca
  Ballasis, Margaret Rosa
MARTYN, Don
  Borbolla, Barbara
MARTYN, Henry
  Perry, Martin

MARTYN, Miles
  Elliott-Cannon, Arthur Elliott
MARVEL, Holt
  Maschwitz, Eric
MARX, Magdeleine
  Paz, Magdeleine
MASON, Carl
  King, Albert
MASON, Chuck
  Rowland, Donald Sydney
MASON, Frank W
  Mason, F Van Wyck
MASON, Michael
  Smith, Edgar
MASSON, Georgina
  Johnson, Marion
MASTERS, Steve
  Mason, Sydney Charles
MASTERS, William
  Cousins, Margaret
MASTERSON, Whit
  Wade, Robert and Miller,
  William
MATELOT
  Uren, Malcolm
MATHER, Anne
  Grieveson, Mildred
MATHER, Berkely
  Davies, John Evan Watson
MATHESON, Hugh
  Mackay, Lewis
MATHESON, Sylvia A
  Schofield, Sylvia Anne
MATT
  Sandford, Matthew
MATTHESON, Rodney
  Creasey, John
MATUSOW, Marshall
  Matusow, Harvey Marshall
MAUGHAM, Robin
  Maugham, Robert Cecil Romer
  (Viscount)
MAURICE, Furnley
  Wilmot, Frank Leslie
  Thompson

MAXWELL, Ann
Pattinson, Lee
MAXWELL, Clifford
Leon, Henry Cecil
MAY, Roberta E
Davidson, Edith May
MAYBURY, Anne
Buxton, Anne
MAYHEW, Elizabeth
Bear, Joan E
MAYNE, Cora
Walker, Emily Kathleen
MAYNE, Rutherford
Waddell, Samuel
MAYO, Arnold
Meredith, Kenneth Lincoln
MAYRANT, Drayton
Simons, Katherine Drayton
Mayrant
MEDHURST, Joan
Liverton, Joan
MEE, Mary
Dean, Mary
MEIKLE, Clive
Brooks, Jeremy
MEINIKOFF, Pamela
Harris, Pamela
MELLOR, Michael
Spooner, Peter Alan
MELMOTH
Tullett, Denis John
MELVILLE, Alan
Caverhill, William Melville
MELVILLE, Jean
Cummins, Mary Warmington
MELVILLE, Lewis
Benjamin, Lewis S
MENANDER
Morgan, Charles
MENDEL, Jo
Bond, Gladys Baker
MENDEL, Jo
Gilbertson, Mildred
MENDL, Gladys
Leslie, Henrietta

MENTOR
Jones, Frank H
MERCER, Frances
Hills, Frances E
MERCURY
Eames, Helen Mary
MEREDITH, Anne
Malleson, Lucy
MEREDITH, Hal
Blyth, Harry
MEREDITH, Peter
Worthington-Stuart, Brian
Arthur
MERLIN, David
Moreau, David
MERRICK, Hugh
Meyer, Harold Albert
MERRICK, Spencer
Mason, Sydney Charles
MERRILL, Lynne
Gibbs, Norah
MERRIMAN, Chad
Cheshire, Gifford Paul
MERRITT, E B
Waddington, Miriam
METHUEN, John
Bell, John Keble
MEURON, Skip
Sands, Leo G
MEWBURN, Martin
Hitchin, Martin
MEYER, H A
Merrick, Hugh
MEYER, Henry J
Hird, Neville
MEYER, June
Jordan, June
MIALL, Robert
Burke, John Frederick
MICHAELS, Barbara
Mertz, Barbara G
MICHAELS, Steve
Avallone, Michael Angelo Jr
MIDLING, Perspicacity
Millward, Pamela

137

MILES, David
  Cronin, Brendan Leo
MILES, John
  Bickham, Jack M
MILES, Miska
  Martin, Patricia Miles
MILES, Susan
  Roberts, Ursula
MILLER, Ellen
  Pattinson, Lee
MILLER, Frank
  Loomis, Noel Miller
MILLER, Margaret J
  Dale, Margaret
MILLER, Mary
  Northcott, Cecil
MILLER, Patrick
  Macfarlane, George Gordon
MILLER, Wade
  Miller, William and Wade,
  Robert
MILLS, Martin
  Boyd, Martin à Beckett
MILLS, Osmington
  Brooks, Vivian Collin
MILNE, Ewart
  Milne, Charles
MILNER, George
  Hardinge, George
MINGSTON, R Gresham
  Stamp, Roger
MINIER, Nelson
  Baker, Laura
MIRYAM
  Yardumian, Miryam
MITCHAM, Gilroy
  Newton, William Simpson
MITCHELL, Ewan
  Janner, Greville
MITCHELL, K L
  Lamb, Elizabeth Searle
MITCHELL, Kerry
  Wilkes-Hunter, Richard

MITCHELL, Scott
  Godfrey, Lionel Robert
  Holcombe
MODELL, Merriam
  Piper, Evelyn
MOKO
  Mead, Sidney
MOLE, William
  Younger, William Anthony
MONIG, Christopher
  Crossen, Kendell Foster
MONKLAND, George
  Whittet, George Sorley
MONMOUTH, Jack
  Pember, William Leonard
MONNOW, Peter
  Croudace, Glyn
MONRO, Gavin
  Monro-Higgs, Gertrude
MONTAGU, Robert
  Hampden, John
MONTGOMERY, Derek
  Simmons, J S A
MONTROSE
  Adams, Charles William
  Dunlop
MONTROSE, David
  Graham, Charles
MONTROSE, Graham
  Mackinnon, Charles Roy
MONTROSE, James St David
  Appleman, John Alan
MONTROSS, David
  Backus, Jean L
MOODIE, Edwin
  De Caire, Edwin
MOOLSON, Melusa
  Solomon, Samuel
MOORE, Frances Sarah
  Mack, Elsie Frances
MOORE, Rosalie
  Brown, Rosalie
MOORHOUSE, E Hallam
  Maynell, Esther H

MORE, Caroline
  Cone, Molly
MORE, Euston
  Bloomer, Arnold
MORENO, Nick
  Deming, Richard
MORESBY, Louis
  Barrington, E
MORETON, John
  Cohen, Morton N
MORGAN, Arlene
  Paine, Lauran Bosworth
MORGAN, Carol McAfee
  Appleby, Carol McAfee
MORGAN, Frank
  Paine, Lauran Bosworth
MORGAN, John
  Paine, Lauran Bosworth
MORGAN, Phyllis
  Thompson, Phyllis
MORGAN, Valerie
  Paine, Lauran Bosworth
MORLAND, Peter Henry
  Faust, Frederick
MORRIS, Ira J
  Jefferies, Ira
MORRIS, John
  Hearne, John and Gargill,
    Morris
MORRIS, Julian
  West, Morris
MORRIS, Ruth
  Webb, Ruth Enid
MORRIS, Sara
  Burke, John Frederick
MORRISON, J Strang
  Thom, William Albert Strang
MORRISON, Peggy
  Morrison, Margaret Mackie
MORROW, Charlotte
  Kirwan, Molly
MORTIMER, June
  Ryder, Vera

MORTON, Anthony
  Creasey, John
MOSES, Ruben
  Wurmbrand, Richard
MOSS, Nancy
  Moss, Robert Alfred
MOSS, Roberta
  Moss, Robert Alfred
MOSSMAN, Burt
  Keevill, Henry John
MOSSOP, Irene
  Swatridge, Irene M M
MOSTYN-OWEN, Gaia
  Servadio, Gaia
MOTTE, Peter
  Harrison, Richard Motte
MOUTHPIECE
  Porter, Maurice
MOWBRAY, John
  Vahey, John George Haslette
MOWERY, Dorothy
  Dunsing, Dee
MOYES, Robin
  Bateman, Robert Moyes C
MUIR, Alan
  Morrison, Thomas
MUIR, Dexter
  Gribble, Leonard Reginald
MUIR, Jane
  Petrone, Jane Gertrude
MUIR, John
  Morgan, Thomas Christopher
MUIR, Willa
  Muir, Wilhelmina Johnstone
MULDOON, Omar
  Matusow, Harvey Marshall
MULLER, Paul
  King, Albert
MULLINS, Ann
  Dally, Ann
MUNDY, Max
  Schofield, Sylvia Anne
MUNDY, V M
  Cunningham, Virginia Myra
    Mundy

MUNRO, C K
   Macmullan, Charles W
   Kirkpatrick
MUNRO, James
   Mitchell, James
MUNRO, Mary
   Howe, Doris
MUNRO, Ronald Eadie
   Glen, Duncan Munro
MUNROE, R
   Cheyne, (Sir) Joseph
MUNTHE, Frances
   Minto, Frances
MURRAY, Edna
   Rowland, Donald Sydney
MURRAY, Geraldine
   Murray, Blanche
MURRAY, Jill
   Walker, Emily Kathleen
MURRAY, Sinclair
   Sullivan, Edward Alan
MURRAY, William
   Graydon, William Murray
MURRELL, Shirley
   Scott-Hansen, Olive
MURRY, Colin
   Murry, John Middleton Jr
MURRY, Colin Middleton
   Murry, John Middleton Jr
MYATT, Nellie
   Kirkham, Nellie
MYERS, Harriet Kathryn
   Whittington, Harry

N D H
   Dick-Hunter, Noel
N O B
   Bettany, F G
NA GOPALEEN, Myles
   O'Nolan, Brian
NADA, John
   Langdon-Davies, John
NAPIER, Mark
   Laffin, John

NASH, Daniel
   Loader, William
NASH, Newlyn
   Howe, Doris
NASH, Simon
   Chapman, Raymond
NAST, Elsa Ruth
   Werner, Elsa Jane
NATHAN, Daniel
   Dannay, Frederic
NAUTICUS
   Seaman, (Sir) Owen
NEAL, Hilary
   Norton, Olive Marion
NEIL, Frances
   Wilson, Christine
NELSON, Chris
   Huff, Darrell
NELSON, Lois
   Northam, Lois Edgell
NELSON, Marguerite
   Floren, Lee
NEMO
   Douglas, Archibald C
NEON
   Acworth, Marion W
NESBIT, Troy
   Folsom, Franklin Brewster
NESS, K T
   Grant, Donald and Wilson,
     William
NETTLETON, Arthur
   Gaunt, Arthur N
NEVILLE, C J
   Franklin, Cynthia
NEVILLE, Margot
   Joske, Neville and Goyder,
     Margot
NEVILLE, Mary
   Woodrich, Mary Neville
NEWCOMB, Norma
   Neubauer, William Arthur
NEWMAN, Margaret
   Betteridge, Anne

NEWTON, David C
    Chance, John Newton
NEWTON, Francis
    Hobsbawn, E J
NEWTON, Macdonald
    Newton, William Simpson
NICHOLAI, C L R
    Clair, Colin
NICHOLAS, F R E
    Freeling, Nicolas
NICHOLLS, Anthony
    Parsons, Anthony
NICHOLS, Fan
    Hanna, Frances
NICHOLSON, John
    Parcell, Norman Howe
NICHOLSON, Kate
    Fay, Judith
NICODEMUS
    Pearce, Melville Chaning
NIELSON, Vernon
    Clarke, Percy A
NIELSON, Virginia
    McCall, Virginia
NIGHTINGALE, Charles
    Duddington, Charles Lionel
NILE, Dorothea
    Avallone, Michael Angelo Jr
NILSON, Bee
    Nilson, Annabel
NINA
    Nelson, Ethel
NIXON, Kathleen
    Blundell, V R
NOBLE, Emily
    Gifford, Janes Noble
NOEL, John
    Bird, Dennis Leslie
NOEL, L
    Barker, Leonard Noel
NONG
    Lobley, Robert
NOON, T R
    Norton, Olive Marion

NOONE, Edwina
    Avallone, Michael Angelo Jr
NORBURN, Martha
    Mead, Martha Norburn
NORDEN, Charles
    Durrell, Lawrence
NORHAM, Gerald
    James, J W G
NORMYX
    Douglas, Norman and
    Fitzgibbon, Elsa
NORRIS, P E
    Cleary, C V H
NORTH, Colin
    Bingley, David Ernest
NORTH, Gil
    Horne, Geoffrey
NORTH, Howard
    Dudley-Smith, Trevor
NORTH, Mark
    Miller, Wright
NORTHE, Maggie
    Lee, Maureen
NORTHERNER
    Hughes, William
NORTHROP, (Capt) B A
    Hubbard, L Ron
NORTHUMBRIAN GENTLEMAN
    Tegner, Henry
NORTON, André
    Norton, Alice Mary
NORTON, Bess
    Norton, Olive Marion
NORTON, Jed
    Lazenby, Norman
NORTON, S H
    Richardson, Mary Kathleen
NORTON, Victor
    Dalton, Gilbert
NORWAY, Kate
    Norton, Olive Marion
NORWICH, John Julius
    Norwich (Viscount)
NORWOOD, Elliott
    Kensdale, W E N

NOSTALGIA
  Bentley, James W B
NOTT, Barry
  Hurren, Bernard
NUDNICK
  Nerney, Patrick W
NUNQUAM
  Blatchford, Robert
NURAINI
  Sim, Katharine Phyllis

O S
  Seaman, (Sir) Owen
OATES, Titus
  Bell, Martin
OBOLENSKY, Ilka
  List, Ilka Katherine
O'BRIEN, Bernadette
  Higgins, Margaret
O'BRIEN, Deirdre
  McNally, Mary Elizabeth
O'BRIEN, Flann
  O'Nolan, Brian
O'BRIEN, John
  Hartigan, Patrick Joseph
O'BYRNE, Dermot
  Bax, (Sir) Arnold
O'CONNELL, Robert Frank
  Gohm, Douglas Charles
O'CONNER, Clint
  Paine, Lauran Bosworth
O'CONNER, Elizabeth
  McNamara, Barbara Willard
O'CONNOR, Dermot
  Newman, Terence
O'CONNOR, Frank
  O'Donovan, Michael Francis
O'CONNOR, Patrick
  O'Connor Wibberley, Leonard
  Patrick
OCTAVIA
  Barltrop, Mabel
ODDIE, E M
  O'Donoghue, Elinor Mary

ODELL, Carol
  Foote, Carol
ODELL, Gill
  Foote, Carol and Gill, Travis
O'DONNELL, Donat
  O'Brien, Conor Cruise
OGDEN, Clint
  King, Albert
O'GRADA, Sean
  O'Grady, John
O'GRADY, Tony
  Clemens, Brian
O'HARA, Kevin
  Cumberland, Marten
O'HARA, Mary
  Sture-Vasa, Mary
OKADA, Hideki
  Glassco, John
OKE, Richard
  Millett, Nigel
OKE, Simon
  Vann, Gerald
OLD COYOTE, Sally
  Old Coyote, Elnora A
OLDCASTLE, John
  Meynell, Wilfred
OLDFIELD, Peter
  Bartlett, Vernon
OLDHAM, Hugh R
  Whitford, Joan
OLGA
  Phillips, Olga
OLIVER, Jane
  Rees, Helen
OLIVER, Laurence
  Brown, Laurence Oliver
OLIVER, Owen
  Flynn, (Sir) J A
OLIVER, Robert
  Carrier, Robert and Dick,
  Oliver Lawson
OLIVIA
  Bussy, Dorothy
OLSEN, D B
  Hitchens, Dolores

142

OLYMPIC
  Hutton, Andrew Nielson
O'MALLEY, Frank
  O'Rourke, Frank
OMAN, Carola
  Lenanton, (Lady)
O'MARA, Jim
  Fluharty, Vernon L
O'NAIR, Mairi
  Evans, Constance May
O'NEILL, Egan
  Linington, Elizabeth
ONIONS, Berta
  Oliver, Amy Roberta
ONIONS, Oliver
  Oliver, George
ORAM, John
  Thomas, John Oram
ORBISON, Keck
  Orbison, Roy and Keck, Maud
ORCHARD, Evelyn
  Swan, Annie S
ORDON, A Lang
  Gordon, Alan Bacchus
O'RILEY, Warren
  Richardson, Gladwell
ORION
  Brooks, Ern
ORME, Alexandra
  Barcza, Alicja
ORR, Mary
  Caswell, Anne
ORWELL, George
  Blair, Eric
O'SHEA, Sean
  Tralins, S Robert
O'SULLIVAN, Seumas
  Starkey, James Sullivan
OUIDA
  Ramé, Marie Louise
OVERY, Claire May
  Bass, Clara May
OVERY, Martin
  Overy, Jillian P J

OWEN, Dean
  McGaughy, Dudley Dean
OWEN, Edmund
  Teller, Neville
OWEN, Hugh
  Faust, Frederick
OWEN, Ray
  King, Albert
OWEN, Roderick
  Fenwick-Owen, Roderic
OWEN, Tom
  Watts, Peter Christopher
OXENHAM, Elsie Jeanette
  Dunkerley, Elsie Jeanette
OXENHAM, John
  Dunkerley, William Arthur
OYVED, Moysheh
  Good, Edward

P B
  Braybrooke, Patrick
P C
  Chalmers, Patrick
PACKER, Vin
  Meaker, Marijane
PADESON, Mary
  Magraw, Beatrice
PADGETT, Lewis
  Kuttner, Henry
PAGE, Eileen
  Heal, Edith
PAGE, Eleanor
  Coerr, Eleanor Beatrice
PAGE, Lorna
  Rowland, Donald Sydney
PAGE, Marco
  Kurnitz, Harry
PAGE, Stanton
  Fuller, Henry B

Cases of a man writing
under a woman's name
are rare. — Cassell's
Encyclopaedia of literature

143

PAGE, Vicki
  Avey, Ruby D
PAGET, John
  Aiken, John
PALMER, John
  Watts, Edgar John Palmer
PAN
  Beresford, Leslie
PANDORA
  Moore, Mary McLeod
PANTOPUCK
  Philpott, Alexis Robert
PARIOS
  Lee, Henry David Cook
PARKER, Seth
  Lord, Phillips H
PARKS, Ron
  Guariento, Ronald
PARR, (Dr) John Anthony
  Anthony, E
PARRISH, Mary
  Cousins, Margaret
PARTRIDGE, Anthony
  Oppenheim, E Phillips
PASSMORE, Aileen E
  Griffiths, Aileen Esther
PASTON, George
  Symonds, E M
PATRICK, Diana
  Wilson, Desemea
PATRICK, John
  Goggan, John Patrick
PATRICK, Q
  Wheeler, Hugh Callingham and
  Webb, Richard Wilson
PATTERSON, Harry
  Patterson, Henry
PATTERSON, Olive
  Rowland, Donald Sydney
PATTERSON, Shott
  Renfrew, A
PAUL, Adrian
  McGeogh, Andrew
PAWNEE BILL
  Lillie, Gordon W

PAXTON, Lois
  Low, Lois
PAYE, Robert
  Campbell, Gabrielle Margaret
  Vere
PEARCE, A H
  Quibell, Agatha
PEARL, Irene
  Guyonvarch, Irene
PECKHAM, Richard
  Holden, Raymond
PEDRICK, Gale
  Pedrick-Harvey, Gale
PEEL, Wallis
  Peel, Hazel
PEGDEN, Helen
  Macgregor, Miriam
PELHAM, Anthony
  Hope, Charles Evelyn Graham
PELHAM, Randolph
  Landells, Richard
PENDER, Marilyn
  Jacobs, Thomas Curtis Hicks
PENDLETON, Ford
  Cheshire, Gifford Paul
PENDOWER, Jacques
  Jacobs, Thomas Curtis Hicks
PENLAKE, Richard
  Salmon, P R
PENMARE, William
  Nisot, Mavis Elizabeth
PENN, Ann
  Jacobs, Thomas Curtis Hicks
PENN, Christopher
  Lawlor, Patrick
PENNAGE, E M
  Finkel, George
PENNY, Rupert
  Thornett, Ernest Basil Charles
PENTECOST, Hugh
  Philips, Judson Pentecost
PEPPER, Joan
  Alexander, Joan
PERCY, Edward
  Smith, Edward Percy

PERCY, Florence
   Akers, Elizabeth
PERKINS, Eli
   Landon, Melville de Lancy
PETERS, Alan
   Spooner, Peter Alan
PETERS, Elizabeth
   Mertz, Barbara G
PETERS, Ellis
   Pargeter, Edith Mary
PETERS, Fritz
   Peters, Arthur A
PETERS, Geoffrey
   Palmer, Madelyn
PETERS, Lawrence
   Davies, Leslie Purnell
PETERS, Ludovic
   Brent, Peter Ludwig
PETERS, Maureen
   Black, Maureen
PETERS, Noel
   Harvey, Peter Noel
PETERS, Roy
   Nickson, Arthur
PHELIX
   Burnett, Hugh
PHILATICUS
   Finlay, Ian
PHILIPPI, Mark
   Bender, Arnold
PHILIPS, Steve
   Whittington, Harry
PHILIPS, Thomas
   Davies, Leslie Purnell
PHILLIP, Alban M
   Allan, Philip Bertram Murray
PHILLIPS, John
   Marquand, John Phillips
PHILLIPS, King
   Perkins, Kenneth
PHILMORE, R
   Howard, Herbert Edmund
PHIPPS, Margaret
   Tatham, Laura

PHIPSON, Joan
   Fitzhardinge, Joan Margaret
PHOENICE, J
   Hutchinson, Juliet Mary Fox
PICKARD, John Q
   Borg, Philip Anthony John
PICTON, Bernard
   Knight, Bernard
PIERCE, Katherine
   St John, Wylly Folk
PIKE, Robert L
   Fish, Robert L
PILGRIM
   Wright, Marjory Beatrice
PILGRIM, Adam
   Webster, Owen
PILGRIM, Anne
   Allan, Mabel Esther
PILGRIM, David
   Palmer, John Leslie and
     Saunders, Hilary Aidan
     St George
PILGRIM, Derral
   Kanto, Peter
PILIO, Gerone
   Whitfield, John
PINDELL, Jon
   Paine, Lauran Bosworth
PINDER, Chuck
   Donson, Cyril
PINE, M S
   Finn, (Sister) Mary Paulina
PIPER, Evelyn
   Modell, Merriam
PIPER, Peter
   Langbehn, Theo
PIPER, Roger
   Fisher, John
PITCAIRN, Frank
   Cockburn, Claud
PITCHFORD, Harry Ronald
   Ebbs, Robert
PLAIDY, Jean
   Hibbert, Eleanor Alice Burford

PLAIN, Josephine
  Mitchell, Isabel
PLAUT, Martin
  Marttin, Paul
PLEDGER, P J
  Tonkin, C B
PLOWMAN, Stephanie
  Dee, Stephanie
PLUMMER, Ben
  Bingley, David Ernest
POLLOCK, Mary
  Blyton, Enid
POMFRET, Joan
  Townsend, Joan
PONT
  Laidler, Graham
POOK, Peter
  Miller, J A
POOLE, Michael
  Poole, Reginald Heber
POOLE, Vivian
  Jaffe, Gabriel
POOTER
  Hamilton, Alex
PORLOCK, Martin
  Macdonald, Philip
PORTER, Alvin
  Rowland, Donald Sydney
PORTOBELLO, Petronella
  Anderson, (Lady) Flavia
POTTER, Beatrix
  Heelis, Beatrix
POTTER, Margaret
  Betteridge, Anne
POWELL, Fern
  Samman, Fern
POWERS, Margaret
  Heal, Edith
POY
  Fearon, Percy
PREEDY, George
  Campbell, Gabrielle Margaret
  Vere

PREEDY, George R
  Campbell, Gabrielle Margaret
  Vere
PRENDER, Bart
  King, Albert
PRENTIS, Richard
  Agate, James
PRENTISS, Karl
  Purdy, Ken
PRESCOT, Julian
  Budd, John
PRESCOTT, Caleb
  Bingley, David Ernest
PRESLAND, John
  Bendit, Gladys
PRESTON, James
  Unett, John
PRESTON, Richard
  Lindsay, Jack
PREVOST, Francis
  Prevost-Battersby, H F
PRICE, Evadne
  Smith, Helen Zenna
PRIESTLEY, Robert
  Wiggins, David
PRIESTLY, Mark
  Albert, Harold A
PROBERT, Lowri
  Jones, Robert Maynard
PROCTER, Ida
  Harris, Ida Fraser
PROCTOR, Everitt
  Montgomery, Rutherford
  George
PROLE, Lozania
  Bloom, Ursula and Eade,
  Charles
PRUTKOV, Kozma
  Snodgrass, W D
PULVERTAFT, Lalage
  Green, Lalage Isobel
PUNDIT, Ephraim
  Looker, Samuel Joseph
PURE, Simon
  Swinnerton, Frank

Q
Quiller-Couch, (Sir) Arthur
QUAD, M
Lewis, Charles Bertrand
QUEEN, Ellery
Dannay, Frederic and Lee,
Manfred B
QUENTIN, Patrick
Webb, Richard Wilson and
Wheeler, Hugh Callingham
QUEX
Nichols, (Captain) G H F
QUILIBET
Fowler, Henry Watson
QUILL
Puddepha, Derek
QUILLET
Fowler, Henry Watson
QUIN, Dan
Lewis, Alfred Henry
QUIN, Shirland
Guest, Enid
QUINCE, Peter
Day, George Harold
QUIRK
Squibbs, H W Q
QUIROULE, Pierre
Sayer, Walter William

R H F
Fairbairn, R H
RACHEN, Kurt von
Hubbard, L Ron
RADYR, Tomos
Stevenson, James Patrick
RAE, Scott
Hamilton, Cecily
RAG MAN
Burrows, Hermann
RAGGED STAFF
Coley, Rex
RAINE, Richard
Sawkins, Raymond Harold
RALSTON, Jan
Dunlop, Agnes M R

RAMAL, Walter
De la Mare, Walter
RAMEAUT, Maurice
Marteau, F A
RAMSAY, Fay
Eastwood, Helen
RAMSEY, Michael
Green, T
RANA, T
Bhatia, June
RAND, Brett
Norwood, Victor George
Charles
RAND, James S
Attenborough, Bernard
George
RANDALL, Clay
Adams, Clifton
RANDALL, Janet
Young, Janet Randall
RANDALL, Rona
Shambrook, Rona
RANDELL, Beverly
Price, Beverly Joan
RANDOM, Alan
Kay, Ernest
RANDOM, Alex
Rowland, Donald Sydney
RANGELY, E R
Kanto, Peter
RANGELY, Olivia
Kanto, Peter
RANGER, Ken
Creasey, John
RANKINE, John
Mason, Douglas Rankine
RANSOME, Stephen
Davis, Frederick Clyde
RAPHAEL, Ellen
Hartley, Ellen R
RASKIN, Ellen
Flanagan, Ellen
RATTRAY, Simon
Dudley-Smith, Trevor

RAVENSCROFT, Rosanne
   Ravenscroft, John R
RAYMOND, Mary
   Keegan, Mary Constance
RAYNER, Richard
   McIlwain, David
READ, Miss
   Saint, Dora Jessie
READE, Hamish
   Gray, Simon
REDMAN, Joseph
   Pearce, Brian
REDMAYNE, Barbara
   Smithers, Muriel
REDWAY, Ralph
   Hamilton, Charles Harold
   St John
REDWOOD, Alec
   Milkomane, George Alexis
   Milkomanovich
REED, Cynthia
   Nolan, Cynthia
REED, Eliot
   Ambler, Eric and Rodda,
   Charles
REES, Dilwyn
   Daniel, Glyn Edmund
REES, J Larcombe
   Larcombe, Jennifer
   Geraldine
REEVES, James
   Reeves, John Morris
REEVES, Joyce
   Gard, Joyce
REILLY, William K
   Creasey, John
REJJE, E
   Hyde, Edmund Errol Claude
REMINGTON, Mark
   Bingley, David Ernest
RENAULT, Mary
   Challans, Mary
RENIER, Elizabeth
   Baker, Betty

RENNIE, Jack
   Spooner, Peter Alan
RENO, Mark
   Keevill, Henry John
RENTON, Cam
   Armstrong, Richard
RENTON, Julia
   Cole, Margaret A
RENZELMAN, Marilyn
   Ferguson, Marilyn
REYNOLDS, Dickson
   Reynolds, Helen Mary
   Greenwood Dickson
REYNOLDS, Jack
   Jones, Jack
REYNOLDS, John
   Fear, William H
RHODE, John
   Street, Cecil John Charles
RHOSCOMYL, Owen
   Vaughan, Owen
RICHARDS, Clay
   Crossen, Kendell Foster
RICHARDS, Francis
   Lockridge, Frances Louise
   and Lockridge, Richard
RICHARDS, Frank
   Hamilton, Charles Harold
   St John
RICHARDS, Hilda
   Hamilton, Charles Harold
   St John
RICHARDS, Paul
   Buddee, Paul
RICHARDS, Peter
   Monger, Ifor
RICHES, Phyllis
   Sutton, Phyllis Mary
RICHMOND, Grace
   Marsh, John
RICHMOND, Mary
   Lindsay, Kathleen
RICKARD, Cole
   Barrett, Geoffrey John

RIDDELL, John
  Ford, Corey
RIDING, Laura
  Gottschalk, Laura Riding
RIFT, Valerie
  Bartlett, Marie
RILEY, Tex
  Creasey, John
RIMMER, W J
  Rowland, Donald Sydney
RING, Basil
  Braun, Wilbur
RING, Douglas
  Prather, Richard S
RINGO, Johnny
  Keevill, Henry John
RINGOLD, Clay
  Hogan, Ray
RIPLEY, Alvin
  King, Albert
RITA
  Humphreys, Eliza M J
RITCHIE, Claire
  Gibbs, Norah
RIVES, Amelia
  Troubetzkoi, (Princess)
RIX, Donna
  Rowland, Donald Sydney
RIXON, Annie
  Studdert, Annie
RIZA, Ali
  Orga, Irfan
ROADSTER
  Bays, J W
ROBBINS, Harold
  Rubins, Harold
ROBERTS, David
  Cox, John
ROBERTS, Desmond
  Best, Rayleigh Breton
  Amis
ROBERTS, Ivor
  Roberts, Irene

ROBERTS, James Hall
  Duncan, Robert Lipscomb
ROBERTS, John
  Bingley, David Ernest
ROBERTS, Ken
  Lake, Kenneth Robert
ROBERTS, Lee
  Martin, Robert Lee
ROBERTS, McLean
  Machlin, Milton
ROBERTSON, Elspeth
  Ellison, Joan
ROBERTSON, Helen
  Edmiston, Helen J M
ROBERTSON, Muirhead
  Johnson, H
ROBIN
  Roberts, Eric
ROCK, Richard
  Mainprize, Don
ROCKWELL, Matt
  Rowland, Donald Sydney
RODD, Ralph
  North, William
ROE, M S
  Thomson, Daisy
ROE, Richard
  Cowper, Francis
ROE, Tig
  Roe, Eric
ROFFMAN, Jan
  Summerton, Margaret
ROGERS, Anne
  Seraillier, Anne
ROGERS, Floyd
  Spence, William
ROGERS, Phillips
  Idell, Albert Edward
ROGERS, Rachel
  Redmon, Lois
ROHMER, Sax
  Wade, Arthur Sarsfield
ROLAND, Walmsley
  Walmsley, Arnold

ROLLS, Anthony
  Vulliamy, Colwyn Edward
ROLPH, C H
  Hewitt, Cecil Rolph
ROMANY
  Evens, George Bramwell
ROMNEY, Steve
  Bingley, David Ernest
RONALD, E B
  Barker, Ronald Ernest
ROOME, Holdar
  Moore, Harold William
ROOS, Kelley
  Roos, William and Kelley,
  Audrey
ROSCOE, Charles
  Rowland, Donald Sydney
ROSCOE, Janet
  Prior, Mollie
ROSCOE, Mike
  Roscoe, John
ROSE, Hilary
  Mackinnon, Charles Roy
ROSE, Phyllis
  Thompson, Phyllis
ROSE, Robert
  Rose, Ian
ROSS
  Martin, Violet Florence
ROSS, Barnaby
  Dannay, Frederic and Lee,
  Manfred B
ROSS, Diana
  Denney, Diana
ROSS, George
  Ross, Isaac
ROSS, J H
  Lawrence, T E
ROSS, Jean
  Hewson, Irene Dale
ROSS, Katherine
  Walter, Dorothy Blake
ROSS, Leonard Q
  Rosten, Leo C

ROSS, Martin
  Martin, Violet Florence
ROSS, Patricia
  Wood, Patricia E W
ROSS, Sutherland
  Callard, Thomas
ROSTRON, Primrose
  Hulbert, Joan
ROTHMANN, Judith
  Black, Maureen
ROWANS, Virginia
  Tanner, Edward Everett
ROWE, Alice E
  Rowe, John Gabriel
ROWLAND, Iris
  Roberts, Irene
ROWLANDS, Effie Adelaide
  Albanesi, Effie Maria
ROWLANDS, Lesley
  Zuber, Mary E L
ROYAL, Dan
  Barrett, Geoffrey John
ROYCE, Kenneth
  Gandley, Kenneth Royce
RUCK, Berta
  Oliver, Amy Roberta
RUDD, Margaret
  Newlin, Margaret
RUDD, Steele
  Davis, Arthur Hoey
RUFFLE
  Tegner, Henry
RUSSELL, Erle
  Wilding, Philip
RUSSELL, Raymond
  Balfour, William
RUSSELL, Shane
  Norwood, Victor George
  Charles
RUTHERFORD, Douglas
  McConnell, John Douglas
  Rutherford
RYAN, J M
  McDermott, John Richard

RYBOT, Doris
  Ponsonby, Doris Almon
RYDER, James
  Pattinson, James
RYLAND, Clive
  Priestley, Clive Ryland

S S
  Sassoon, Siegfried
SABBAH, Hassan i
  Butler, Bill
SABIAD
  White, Stanhope
SABRE, Dirk
  Laffin, John
SABRETACHE
  Barrow, Albert Stewart
SACKERMAN, Henry
  Kahn, H S
SADBALLS, John
  Matusow, Harvey Marshall
SADDLER, K Allen
  Richards, Ronald C W
SAGITTARIUS
  Katzin, Olga
ST CLAIR, Philip
  Howard, Munroe
ST CLAIRE, Yvonne
  Hall, Emma L
SAINT-EDEN, Dennis
  Foster, Donn
ST GEORGE, Arthur
  Paine, Lauran Bosworth
ST JOHN, David
  Hunt, E Howard
SAKI
  Munro, Hector Hugh
SALT, Johathan
  Neville, Derek
SALTEN, Felix
  Saltzmann, Sigmund
SALTER, Cedric
  Knight, Francis Edgar
SALTER, Mary D
  Ainsworth, Mary Dinsmore

SALTER AINSWORTH, Mary D
  Ainsworth, Mary Dinsmore
SAMPSON, Richard Henry
  Hull, Richard
SANBORN, B X
  Ballinger, William Sanborn
SANDERS, Brett
  Barrett, Geoffrey John
SANDERS, Bruce
  Gribble, Leonard Reginald
SANDERS, Jeanne
  Rundle, Anne
SANDERS, Winston P
  Anderson, Poul
SANDS, Martin
  Burke, John Frederick
SANDYS, Oliver
  Evans, Marguerite Florence
SANTA MARIA
  Powell-Smith, Vincent
SANTEE, Walt
  King, Albert
SAPPER
  Fairlie, Gerard
SAPPER
  McNeile, H C
SARA
  Blake, Sally Mirliss
SARAC, Roger
  Caras, Roger
SARASIN, J G
  Salmon, Geraldine Gordon
SARBAN
  Wall, John W
SARGENT, Joan
  Jenkins, Sara Lucile
SARNIAN
  Falla, Frank
SASHUN, Sigma
  Sassoon, Siegfried
SAUNDERS, Anne
  Aldred, Margaret
SAUNDERS, Ione
  Cole, Margaret A

SAUNDERS, John
  Nickson, Arthur
SAVA, George
  Milkomane, George Alexis
    Milkomanovich
SAVAGE, Leslie
  Duff, Douglas Valder
SAVAGE, Richard
  Roe, Ivan
SAVAGE, Steve
  Goodavage, Joseph F
SAWLEY, Petra
  Marsh, John
SAXON
  Matthews, Edith J
SAXON, John
  Gifford, James Noble
SAXON, John
  Rumbold-Gibbs, Henry
    St John C
SCARLETT, Roger
  Blair, Dorothy and Page,
    Evelyn
SCARLETT, Susan
  Streatfeild, Noel
SCHAW, Ruth
  Drummond, Alison
SCHWARTZ, Bruno
  Mann, George
SCIENCE INVESTIGATOR
  Speck, Gerald Eugene
SCOBEY, Marion
  Coombs, Joyce
SCOT, Neil
  Grant, (Lady) Sybil
SCOTT, Agnes Neill
  Muir, Wilhelmina Johnstone
SCOTT, Bradford
  Scott, Leslie
SCOTT, Bruce
  McCartney, R J
SCOTT, Casey
  Kubis, Patricia Lou

SCOTT, Denis
  Means, Mary and Saunders,
    Theodore
SCOTT, Douglas
  Thorpe, John
SCOTT, Elizabeth
  Capstick, Elizabeth
SCOTT, Grover
  King, Albert
SCOTT, Norford
  Rowland, Donald Sydney
SCOTT, O R
  Gottliebsen, Ralph J
SCOTT, Valerie
  Rowland, Donald Sydney
SCOTT, Warwick
  Dudley-Smith, Trevor
SCOTT-MORLEY, A
  Oakley, Eric Gilbert
SCROPE, Mason
  Mason, Arthur Charles
SEAFARER
  Barker, Clarence Hedley
SEAFORTH
  Foster, George Cecil
SEA-LION
  Bennett, Geoffrey Martin
SEA-WRACK
  Crebbin, Edward Horace
SEDGWICK, Modwena
  Glover, Modwena
SEFTON, Catherine
  Waddell, Martin
SEGUNDO, Bart
  Rowland, Donald Sydney
SEIFERT, Elizabeth
  Gasparotti, Elizabeth
SELDEN, George
  Thompson, George Selden
SELL, Joseph
  Haley, W J
SELMARK, George
  Seldon Truss, Leslie

SENCOURT, Robert
    George, Robert Esmonde
    Gordon
SERAFIAN, Michael
    Martin, Malachi
SERJEANT, Richard
    Van Essen, W
SERNICOLI, Davide
    Trent, Ann
SETH, Andrew
    Pattison, Andrew Seth P
SETON, Graham
    Hutchison, Graham Seton
SETOUN, Gabriel
    Hepburn, Thomas Nicoll
SEUFFERT, Muir
    Seuffert, Muriel
SEVERN, David
    Unwin, David Storr
SEVERN, Forepoint
    Bethell, Leonard Arthur
SEVERN, Richard
    Ebbs, Robert
SEYMOUR, Henry
    Hartmann, Helmut Henry
SHALIMAR
    Hendry, Frank Coutts
SHALLOW, Robert
    Atkinson, Frank
SHAN
    McMordie, John Andrew
SHANE
    Richardson, Eileen
SHANE, John
    Durst, Paul
SHANE, Martin
    Johnston, George Henry
SHANE, Rhondo
    Norwood, Victor George
    Charles
SHANNON, Carl
    Hogue, Wilbur Owings
SHANNON, Dell
    Linington, Elizabeth

SHANNON, Monica
    Katchamakoff, Atanas
SHANWA
    Haarer, Alec Ernest
SHARMAN, Miriam
    Bolton, Miriam
SHARP, Helen
    Paine, Lauran Bosworth
SHAUL, Frank
    Rowland, Donald Sydney
SHAW, Artie
    Arshavsky, Abraham Isaac
SHAW, Irene
    Roberts, Irene
SHAW, Jane
    Evans, Jean
SHAW, Jill A
    Keeling, Jill Annette
SHAW, T E
    Lawrence, T E
SHAYNE, Nina
    Gibbs, Norah
SHEARING, Joseph
    Campbell, Gabrielle Margaret
    Vere
SHELBY, Cole
    King, Albert
SHELLEY, Frances
    Wees, Frances Shelley
SHELTON, Michael
    Stacey, P M de Cosqueville
SHEPHERD, Neal
    Morland, Nigel
SHERATON, Neil
    Smith, Norman Edward
    Mace
SHERMAN, George
    Moretti, Ugo
SHERRY, Gordon
    Sheridan, H B
SHIEL-MARTIN
    Old, Phyllis Muriel Elizabeth
SHONE, Patric
    Hanley, James

SHORE, Norman
  Smith, Norman Edward Mace
SHORE, Philippa
  Holbeche, Philippa
SHORT, Luke
  Glidden, Frederick Dilley
SHOTT, Abel
  Ford, T W
SHROPSHIRE LAD
  Barber-Starkey, Roger
SHUTE, Nevil
  Norway, Nevil Shute
SHY, Timothy
  Wyndham Lewis, D B
SIBLEY, Lee
  Landells, Anne
SIDNEY, Neilma
  Gantner, Neilma B
SIGMA SASHUN
  Sassoon, Siegfried
SILVER, Nicholas
  Faust, Frederick
SILVESTER, Frank
  Bingley, David Ernest
SIMMONDS, Mike
  Simmonds, Michael Charles
SIMMONS, Catherine
  Duncan, Kathleen
SIMMONS, Kim
  Duncan, Kathleen
SIMON, Robert
  Musto, Barry
SIMON, S J
  Skidelsky, Simon Jasha
SIMONS, Roger
  Punnett, Margaret and
    Punnett, Ivor
SIMPLE, Peter
  Herbert, John; Hogg, Michael;
    Welch, Colin and Wharton,
    Michael
SIMPLEX, Simon
  Middleton, Henry Clement
SIMPSON, Warwick
  Ridge, William Pett

SIMS, John
  Hopson, William L
SIMS, (Lieut) A K
  Whitson, John Harvey
SINBAD
  Dingle, Aylward Edward
SINDERBY, Donald
  Stephens, Donald Ryder
SINJOHN, John
  Galsworthy, John
SION, Mari
  Jones, Robert Maynard
SKEEVER, Jim
  Hill, John Alexander
SLADE, Gurney
  Bartlett, Stephen
SLAUGHTER, Jim
  Paine, Lauran Bosworth
SMALL, Ernest
  Lent, Blair
SMEE, Wentworth
  Burgin, G B
SMEED
  Taylor, Deems
SMEED, Frances
  Lasky, Jesse L
SMITH, Dodie
  Smith, Dorothy Gladys
SMITH, Harriet
  Scott, Hilda R
SMITH, Jessica
  Penwarden, Helen
SMITH, S S
  Williamson, Thames
SMITH, Shelley
  Bodington, Nancy Hermione
SMITH, Surrey
  Dinner, William
SMITH, Wade
  Snow, Charles Horace
SMITH, Z Z
  Westheimer, David
SNAFFLES
  Payne, Charles J

SNOW, Lyndon
  Ansle, Dorothy Phoebe
SOMERS, J L
  Stickland, Louise Annie
    Beatrice
SOMERVILLE
  Somerville, Edith Oenone
SOSTHENES
  Coad, Frederick R
SOUTHCOTE, George
  Aston, (Sir) George
SOUTHWORTH, Louis
  Grealey, Tom
SOUTTER, Fred
  Lake, Kenneth Robert
SPADE, Mark
  Balchin, Nigel
SPAIN, John
  Adams, Cleve Franklin
SPALDING, Lucille
  Jay, Marion
SPARLIN, W
  Spratling, Walter Norman
SPENCE, Betty E
  Tettmar, Betty Eileen
SPENCE, Duncan
  Spence, William
SPERLING, Maria Sandra
  Floren, Lee
SPIEL, Hilde
  De Mendelssohn, Hilde
SPINELLI, Marcos
  Spinelli, Grace
SPOONHILL
  Reaney, James
SPRINGFIELD, David
  Lewis, Roy
SPROSTON, John
  Scott, Peter Dale
SPROULE, Wesley
  Sproule, Howard
SPURR, Clinton
  Rowland, Donald Sydney
SQUARE, Charlotte
  Haldane, Robert Ayllner

SQUIRES, Phil
  Barker, S Omar
STAFFORD, Ann
  Pedlar, Ann
STAFFORD, Peter
  Tabori, Paul
STAGGE, Jonathan
  Webb, Richard Wilson and
    Wheeler, Hugh Callingham
STAMPER, Alex
  Kent, Arthur
STAN, Roland
  Rowland, Donald Sydney
STAND, Marguerite
  Stickland, M E
STANDISH, Buck
  Paine, Lauran Bosworth
STANDISH, Burt L
  Patten, Gilbert
STANDISH, J O
  Horler, Sydney
STANDISH, Robert
  Gerahty, Digby George
STANGE, Nora Kathleen
  Begbie
  Stanley, Nora K B
STANHOPE, Douglas
  Duff, Douglas Valder
STANHOPE, John
  Langdon-Davies, John
STANLEY, Arthur
  Megaw, Arthur Stanley
STANLEY, Bennett
  Hough, Stanley Bennett
STANLEY, Chuck
  Strong, Charles Stanley
STANLEY, Margaret
  Mason, Sydney Charles
STANLEY, Michael
  Hosie, Stanley William
STANLEY, Warwick
  Hilton, John Buxton
STANSBURY, Alec
  Higgs, Alec S

STANTON, Borden
Wilding, Philip
STANTON, Coralie
Hosken, Alice Cecil
Seymour
STANTON, Vance
Avallone, Michael Angelo Jr
STARK, Joshua
Olsen, Theodore Victor
STARK, Richard
Westlake, Donald Edwin
STARR, Henry
Bingley, David Ernest
STARR, Leonora
Mackesy, Leonora Dorothy
Rivers
STAVELEY, Robert
Campbell, R O
STEEL, Byron
Steegmuller, Francis
STEEL, Kurt
Kagey, Rudolf
STEEN, Frank
Felstein, Ivor
STEER, Charlotte
Hunter, Christine
STERLING, Maria Sandra
Floren, Lee
STERLING, Stewart
Winchell, Prentice
STERN, Elizabeth
Uhr, Elizabeth
STEVENS, Christopher
Tabori, Paul
STEVENS, Dan J
Overholser, Wayne D
STEVENS, J B
Rowland, Donald Sydney
STEVENS, Jill
Mogridge, Stephen
STEVENS, S P
Palestrant, Simon
STEVENS, William Christopher
Allen, Stephen Valentine

STEVENSON, Christine
Kelly, Elizabeth
STEWART, C R
Adam, C G M
STEWART, Jean
Newman, Mona A J
STEWART, Logan
Savage, Lee
STEWART, Logan
Wilding, Philip
STEWART, Marjorie
Huxtable, Marjorie
STEWART, Will
Williamson, Jack
STEWER, Jan
Coles, Albert John
STITCH, Wilhelmina
Collie, Ruth
STODDARD, Charles
Strong, Charles Stanley
STOKES, Cedric
Beardmore, George
STONE, Eugene
Speck, Gerald Eugene
STONE, Hampton
Stein, Aaron Marc
STONE, Simon
Barrington, Howard
STORM, Lesley
Clark, Mabel Margaret
STORM, Virginia
Swatridge, Irene M M
STORME, Peter
Stern, Philip Van Doren
STRAND, Paul E
Palestrant, Simon
STRANG, Herbert
L'Estrange, C James and
Ely, George Herbert
STRANGE, John Stephen
Tillett, Dorothy Stockbridge
STRATEGICUS
O'Neill, Herbert Charles
STRATTON, John
Alldridge, John Stratten

STRATTON, Thomas
  Coulson, Robert Stratton and
  De Weese, T Eugene
STRONG, Susan
  Rees, Joan
STRUTHER, Jan
  Maxtone-Graham, Joyce
STRYDOM, Len
  Rousseau, Leon
STUART, Alan
  Weightman, Archibald John
STUART, Alex
  Mann, Violet Vivian
STUART, Brian
  Worthington-Stuart, Brian
  Arthur
STUART, Charles
  Mackinnon, Charles Roy
STUART, Clay
  Whittington, Harry
STUART, Don A
  Campbell, John Wood Jr
STUART, Florence
  Stonebreaker, Florence
STUART, Frederick
  Tomlin, Eric
STUART, Gordon
  Wood, James
STUART, Ian
  Maclean, Alistair
STUART, John Roy
  McMillan, Donald
STUART, Logan
  Wilding, Philip
STUART, Margaret
  Paine, Lauran Bosworth
STUART, Matt
  Holmes, Llewellyn Perry
STUART, Sheila
  Baker, Mary Gladys Steel
STUART, Sidney
  Avallone, Michael Angelo Jr
STUART, Vivian
  Mann, Violet Vivian

STURGEON, Theodore
  Waldo, Edward Hamilton
STURGUS, J B
  Bastin, John
STUYVESANT, Polly
  Paul, Maury
SUBHADRA-NANDAN
  Prafulla, Das
SUBOND, Valerie
  Grayland, Valerie M
SULLIVAN, Eric Harrison
  Hickey, Madelyn E
SUMMERHAYES, Prudence
  Alan Turner, Violet
  Prudence
SUMMERS, D B
  Barrett, Geoffrey John
SUMMERS, Gordon
  Hornby, John W
SUMMERSCALES, Rowland
  Gaines, Robert
SURREY, Kathryn
  Matthewman, Phyllis
SUTHERLAND, Joan
  Collings, Joan
SUTTLING, Mark
  Rowland, Donald Sydney
SUTTON, Henry
  Slavitt, David
SUTTON, John
  Tullett, Denis John
SUTTON, Rachel B
  Sutton, Margaret
SWAN, Annie S
  Burnett-Smith, Annie S
SWAYNE, Geoffrey
  Campion, Sidney
SWIFT, Benjamin
  Paterson, W R
SWIFT, Julian
  Applin, Arthur
SWIFT, Rachelle
  Lumsden, Jean

SYLVESTER, Philip
  Worner, Philip A I
SYLVIA
  Ashton-Warner, Sylvia

T
  Thorp, Joseph
T P
  O'Connor, T P
TAAFFE, Robert
  Maguire, Robert A J
TABARD, Peter
  Blake, Leslie James
TAFFRAIL
  Dorling, Henry Taprell
TAGGART, Dean
  King, Albert
TAINE, John
  Bell, Eric Temple
TALBOT, Henry
  Rothwell, Henry Talbot
TALBOT, Hugh
  Alington, Argentine Francis
TALBOT, Kay
  Rowland, Donald Sydney
TAPER
  Levin, Bernard
TATE, Ellalice
  Hibbert, Eleanor Alice Burford
TAYLOR, Ann
  Brodey, Jim
TAYLOR, H Baldwin
  Waugh, Hillary Baldwin
TAYLOR, John
  Magee, James
TAYLOR, Sam
  Goodyear, Stephen Frederick
TEARLE, Christian
  Jacques, Edward Tyrrell
TEG, Twm
  Vulliamy, Colwyn Edward
TELSTAR
  Goodwin, Geoffrey
TEMPEST, Jan
  Swatridge, Irene M M

TEMPLE, Paul
  Durbridge, Francis and
    McConnell, James Douglas
    Rutherford
TEMPLE, Robin
  Wood, Samuel Andrew
TEMPLE-ELLIS, N A
  Holdaway, Neville Aldridge
TEMPLETON, Jesse
  Goodchild, George
TENNANT, Catherine
  Eyles, Kathleen Muriel
TENNENBAUM, Irving
  Stone, Irving
TERAHATA, Jun
  Kirkup, James
TERRY, C V
  Slaughter, Frank Gill
TEW, Mary
  Douglas, Mary
TEY, Josephine
  Mackintosh, Elizabeth
THANE, Elswyth
  Beebe, Elswyth Thane
THANET, Octave
  French, Alice
THAYER, Jane
  Woolley, Catherine
THETA, Eric Mark
  Higginson, Henry Clive
THIRLMERE, Rowland
  Walker, John
THOMAS, Carolyn
  Duncan, Actea
THOMAS, G K
  Davies, Leslie Purnell
THOMAS, Gough
  Garwood, Godfrey Thomas
THOMAS, J Bissell
  Stephen, Joyce Alice
THOMAS, Jim
  Reagan, Thomas B
THOMAS, Joan Gale
  Robinson, Joan Gale

THOMAS, Lee
    Floren, Lee
THOMAS, Michael
    Benson, Michael
THOMPSON, Buck
    Paine, Lauran Bosworth
THOMPSON, China
    Lewis, Mary Christianna
THOMPSON, Eileen
    Panowski, Eileen Janet
THOMPSON, Russ
    Paine, Lauran Bosworth
THOMSON, Audrey
    Gwynn, Audrey
THOMSON, Joan
    Charnock, Joan
THOMSON, Jon H
    Thomson, Daisy
THOMSON, Neil
    Johnson, Henry T
THORN, Barbara
    Paine, Lauran Bosworth
THORNTON, Maimee
    Jeffrey-Smith, May
THORNTON, W B
    Burgess, Thornton W
THORP, Ellen
    Robertson, Margery Ellen
THORP, Morwenna
    Robertson, Margery Ellen
THORPE, Sylvia
    Thimblethorpe, June
THURLEY, Norgrove
    Stoneham, Charles Thurley
THURLOW, Robert
    Griffin, Jonathan
TIBBER, Robert
    Friedman, Eve Rosemary
TIBBER, Rosemary
    Friedman, Eve Rosemary
TILBURY, Quenna
    Walker, Emily Kathleen
TILLEY, Gene
    Tilley, E D

TILTON, Alice
    Taylor, Phoebe Atwood
TIM
    Martin, Timothy
TODHUNTER, Philippa
    Bond, Grace
TOKLAS, Alice B
    Stein, Gertrude
TOLER, Buck
    Kelly, Harold Ernest
TOLLER
    Lyburn, Eric Frederic St John
TOMLINE, F Latour
    Gilbert, William Schwenck
TONKONGY, Gertrude
    Friedberg, Gertrude
TOPICUS
    Goodwin, Geoffrey
TORQUEMADA
    Mathers, Edward Powys
TORR, Iain
    Mackinnon, Charles Roy
TORRIE, Malcolm
    Mitchell, Gladys
TORROLL, G D
    Lawson, Alfred
TOWERS, Tricia
    Ivison, Elizabeth
TOWNSEND, Timothy
    Robey, Timothy Lester
    Townsend
TOWRY, Peter
    Piper, David Towry
TRACEY, Grant
    Nuttall, Anthony
TRACEY, Hugh
    Evans, Kay and Evans, Stuart
TRACY, Catherine
    Story, Rosamond Mary
TRAFFORD, Jean
    Walker, Edith

> No names, no pack drill
> —British Army saying

TRAILL, Peter
  Morton, Guy Mainwaring
TRAPROCK, Walter E
  Chappell, George S
TRAVER, Robert
  Voelker, John Donaldson
TRAVERS, Hugh
  Mills, Hugh Travers
TRAVERS, Will
  Rowland, Donald Sydney
TRAVIS, Gretchen
  Mockler, Gretchen
TRAWLE, Mary Elizabeth
  Elwart, Joan Frances
TREHEARNE, Elizabeth
  Maxwell, Patricia Anne
TRENT, Lee
  Nuttall, Anthony
TRENT, Paul
  Platt, Edward
TRESILIAN, Liz
  Green, Elizabeth Sara
TRESSALL, Robert
  Noonan, Robert
TRESSELL, Robert
  Noonan, Robert
TRESSIDY, Jim
  Norwood, Victor George
  Charles
TREVENA, John
  Henham, E J
TREVES, Kathleen
  Walker, Emily Kathleen
TREVOR, Elleston
  Dudley-Smith, Trevor
TREVOR, Glen
  Hilton, James
TREVOR, Ralph
  Wilmot, James Reginald
TREW, Cecil G
  Ehrenborg, (Mrs) C G
TRING, A Stephen
  Maynell, Laurence Walter
TRIPP, Karen
  Gershon, Karen

TRITON, A N
  Barclay, Oliver Rainsford
TROTTER, Sallie
  Crawford, Sallie
TROTWOOD, John
  Moore, John
TROY, Katherine
  Buxton, Anne
TROY, Simon
  Warriner, Thurman
TRUSCOT, Bruce
  Peers, Edgar Allison
TSUYUKI SHIGERU
  Kirkup, James
TUCKER, Lael
  Wertenbaker, Lael Tucker
TUCKER, Link
  Bingley, David Ernest
TURNER, C John
  Whiteman, William Meredith
TURNER, Len
  Floren, Lee
TURNER, Mary
  Lambot, Isobel Mary
TURVEY, Winsome
  Rusterholtz, Winsome Lucy
  Austel
TUSTIN, Elizabeth
  White, Celia
TWEEDALE, J
  Bickle, Judith
TYLER, Clarke
  Brookes, Ewart Stanley
TYLER, Ellis
  King, Albert
TYSON, Teilo
  McFarlane, David

UBIQUE
  Guggisberg, (Sir) F G
UNCLE HENRY
  Wallace, Henry
UNCLE MAC
  McCulloch, Derek

UNCLE MONTY
  Hamilton-Wilkes, Edwin
UNCLE REG
  Woodcock, E Page
UNCUT CAVENDISH
  Meares, John Willoughby
UNDERWOOD, Keith
  Spooner, Peter Alan
UNDERWOOD, Michael
  Evelyn, John Michael
UNDERWOOD, Miles
  Glassco, John
UNDINE, P F
  Paine, Lauran Bosworth
UNOFFICIAL OBSERVER
  Carter, John Franklin
URIEL, Henry
  Faust, Frederick
URQUHART, Paul
  Black, Ladbroke Lionel Day
USHER, Margo Scegge
  McHargue, Georges

V V V
  Lucas, E V
VAIL, Amanda
  Miller, Warren
VAIL, Philip
  Gerson, Noel Bertram
VALE, Keith
  Clegg, Paul
VALENTINE
  Pechey, Archibald Thomas
VAN BUREN, Abigail
  Phillips, Pauline
VAN DINE, S S
  Wright, Willard Huntington
VAN DYKE, J
  Edwards, Frederick Anthony
VAN HELLER, Marcus
  Kanto, Peter
VANCE, Ethel
  Stone, Grace Zaring
VANCE, Jack
  Kuttner, Henry

VANE, Brett
  Kent, Arthur
VANE, Michael
  Humphries, Sydney
VANSITTART, Jane
  Moorhouse, Hilda
VARDRE, Leslie
  Davies, Leslie Purnell
VAUGHAN, Carter A
  Gerson, Noel Bertram
VAUGHAN, Julian
  Almond, Brian
VAUGHAN, Richard
  Thomas, Ernest Lewys
VEDETTE
  Fitchett, W H
VEHEYNE, Cherry
  Williamson, Ethel
VEITCH, Tom
  Padgett, Ron
VENNING, Hugh
  Van Zeller, Claud H
VERNON, Claire
  Breton-Smith, Clare
VERNON, Kay
  Vernon, Kathleen Rose
VERNON, Marjorie
  Russell, Shirley
VERONIQUE
  Fisher, Veronica Suzanne
VERWER, Hans
  Verwer, Johanne
VESTAL, Stanley
  Campbell, Walter Stanley
VICARY, Dorothy
  Rice, Dorothy
VICTOR, Charles B
  Puechner, Ray
VIDENS
  Mumford, A H
VIGILANS
  Partridge, Eric
VIGILANS
  Rice, Brian Keith

VIGILANTES
Zilliacus, Konni
VILLIERS, Elizabeth
Thorne, Isabel Mary
VINCENT, Heather
Walker, Emily Kathleen
VINCENT, Honor
Walker, Emily Kathleen
VINCENT, Jim
Foxall, P A
VINCENT, John
Farrow, R
VINCENT, Mary Keith
St John, Wylly Folk
VINSON, Elaine
Rowland, Donald Sydney
VINSON, Kathryn
Williams, Kathryn
VIPONT, Charles
Foulds, Elfrida Vipont
VIPONT, Elfrida
Foulds, Elfrida Vipont
VISIAK, E H
Physick, Edward Harold
VIVIAN, Francis
Ashley, Ernest
VOX, Agnes Mary
Duffy, Agnes Mary
VOYLE, Mary
Manning, Rosemary
VUL' INDLELA
Becker, Peter

WADE, Bill
Barrett, Geoffrey John
WADE, Henry
Aubrey-Fletcher, (Sir)
Henry Lancelot
WADE, Robert
McIlwain, David
WADE, Thomas
Looker, Samuel Joseph
WAGNER, Peggy
Wagner, Margaret Dale

WAKE, G B
Haynes, John Harold
WALDO, Dave
Clarke, David
WALDRON, Simon
King, Albert
WALES, Hubert
Piggott, William
WALES, Nym
Snow, Helen Foster
WALFORD, Christian
Dilcock, Noreen
WALKER, Holly Beth
Bond, Gladys Baker
WALKER, Jean Brown
Walker, Edith
WALLACE, Agnes
King, Albert
WALLACE, Doreen
Rash, Dora
WALTER, Katherine
Walter, Dorothy Blake
WALTER, Kay
Walter, Dorothy Blake
WALTERS, Hugh
Hughes, Walter Llewellyn
WALTERS, Rick
Rowland, Donald Sydney
WALTERS, T B
Rowe, John Gabriel
WAND, Elizabeth
Tattersall, Muriel Joyce
WANDERER
Smith, Lily
WARD, Artemus
Browne, Charles Farrar
WARD, Brad
Peeples, Samuel Anthony
WARD, Kate
Cust, Barbara Kate
WARD, Kirwan
Kirwan-Ward, Bernard
WARDEN, Florence
Price, Florence Alice

WARE, Monica
  Marsh, John
WARNER, Frank
  Richardson, Gladwell
WARNER, Leigh
  Smith, Lillian M
WARRE, Mary D
  Greig, Maysie
WARREN, Andrew
  Tute, Warren
WARREN, Wayne
  Braun, Wilbur
WASH, R
  Cowlishaw, Ranson
WATER, Silas
  Loomis, Noel Miller
WATSON, C P
  Agelasto, Charlotte Priestley
WATSON, Frank
  Ames, Francis H
WATSON, Will
  Floren, Lee
WAVERLEY, John
  Scobie, Stephen Arthur Cross
WAYLAN, Mildred
  Harrell, Irene Burk
WAYLAND, Patrick
  O'Connor, Richard
WAYNE, Heather
  Gibbs, Norah
WAYNE, Joseph
  Overholser, Wayne D
WAYNE, Marcia
  Best, Carol Anne
WEALE, B Putnam
  Simpson, Bertram L
WEAVER, Ward
  Mason, F Van Wyck
WEBB, Christopher
  O'Connor Wibberley, Leonard
  Patrick
WEBB, Neil
  Rowland, Donald Sydney

WEBSTER, Jean
  Webster, Alice Jane Chandler
WEBSTER, Noah
  Knox, Bill
WEIR, Jonnet
  Nicholson, Joan
WELBURN, Vivienne C
  Furlong, Vivienne
WELCH, Ronald
  Felton, Ronald Oliver
WELCH, Rowland
  Davies, Leslie Purnell
WELCOME, John
  Brennan, John
WELLS, Hondo
  Whittington, Harry
WELLS, John J
  Coulson, Juanita and Bradley,
  Marion Z
WELLS, Tobias
  Forbes, Stanton
WELLS, Tracey
  Nuttall, Anthony
WENTWORTH, John
  Child, Philip A G
WERNER, Jane
  Watson, Jane Werner
WERNER, Peter
  Booth, Philip Arthur
WERRERSON, Talbot
  Robertson, Walter George
WESLEY, James
  Rigoni, Orlando Joseph
WESSEX, Martyn
  Little, D F
WESSEX REDIVIVUS
  Dewar, Hubert Stephen
  Lowry
WEST, Anna
  Edward, Ann
WEST, Keith
  Lane, Kenneth Westmacott
WEST, Laura M
  Hymers, Laura M

WEST, Mark
Huff, Darrell
WEST, Nathaniel
Weinstein, Nathan Wallenstein
WEST, Tom
Reach, James
WEST, Trudy
West, Gertrude
WESTALL, Lorna
Houseman, Lorna
WESTERN, Barry
Evans, Gwynfil Arthur
WESTERN-HOLT, J C
Heming, Jack C W
WESTGATE, John
Bloomfield, Anthony John
Westgate
WESTLAND, Lynn
Joscelyn, Archie Lynn
WESTMACOTT, Mary
Christie, (Dame) Agatha
WESTRIDGE, Harold
Avery, Harold
WETZEL, Lewis
King, Albert
WEYMOUTH, Anthony
Cobb, Ivo Geikie
WHARTON, Anthony
Macallister, Alister
WHEEZY
Hounsfield, Joan
WHETTER, Laura
Mannock, Laura
WHITAKER, Ray
Davies, John
WHITBY, Sharon
Black, Maureen
WHITE, Dale
Place, Marian Templeton
WHITE, Harry
Whittington, Harry
WHITE, Heather
Foster, Jess Mary Mardon
WHITE, Jane
Brady, Jane Frances

WHITEFRIAR
Hiscock, Eric
WHITEHAND, Satherley
Satherley, David and
Whitehand, James
WHITEHOUSE, Peggy
Castle, Frances Mundy
WHITINGER, R D
Place, Marian Templeton
WHITLEY, George
Chandler, Arthur
WHITNEY, Hallam
Whittington, Harry
WHITTINGHAM, Sara
Gibbs, Norah
WHYE, Felix
Dixon, Arthur
WIBBERLEY, Leonard
O'Connor Wibberley, Leonard
Patrick
WICKLOE, Peter
Duff, Douglas Valder
WIGAN, Christopher
Bingley, David Ernest
WIGG, T I G
McCutchan, Philip D
WILDE, Hilary
Breton-Smith, Clare
WILDE, Leslie
Best, Rayleigh Breton Amis
WILKINSON, Tim
Wilkinson, Percy F H
WILLEY, Robert
Ley, Willy
WILLIAMS, Beryl
Epstein, Beryl
WILLIAMS, F Harald
Orde-Ward, F W
WILLIAMS, J R
Creasey, Jeanne
WILLIAMS, Jeanne
Creasey, Jeanne
WILLIAMS, Michael
St John, Wylly Folk

WILLIAMS, Patry
  Williams, D F and Patry, M
WILLIAMS, Rex
  Wei, Rex
WILLIAMS, Richard
  Francis, Stephen D
WILLIAMS, Roth
  Zilliacus, Konni
WILLIAMS, Violet M
  Boon, Violet Mary
WILLIAMSON, Paul
  Butters, Paul
WILLOUGHBY, Hugh
  Harvey, Charles
WILLS, Chester
  Snow, Charles Horace
WILSON, Ann
  Baily, Francis Evans
WILSON, Christine
  Geach, Christine
WILSON, D M
  Bentley, Frederick Horace
WILSON, Edwina H
  Brookman, Laura L
WILSON, Elizabeth
  Ivison, Elizabeth
WILSON, John Burgess
  Wilson, John Anthony Burgess
WILSON, Martha
  Morse, Martha
WILSON, Yates
  Wilson, Albert
WINCH, John
  Campbell, Gabrielle Margaret
    Vere
WINDER, Mavis
  Winder, Mavis Areta
WINCHESTER, Kay
  Walker, Emily Kathleen
WINDSOR, Rex
  Armstrong, Douglas
WINFIELD, Allen
  Stratemeyer, Edward
WINFIELD, Arthur M
  Stratemeyer, Edward

WINGFIELD, Susan
  Reece, Alys
WINN, Alison
  Wharmby, Margot
WINN, Patrick
  Padley, Arthur
WINSLOWE, John R
  Richardson, Gladwell
WINSTAN, Matt
  Nickson, Arthur
WINTER, John Strange
  Stannard, Eliza Vaughan
WINTERS, Bernice
  Winters, Bayla
WINTERS, Mary K
  Hart, Caroline Horowitz
WINTON, John
  Pratt, John
WITHERBY, Diana
  Cooke, Diana
WITHERS, E L
  Potter, George William
WODEN, George
  Slaney, George Wilson
WOLFENDEN, George
  Beardmore, George
WONG, Elizabeth
  Chi Lien
WOOD, J Claverdon
  Carter, Thomas
WOOD, Mary
  Bamfield, Veronica
WOOD, Quality
  Wood, Violet
WOODCOTT, Keith
  Brunner, John
WOODFORD, Cecile
  Woodford, Irene-Cecile
WOODROCK, R A
  Cowlishaw, Ranson
WOODRUFF, Philip
  Mason, Philip
WOODS, Jonah
  Woods, Olwen
WOODS, Ross
  Story, Rosamond Mary

WOODWARD, Lillian
  Marsh, John
WOOLLAND, Henry
  Williams, Guy Richard Owen
WORTH, Martin
  Wigglesworth, Martin
WORTH, Maurice
  Bosworth, Willan George
WRAITH, John
  Devaney, Pauline and Apps,
  Edwin
WRIGHT, Elnora A
  Old Coyote, Elnora A
WRIGHT, Sally
  Old Coyote, Elnora A
WRIGHT, Ted
  Wright, George T
WRIGHT, Wade
  Wright, John
WYANDOTTE, Steve
  Thomas, Stanley A C
WYLCOTES, John
  Ransford, Oliver
WYNDER, Mavis Areta
  Winder, Mavis Areta
WYNDHAM, Esther
  Lutyens, Mary
WYNDHAM, John
  Harris, John Beynon
WYNMAN, Margaret
  Dixon, Ella Hepworth
WYNNE, Anthony
  Wilson, Robert McNair
WYNNE, May
  Knowles, Mabel Winifred
WYNNE, Pamela
  Scott, Winifred Mary

Y Y
  Lynd, Robert
YARBO, Steve
  King, Albert
YATES, Dornford
  Mercer, Cecil William
YERUSHALMI, Chaim
  Lipschitz, (Rabbi) Chaim
YES TOR
  Roche, Thomas
YLLA
  Koffler, Camilla
YORK, Andrew
  Nicole, Christopher
YORK, Jeremy
  Creasey, John
YORKE, Margaret
  Nicholson, Margaret Beda
YORKE, Roger
  Bingley, David Ernest
YOUNG, Filson
  Bell, Alexander
YOUNG, Jan
  Young, Janet Randall
YOUNG, Kendal
  Young, Phyllis Brett
YOUNG, Robert
  Payne, Pierre Stephen Robert
YOUNG, Rose
  Harris, Marion Rose

ZED
  Dienes, Zoltan
ZINKEN
  Hopp, Signe

166